LURECRAFT

How to Make Plugs, Spinners, Spoons, and Jigs to Catch More Fish

Written and illustrated by

RUSS MOHNEY

With contributions from Rich Rousseau, author of *Making Wooden Fishing Lures*

FOX CHAPEL
PUBLISHING

Award-winning woodcarver, lurecrafter, and angler Rich Rousseau of northern Michigan generously provided expert advice to update this classic book for the twenty-first century fisherman. Rousseau has been carving wood for more than 50 years, carving lures and decoys for more than 25 years, and fishing since he was four years old His beautiful and functional hand-carved lures, all following the patterns found in this book, are featured in the color gallery, along with his illuminating step-by-step photography for lurecrafting from start to finish. Rousseau has also authored his own book, "Making Wooden Fishing Lures" (2010), which covers carving, painting, tools, and materials and is another great resource for the crafty fisherman.

ISBN 978-1-56523-780-3

Library of Congress Cataloging-in-Publication Data

Mohney, Russ.
  [Complete book of lurecraft]
  Lurecraft.
     pages cm
Reprint of: The complete book of lurecraft. New York, NY : Outdoor Life Books, c1987.
Includes index.
ISBN 978-1-56523-780-3
1. Fishing lures--Design and construction. I. Title.
SH449.M64 2013
799.12028'4--dc23
                        2012045486

To learn more about the other great books from Fox Chapel Publishing, or to find a retailer near you,
call toll-free 800-457-9112 or visit us at *www.FoxChapelPublishing.com*.

Note to Authors: We are always looking for talented authors to write new books. Please send a brief letter
describing your idea to Acquisition Editor, 1970 Broad Street, East Petersburg, PA 17520.

Printed in China
First printing

This book is dedicated to my father, who taught me to appreciate the quiet beauty of the places where fish are found, and to judge the value of an angling experience by the challenge rather than the catch; and to my daughter Katie, to whom I am privileged to pass along whatever wisdom I may have acquired.

CONTENTS

Publisher's Note

In 1987, Russ Mohney published this comprehensive book on lurecraft and lure science to rave reviews. I am now pleased to reintroduce Mohney's work with all of the original content and lure designs plus an updated photo gallery of hand-carved lures and step-by-step lure making instructions.

Russ Mohney passed away in 2010, but left a legacy that his children, friends, coworkers, and readers all over the country and world carry with them. Mohney got his start in angling and lure making while growing up in a family of outdoor enthusiasts. Fishing and his various occupations took him to several continents throughout his life, but he always returned to his native Washington, which was the true origin of his lifelong love of the outdoors. Mohney wrote for the Chronicle of Lewis County, Washington, for more than a decade before the end of his life, faithfully contributing a weekly column "The Backyard Naturalist" where every Tuesday he shared his extensive knowledge of the outdoors, instructing on everything from fishing and game to berries and nettle soup. Mohney also published more than ten books on outdoor pursuits, covering topics such as camping, backpacking, game cooking, and even a little regional history. One of his best-selling books was "Why Wild Edibles? The Joys of Finding, Fixing, and Tasting West of the Rockies." He also wrote a book of personal essays titled "A Simple Song: Recollections from a Backwoods County."

During the course of his 75 years, Mohney didn't just hone his powerful knowledge of the outdoors. He also worked in many diverse occupations: as a free speech radio broadcaster; as an artist who mastered the study of Native American art and created an impressive portfolio of tribal artwork; as a public relations staff member at Centralia College; and as an employee of the Forest Service. Near the end of his life, Mohney, the Lewis County Economic Development Council, and the Lewis County Chronicle created the Russ Mohney Recreation Resource Stewardship Award, which is awarded annually to a person or group for outstanding contributions to outdoor recreation. The award is now just one more remembrance for a well-remembered man. Author, angler, activist; cancer survivor, father, philanthropist: Mohney lives on in the works that he shared with the world and that we now share with you.

Alan Giagnocavo

Preface

The first lure I can remember making was a round ball of cedar whittled from a stick of kindling, fitted with a hammered spinner blade made from a candy tin, and trailed with a galvanized hook wrapped with some white feather. It looked cob-rough and illogical, but it caught a half-dozen Puget Sound salmon before it finally succumbed to an underwater snag. It was immediately replaced by another, slicker version. It, in turn, was followed by a succession of modifications of the same basic lure. Some were larger, some smaller, some had different color combinations…until eventually I had modified my early Cherry Bobber to a point where it was the most effective.

My interest in—and enjoyment from—homemade lures continued to grow throughout my fishing career. I remember in particular a trolling plug I made in preparation for a trout-fishing trip into Canada. It was designed along the lines of the famous Flatfish but was fuller bodied and carved to run shallower. I'll always remember the husky lake trout I took on it because the fish responded to features I had purposely designed into the lure.

Over the years I have designed and built hundreds of lures, not all of them successful by any means. But as I gained greater knowledge of the fish and studied the science of fish behavior, the failures became fewer and farther between. Today, I have tackleboxes stuffed with lures for every conceivable type of fishing—and I'd be willing to bet on almost any of them at the proper time and place. They represent a lot of time, study, and fun.

At the outset, making your own lures may seem unnecessary. As you browse through a well-stocked tackle shop, you may wonder why anyone would need to make his own lures. Surely it isn't because the tackle makers don't offer us a sufficient choice.

In reality, there are a lot of gaps in the seemingly endless array of tackle on the commercial market. These lures are made to serve millions of anglers under a wide variety of conditions. Mass-market demands cannot allow for variation to suit local habitat. The truth is, many of the lures on those shelves aren't very good under any angling conditions. Although most manufacturers are responsible people trying to produce useful tackle, there are hundreds of firms that put a lot more research into their packaging and marketing than into their lures. Thousands of imported gadgets have been designed and built by people who have never even seen a trout or bass, much less fished for one.

In recent years, many fishing experts have been telling us how to "tune" a factory lure to make it work under certain fishing conditions. It is really necessary if the lure is going to catch fish in our favorite spot. A better alternative is to carry a lure that is specifically designed for our hometown water. That means making your own lures—and that's what this book is all about.

Making lures that work better than the best commercial tackle requires an understanding of the biological factors that cause a fish to respond to a lure. Most anglers already have some background in the habits and preferences of their favorite fish, and this book will round out that education.

Beyond the practical value of making lures that are really effective, there are other benefits to be derived from making your own terminal tackle. One is the satisfaction that all of us feel after taking a trophy with a lure of our own design. Another factor to consider is economy. You've probably discovered that factory-made lures aren't cheap. It is possible to pay from five to ten dollars for a decent troll rig or bass plug. The do-it-yourself equivalent may work better and cost only a few pennies. It may also provide a lot of pure enjoyment in the time spent crafting it. A great many of us begin to look at our handicraft with the critical eye of an artist, thoroughly enjoying the lure itself, quite aside from its value as a device that might catch a fish. More often than not, the hours spent at the tackle bench are filled with plans and fantasies of fishing trips still to come, the fond recollections of outings long past, and the careful analysis of tackle and technique that produced an especially rewarding experience. Almost every home lurecrafter becomes a better angler through this study and reflection.

Making your own lures is something of a specialized hobby, but the tools, techniques, and materials involved are surprisingly simple. You can make very effective and professional lures with everyday tools and the commonest of materials. In this book you'll find many excellent designs that have been built from everyday items with a minimum of technical skill—yet they are fun to make and they catch fish.

The lures described in this book have proved effective in a lot of different waters. Still, the homecrafter eventually becomes a dedicated experimenter, chopping a bit here and adding a touch there to make the lure work better. You will unquestionably produce new lures that will work in many of the special circumstances you'll face in your own angling future. When you develop a lure that is spectacularly successful, I hope you'll share it with the rest of the growing fraternity of home lurecrafters.

—*Russ Mohney*

chapter ONE

THE HISTORY OF THE LURE

There are two men of history to whom we owe an enormous debt of gratitude. The first was that adventurous soul who discovered that oysters are edible—thereby proving that uncommon vision in the face of convention was an acceptable, even admirable human quality. The second was the pioneer with enough imagination and faith to catch a fish on an artificial lure. In a world where everyone used bait to take fish with annoying regularity, one solitary figure had the courage, conviction, and patience to finally hook a fish on a painted stick of wood.

Man was an angler long before his activities were first scratched on the walls of history. Many of his cultures were built upon the catching of fish, usually by abysmally unsportsmanlike means, but he prospered and multiplied anyway. Early man's existence was governed by eating, catching fish or game, and sex—though not necessarily in that order. It is not hard to imagine that long-ago day when some primitive—his larder filled with fish and his other appetites forgotten— decided to go fishing just for fun. Putting away his nets and clubs, he laboriously fashioned a small spear. Satisfied with the implement, he waded into a shallow pool and attempted to meet a fish on a more-or-less equal footing. Mankind has never quite recovered from that experience!

It isn't difficult to carry the imagination a step further. Around the campfire gutteral arguments raged over the relative merits of the bamboo spear and the ultralight willow lance. The nights were punctuated by animated accounts of grand specimens that were struck but managed to escape through great courage and incredible strength. Tousled heads nodded in assent, each angler having shared the experience at one time or another. A few of the tales may have been embellished in the telling to clarify some particularly important point, but most were quite accurate. Anglers were—then as today—mostly virtuous and honest men.

Somewhere along the evolutionary footpath man finally surpassed the fish in intelligence, thus setting the stage for a momentous breakthrough. One auspicious day the notion occurred to someone that fish had to eat, too. The fishhook and baitfishing would soon follow.

Development of Lure Fishing

In reality, the artificial lure was born nearly nineteen centuries ago in the form of the angling fly. The exact origin of the fly is obscured by time, but we know there was generally widespread use of the device by the second century A.D. in Europe and the Mediterranean. No drawings or accurate descriptions of those flies survive, except for a few references to feathers and fabrics tied to a hook. By the mid-1400s, however, the fly was surprisingly well developed. A British publication from 1496 included drawings of several patterns that would serve well on today's trout streams. The fly was a successful departure from common bait angling, but the limitations of early tackle and technique confined flyfishing even more severely than the common hook-and-line bait methods of that era.

In the purest sense, the first artificial lures were probably wooden jigs used by Eskimos and northern Indians for ice fishing. Relics of these earliest rigs still survive in parts of Alaska and Canada, where their use was described in several accounts of the gold-rush days. Those rustic lures didn't include any of the attraction elements we normally associate with a useful lure. They were employed during the sparse winter months on the northern ice, where the fish would strike at almost anything—edible or not!

The first record of an artificial that actually incorporated effective attraction elements was recorded in the journals of explorer Captain James Cook. In his 1770 expedition to Hawaii, Cook found the natives using a trolling spoon fashioned from natural mother-of-pearl. The seashell had the curve necessary to impart "action" and the iridescent material on the inside of the shell provided an attractant to the fish. According to the accounts, the spoon apparently worked very well.

The modern metal spoon appeared shortly afterward in both England and North America, undoubtedly developed independently of the Polynesian pearl spoon. Several records indicate it was used extensively for pike and muskies in the northern lakes and rivers of the United States and Canada by the year 1801.

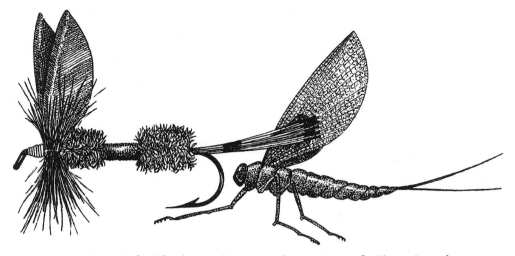

A typical modern dry fly (left), designed to imitate the aquatic mayfly. The earliest of recorded artificial lures, flies were known to have been used in Europe by the second century A.D.

By 1846 a polished and very effective spoon was being commercially produced in Whitehall, New York, by Julio T. Buell. Buell is generally credited with inventing the modern spoon blade, complete with the proper curves to effect a "wobbling" action. Buell's design is virtually unchanged today and is still a deadly lure. In any of several forms it can be found in almost every phase of modern fishing.

Anglers of the Civil War period in America discovered that the spoon could be combined with bait in some areas to improve the catch rate. The added weight of a nightcrawler or porkrind adversely affected the action, though, and around 1865 a tinkerer named William T. J. Lowe achieved angling immortality by inventing the spinner. Lowe's discovery was far more than a mere modification of Buell's spoon. The spinner—on which the blade could rapidly rotate about a fixed shaft—was designed to attract the fish but not to elicit the strike. That important function was assigned to the bait which followed. Buell's spoon, which was directly struck by the fish—and Lowe's attractor spinner to complement a natural bait—were the first halting steps toward the development of the modern arsenal of lures. The lake troll, flasher string, dodger, buzzer-bait, and several generations of bladed spinning lures owe their creation to the principles set forth by those two American experimenters.

The familiar wooden plug first appeared in England in about 1870. For many years British anglers had been dragging wounded to dead minnows through the water, relying on the action and flash to invoke a strike. It was a natural step to devise an artificial lure that would provide the same movement and attractive color to the business end of a fishing line. The first artificial lure in England was probably a plug known as the Caledonian, though others became more popular. The Phantom, the Protean, and the famed Devon Minnow have a long and colorful history in British angling. The Devon in particular proved to be successful and adaptable. It is still used on some waters in Scotland, England, and Wales.

Nobody can be perfectly sure when the bass plug appeared in America, but a cigar-shaped lure whittled by James Heddon in 1896 is generally accepted as our first successful plug. Heddon's lure was quickly adapted by a growing band of bass anglers who—in typical fisherman fashion—immediately changed the shape, size, and color according to their own whims. They eventually found—more by accident than design—many of the attraction principles that are incorporated in today's lures.

Heddon's lure and William Lowe's spinner blade were combined in the early days of this century by West Coast salmon anglers. They began trolling the "cherry bobber" in U.S. and Canadian waters, catching salmon almost as easily as with traditional fresh herring baits.

The artificial lure would not have been developed without the invention of the geared, multiplier reel—from which the lure could be cast and retrieved over considerable distances. Prior to the appearance of the casting reel, lures and spoons had been dragged from a boat on handlines or stiff fixed tackle similar to stubby outriggers. It was the Kentucky reel that allowed shorebound anglers to begin using the newfangled spoons, spinners, and plugs that had added a startling new dimension to common fishing.

The first reels were made almost exclusively in the state of Kentucky by early watchmakers. The very first geared reel is attributed to George Snyder of Paris, Kentucky, around 1805. There was sort of a backward time element in this marriage of lure and reel, owing largely to the fact that the first reels were rare, expensive, and virtually unknown outside of the hills of Appalachia.

The early Kentucky reels were remarkably well designed and built, but were reserved for a few wealthy anglers in the neighborhood. They had yet to be fitted with jeweled bearings and adjustable drags, but they were a profound improvement over the single-action reels of the preceding centuries. The single-action had been around since at least the 13th century, but was little more than a spool on which line could be stored. The multiplier, from which a heavy bait or lure could be cast directly from the reel, was perhaps the most significant change in fishing technique ever developed. It was eventually adapted to every known form of angling.

Snyder's reels were followed by improved models built by other watchmakers in that region. Excellent multipliers, doublers, and quadruplers were produced by Kentuckians Jonathan Meeks and S.L. Sage in the post-Civil War era.

The fishhook was the last piece of the modern tackle puzzle to be fitted in place, and it followed the somewhat reverse development pattern. It had been invented eons before by some unknown aboriginal, but was not adapted to artificial lures until the 1880's—which seemed reasonable enough. There was little need for special hooks until the lure had been around long enough to prove it would last. The mass production of modern steel hooks had begun in England around 1650 when Charles Kirby opened a shop and made hooks for the sport and commercial markets. Kirby's long-shank design was superb and is still widely used by the longline cod fleets around the world. Kirby's hooks are great for bait, but not particularly good for spoons or plugs. By the time Buell and Heddon were producing lures commercially, however, O. Mustad and Sons Company was furnishing a variety of hook designs in Oslo. The Mustads soon became the standard of the lure industry, supplying special hook designs for the new terminal tackle.

In the relatively short period from Snyder's geared reel through Julio T. Buell's polished spoon to James Heddon's modern plug, fishing had moved from a hit-or-miss pastime to a serious technological pursuit. Many observers during that period believed all the newly developed gadgets would simply ruin the sport. The doomsayers, happily, were all wrong. Instead of wrecking the whole experience, the new developments provided us infinitely more water, more species to chase, and virtually an unlimited opportunity for enjoyment. As the world produces more and more people (and more anglers!) it is this proliferation of tackle and technique that has allowed fishing to remain the common man's relaxation. Our technological development has continued unabated, but now we are fine-tuning our instruments instead of discovering altogether new principles. We probably will never see the sort of raw progress that occurred in that illustrious century—at least not in sport fishing. It was surely angling's golden age.

Modern Lures

When you start looking critically at the dazzling array of plugs and lures in a tackle shop or in a mail-order catalog, you'll find they can be reduced to no more than a couple of dozen basic shapes and relatively few sizes. These are the essence of the progress made since the days of Buell and Heddon by an army of experimenters. Despite an intense effort to build a better lure— and attract billions of fishing dollars—the shapes of the basic lures and spinner blades have changed very little since the beginning. It is quite possible to buy a plug this week that is almost exactly the size and shape of Heddon's first effort. The materials and paint have changed radically, but it remains quite the same lure in practical use. Over the years a few grand breakthroughs have occurred, but they have been precious scarce when viewed from the perspective of history.

Every year a number of outrageous departures appear in the tackle catalogs, but after a couple of seasons they drift into deserved obscurity. History remembers only those lures that have proven their ability to catch fish under varying conditions.

Modern development has been the slightest in the general area of plugs— as opposed to other artificials—but every year some manufacturer claims a startling improvement that will revolutionize the sport of fishing. Upon close examination we find the glittering new lure is really only a modification of a proven performer. More often than not, the real changes are in finish and detail. These are quite important facets in fish attraction and may even justify the glowing advertisements. Still, the basic plug collection consists of only a handful of shapes and designs.

Our inventiveness has brought about a greater change in the specialized plugs known as crankbaits, poppers, or surface lures. There are any number of applications for these rigs, though they are not necessarily interchangeable. This group of lures is relatively new in the history of tackle development, and they offer the angler an opportunity to take fish from very difficult waters, places we couldn't have fished with other tackle. There are only a few basic designs in these groups of artificials, but we can probably expect a number of excellent new lures to appear in the decades ahead. It may be true that the discovery of new principles in fishing has already happened, but the refinements and variations continue to occur with predictable regularity.

There has been an interesting digression in the field of spinner lures. In the past few years a number of plug bodies and crankbaits have been enhanced through the use of center-shafted spinners known as "buzzers" or "darts." They consist of a basic plug to which has been added a fore-or-aft attractor blade on a central shaft. They carry names like Buzz Bombs and Delta Darts, but they are really no more than adaptations of the old British spinning harness. They reinforce the contention that little really new is being done in tackle development.

It isn't my intent to belittle this type of lure; in some places and under certain conditions it can be among the most effective of lures for taking bass, trout, and a variety of other fish. I only point out the origin of this device as a means of illustrating the difference between an adaptation and an entirely new idea in angling paraphernalia.

We have noted that the very first artificial was a kind of jig fished through the ice. Modern angling has followed that first principle with literally hundreds of casting jigs on today's market. They range from tiny crappie and coarse-fish pieces to great saltwater jigs weighing 2 pounds or more when fully rigged. The

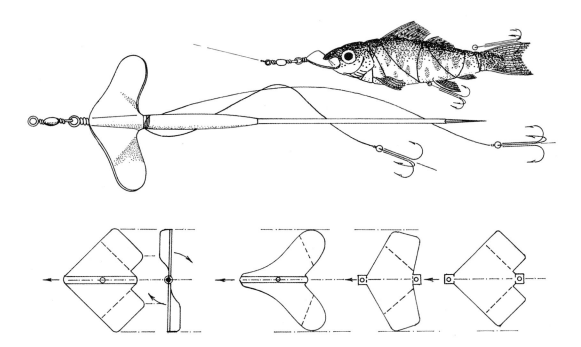

We like to think of modern advances in fishing tackle as being our own. The newest of spinning devices, however, are really only newfangled modifications of earlier inventions. This buzzer blade comes from a British spinning harness, circa 1845.

vary as greatly in appearance as in size, but they remain true to the single original angling concept. The difference in attraction from one to another is the result of modifications for certain species and to accommodate differing techniques for use.

Angling progress in the area of trolled lures has been intense through the past fifty years. We use the trolling technique today in both freshwater and salt for a variety of fish ranging from tiny to the giants of the tropical seas. The lures, actually, are almost exclusively modern modifications of rigs that have been proven in other forms of fishing. The addition of diving planes, internal weights, illumination, and prey-specie triggers such as claws, tails, and fins has improved the lures for specific trolling applications, but the basic lure is still pretty much the way the early experimenters left it.

The Age of Realism

The first modern lures were silver, red, white, or some combination of those colors. They were almost universally painted with a vertical or diagonal separation of color. Most anglers periodically freshened the lures with new paint and some were bold enough to change the color pattern. The manufacturers stayed with the barest of basics, following the cue of Henry Ford, who would sell his Model-T in any color, so long as it was black!

The first lures that were manufactured in other colors didn't vary much from the original effect. Builders might use yellow instead of white, blue in place of red, but they didn't get very creative. Most anglers considered fish totally color blind, so the actual hue didn't seem to matter. A few salmon fishermen distinguished between those lures intended to be seen in the light instead of silhouetted against it, and darkened the underside of those plugs that were fished shallow—above the fish. It was just another tiny step in the historical development of the artificial lure, but today nearly all plug manufacturers design their color schemes from the viewpoint of the fish. A lot of lures, of course, are designed to catch fishermen instead of fish—but we'll dispense with those as we move forward into making our own lures.

chapter
· TWO ·

THE SCIENCE OF FISH ATTRACTION

For a fishing lure to accomplish its intended purpose, it must perform two critical functions. Assuming it is mechanically capable of being trolled or cast through water in which fish are present, it must first attract the attention of any fish that are nearby and then cause them to strike at it. In the simplest of terms, those are the only things a lure can be expected to do. If it does, the ultimate result will be reduced to a conflict between the skill and equipment of the angler and the strength and spirit of the fish. I choose to think of the conflict—rather than the outcome—as the culminating step in an experience that began with the design and choice of a lure.

The ability of a lure to catch a fish's attention, through whatever means it may employ, is known as fish attraction. It has long been the subject of both scientific and practical study, and at least a few proven principles lie among the clouds of conjecture that surround the question.

The characteristic of a lure that causes a fish to strike is called the response trigger. Any of several factors may be involved in stirring the instinct to bite, and this subject has been perhaps more deeply studied than any other element in the science of fishing with artificial lures.

Lures fall into three broad classes in their design and construction. The first of these is a group of lures considered "realistic" in appearance and conformity, designed and built to closely approximate the natural forage or prey item of the fish being sought. The second class is the "impressionistic" lure. It uses design factors that are not at all realistic, yet cause fish to consider it prey. The third—and most important to the amateur luremaker—is the "representative" lure, which may employ features of both the other lure classes. An effective lure may be any of these three, but it must possess the twin attributes of fish attraction and response trigger to produce the strike reaction from a fish.

In recent years the development of the realistic lure has entered an era of almost impossible perfection. Manufacturers have used new materials and highly technical processes that very accurately duplicate the look, texture, and color of actual food sources for target gamefish. The search for the ultimate lure continues; lure manufacturers are experimenting with newer materials, processes, and even chemical impregnants that will make the lure taste and smell just like real food. One cannot help but wonder if it wouldn't be easier to just use a real worm!

Despite these advancements in lure technology, even the most casual observer will note that many skilled anglers in almost every fishing field use representative lures more than any other kind—and with great success. The blaring advertisements notwithstanding, the present realistic lures really aren't any more effective than

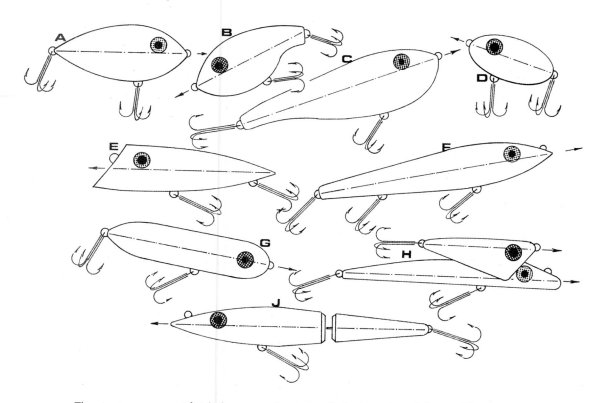

The most common artificial plugs come in a rather limited number of shapes. These are: (A) Shad, (B) Minnie, (C) Scat, (D) Torpo, (E) Piker, (F) Magnum or Winchester, (G) Heddon or Nugget, (H) Triangle, (J) Jointed. There are dozens of variations of each.

the representative and impressionistic models that have been the backbone of artificial angling since Julio Buell began startling fish with his newfangled spoon more than a century ago.

There is little doubt that the first artificial lures were meant to approximate food elements that were difficult to find or use. The first flies, for example, were tied to look like the bugs that fish ate. They weren't perfectly realistic, but they resembled the actual insect or nymph in size, shape, and color. The early fly technicians had stumbled onto the first secrets of fish attraction.

Pioneer lure-makers took a cue from the flyfishers and set out to duplicate —as much as was practical—the basic elements of the preferred food of their target fish. It was unquestionably more difficult to build something that looked like a minnow than to reproduce a lifelike mosquito, so a few of the early experimenters incorporated impressionistic features into their designs that produced an instinctive strike reaction. It's unlikely that the use of correct impression elements occurred by accident or coincidence. I think the anonymous developer of the Devon Minnow and America's James Heddon had some essential understanding of their quarry when they whittled their first wooden lures.

An understanding of the fish was helpful to the early success of the angler using artificials and it is no less important to the fisherman or amateur lure builder today. It is from this basic knowledge of the gamefish that we begin to appreciate the elements of fish attraction that must be incorporated into the lure.

Fish Attraction

Fish attraction is simply the characteristic of a lure to appeal to one of several instinctive senses of the fish. In the most general of terms, the lure must cause a reaction through physical stimulation. It may be the color, shape, movement, scent, sound, or even the taste of the lure that attracts a fish. Most often it is a combination of these factors that creates the desired response. Once attracted, the lure must then produce a more primal response in the fish to cause it to strike. For the time being, we'll concentrate on the first element of a successful lure—attraction.

To fully understand the science of fish attraction, we must first know something of the fish. And the first thing we have to realize is that the fish is purely a creature of dictatorial instinct. While there are some differences in cerebral ability in various species, even the brightest of fish is incapable of independent thought. Compared with even the slowest-witted of land vertebrates, the fish is as stupid as a stick. Nature has compensated for this utter stupidity by providing especially keen instincts and well-defined instinctive responses. It's a fact we can use!

The forebrain of all vertebrates can be divided into three essential parts; the forebrain (olfactory lobes and cerebral hemispheres), the midbrain including the optic lobes, and a hindbrain—the cerebellum and medulla oblongata. Up in the forebrain we find the great distinction between the fishes and other animals. In most fishes the forebrain is almost entirely concerned with olfactory functions. The most primitive of logical or rational thought appears to be missing—or at least non-functional—in the world of fishes. The signals we send through our lures, then, must appeal exclusively to the physical senses of our target.

Almost all lure designers agree that the most effective attraction elements are visual. Consequently, a great deal of experimentation has been done with color, color combinations, reflective and refractive components, contrast enhancement, shape, and size. These are all visual factors that can add or detract from the effectiveness of a lure.

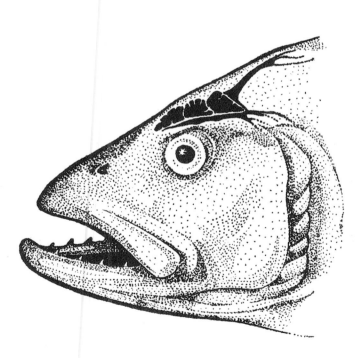

By comparison to even the stupidest of land mammals, the fish hasn't a lot of brainpower. Instead, it's driven by pure instinct—a factor in favor of the knowledgeable luremaker.

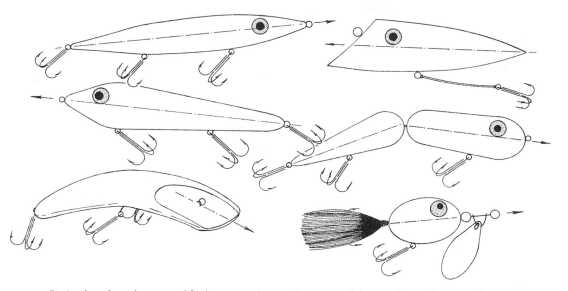

Basic plugs have been modified to meet the requirements of the trophy angler. Large lures are designed to attract the biggest fish.

The dominance of visual elements in a lure stems from the fish's eye, which differs substantially from that of terrestrial animals. We must consider the rather unique vision capabilities of the fish when designing or choosing a lure. The most striking feature of the eye is that the lens is round, rather than flattened like the human eye. In practical terms, this means that the fish has a wider field of vision, can see very clearly for certain distances, and can use the reflective undersurface of the water as a visual backup to direct vision. Some research indicates that this unusual ability allows the fish to see all the way around a shallow-swimming lure. In effect, he can simultaneously see the top, sides, bottom, head, and tail of his prey. He gets a very good look at our lure in a very short time, a factor we have to consider when we make or choose a lure.

The most important difference in vision to the angler is the fixed-focus aspect of a fish's eye. While most mammals are able to adjust the retina to allow a clear view of either nearby or distant objects, the fish has a limited depth of field in which he can see distinctly. The range of vision varies with species and can generally be judged by the habitat in which the fish functions best. Most fishes that are found in rivers, small lakes, and other bodies with strict size limitations have relatively short-range vision. Pelagic ocean fishes and sharks, on the other hand, are decidedly far-sighted.

The fixed-focus characteristic of a fish's vision increases our need for very deliberate attraction devices, but provides us an important advantage in the area of "triggers" which we will discuss in detail a bit later.

In behavioral terms, the extraordinary vision of fish—at least some fish—means that the size of the lure is critical in certain circumstances. Almost every fly fisherman has had the experience of a dramatic turnaround by simply changing the size of a particular pattern. A size 10 nymph may prove fruitless on a certain day, but a number 14 of an identical pattern and color may draw a strike on nearly every cast. Exactly the same visual discrimination applies to artificial lures…and explains why many experienced anglers carry several sizes of the same basic lure in their tacklebox.

The color of a lure is second in importance only to size in effectiveness, but the question of color is one to which there are no hard-and-fast answers. Only a few years ago it was generally accepted that all fish were color-blind. A few biologists still hold that line, but most behavioral scientists agree that many species have at least some color recognition and respond differently when subjected to different colors of lights, food, and backgrounds. Another group believes that fish don't see color the same way that land animals do, but rather measure the contrast values and react accordingly. Perhaps someday we will hook a computer to a fish's eye and see precisely what he sees, but for the time being we must consider the purely practical aspects of what works and what doesn't.

The olfactory senses of fish have been specifically determined and measured—and they are remarkable. Fish use their sense of smell much the same way other animals do, by recognizing chemicals that touch special nerve receptacles in the olfactory system. In the medium of water, though, the chemicals tend to be less erratic and more concentrated. That means the fish can distinguish almost infinite changes in the chemical composition of the water, "smelling" the tiniest of changes. The portion of a fish's brain that decodes these chemical signals is very well developed in many species. The Pacific salmon, for example, depend for their homing direction on the precise chemical composition of the water in their ancestral rivers. Even from distances of several thousand miles away, the salmon literally "smells" his way home. Large-scale tests at the University of Washington have conclusively proven that Coho salmon, artificially imprinted with the chemical matrix of a river other than that in which they were hatched, will unerringly return to the "new" river. Northern pike, on the other hand, have almost no sense of smell at all. They will ignore food hidden in laboratory tanks, even though they've been deprived of food for long periods of time.

At this stage of lure development we are not so concerned with making a lure smell attractive as the reverse. With the acute olfactory sense that most gamefish possess, the angler must be careful not to negate the attraction value of his lure by putting a foreign or "warning" scent on it. A fisherman who allows his minnow or nightcrawler to drag through old fuel and other chemicals in the bottom of his boat is reducing the effectiveness of that bait. There have been several commercially successful scent compounds sold to anglers over the years, and there is little doubt they are of value in increasing the action. Some camouflage distasteful scents; others are designed to attract fish. Whichever principle they employ, they can add substantially to the effect of the lure.

The matter of taste is probably one of the minimal factors in the design of a lure, but it may become more important in some of the super-lures that we are approaching in our technological approach to fishing. The taste organs of most fish are fairly well developed and many species have evolved a list of preferred foods that is probably based—at least partly—on flavor. We aren't likely to develop a lure that tastes like a herring, but knowing the herring is the preferred food of some saltwater species gives us an edge in developing effective lures. Taste is definitely not a factor that the amateur lure-builder has to consider, but taste preferences have led to some behavioral characteristics of fish that we will have to think about.

For many fish, the sound of a lure can definitely be a designed element of attraction. Most fish have reasonably well-developed ears located on either side of the head. Tests indicate fish hear quite well in the range of 100–10,000 cycles per second. A few species have a sound-link between their ears and their swim bladders, allowing the large organ to act as sort of a biological hydrophone. As you might expect, these fish are especially sensitive to sounds in the water. At least a few lures are on the market that capitalize on sound as one of their attraction features, in chorus with other attraction elements. So far, no designer has produced a lure that uses sound exclusively for attraction, although some shark researchers are able to call sharks to a test area with suspended hydrophonic devices. Some lures use sound as an additional means of attracting fish and many others accidentally incorporate a sonic factor that draws attention to itself.

The final area of sense attraction that we'll discuss is that of action and movement. The motion of a lure in water is a visual component, of course, but the motion also sets up short pressure waves in the water that many anglers fail to appreciate. These waves are felt by a unique set of receptors along the lateral line, under the fish's skin. It is an extension of the fish's sense of touch.

Most fish have very critical free-nerve endings in several parts of their bodies that allow them to be aware of infinitely small touch messages. Nearly all species have these highly discriminatory touch receptors along their lateral line, allowing them to feel very slight changes in water pressure. In laboratory tests, surgically blinded fish are able to discern the presence of other fishes nearby through these tiny pressure sensors. If a lure produces waves at the same frequency as a prey species or a fish in distress, predators may be attracted initially by their sense of touch. It is then the function of the lure to present other attraction elements and the final response trigger to cause a strike.

The fish is not the smartest of creatures, but the advantage to the angler is that he will respond dependably to certain physiological stimuli according to a rigid set of instincts. As a user of artificial lures, the angler is put upon to know the instinctive responses of his quarry, make certain judgements about the conditions under which he fishes, and then choose a lure that most correctly balances the formula. The conclusions surrounding water, temperature, and surface weather are variables best learned from experience...but even the newest of novices can make an educated guess as to the lure if he understands the principles of fish attraction.

Let's put these principles into practice by considering the means by which our lure can accomplish a high level of attraction. While the home lure-designer will exhibit an understandable interest in using the attraction principles in building a lure, these factors are equally important to the angler about to plunk down his hard-earned cash for a factory-made bit of terminal tackle.

Visual Attraction

Visual attraction is the most important, reliable, and demonstrable component of the artificial lure. For the most part, visual attraction is a complex combination of size, shape, color, action, and reflective or refractive elements. Many lures use only one or two of these to their best advantage. Some use most of these and are often more effective. We must remember that there are times when the visual aspects of the lure have been overdone and it is too active for good response. Many of the lures that have been successful for generations have achieved an exceptional balance of visual components—and no amount of tinkering has improved them at all.

The amateur luremaker is limited to impressionistic or representative visual effects in his lure by purely practical constraints. The ultrarealistic models in the marketplace require very expensive equipment and techniques to produce—factors quite unsuited to one-of-a-kind backporch lure production. Almost any amateur lure enthusiast, however, can make superb lures in other styles. Just as the impressionist painter uses recognizable key elements in a scene to paint his picture, the luremaker takes the essential components of size, shape, color, and

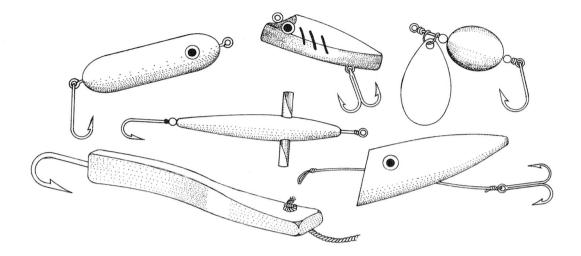

From these humble beginnings have sprung the vast array of modern plugs. These six plugs are the first known patterns. They include, clockwise from upper left; Heddon's Cigar, Heddon's River Runt, the famous Cherry Bobber, the J-Plug or squid-plug, and the Tin Squid. At center is the British Devon Minnow.

contrast to build his impression. It might be best to illustrate this premise by designing a saltwater lure to represent a shrimp or prawn.

Obviously, the actual shape of the animal is too complex for a very exact reproduction of the body. But we can make a fairly decent likeness of the characteristic head and can rather easily duplicate the overall shape of the shrimp. The several paired legs and swimming flukes are much too intricate to duplicate exactly, but we can represent them with plastic wands on either side and some painted slashes to fill in the impression. The addition of a tail fluke completes the effect; the addition of paint and hooks completes the lure. Except for the paint scheme, the first of our examples is nearly a realistic lure —but the other examples show how representative and impressionistic treatments can produce very useful, workable lures. By the way, in open water tests, the second model—the representative lure—proved to be the most effective.

The science of designed attraction is—as you might expect—terribly involved. It seems practical to limit our investigation of attraction elements to those lures the home craftsman is likely to make for himself. Certainly the modern, highly-detailed lures are effective, but in almost every circumstance the representative

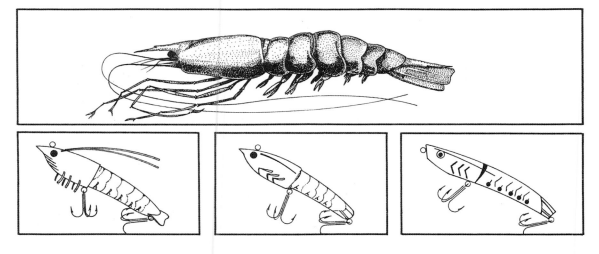

There are three essential ways to build a lure that approximates a food source, in this case, a crayfish. From left: realistic, representative, and impressionistic. All have definite applications in lure design.

lures are just as good. Many anglers get an extra surge of satisfaction from taking fish on a well-designed and carefully made impressions. I rather tend to think that we might as well be using a real minnow as an imitation that even its mother wouldn't know from the real thing!

If the home crafter is an accomplished artist, he might painstakingly produce a highly realistic presentation of a natural prey animal. I suspect the effort would take many hours and the artist would understandably be reluctant to subject his creation to the loss or damage of actually fishing with it. A set of huge teethmarks might be a grand badge of honor, but it probably still wouldn't be worth the risk. From a practical standpoint we are all more likely to build and use somewhat simpler attractors.

Color Attraction

A lot has been said and written about the role of color in attracting fish, but the truth is we don't yet know everything about this complex subject. Whether a lure is realistic, representative, or impressionistic, it must be finished in a combination of colors that will attract fish. There is a lot of evidence to suggest that the actual colors are less important than the contrast between those colors and the pattern in which they are applied. In actual field tests a common red-and-white plug was fished alongside a green-and-pale yellow lure of identical design. The catch rate was about the same, and when the two were photographed in black-and-white there was really very little difference between them.

We can achieve the proper contrast in a lure by learning to use color combinations that produce definite contrast patterns when applied. It doesn't matter whether the lure is realistic, representative, or an impression—as long as the proper contrast appears in the patter. In this example, we have painted a "frog" finish and a "perch" finish in all three styles. It is easy to see that we have enhanced the contrast on all of them in the same way. In practice, all three lures work about the same.

Nobody has given us a chart that will provide guidelines for choosing lure colors, but we will deal with the subject extensively in Chapter 5. One of the best

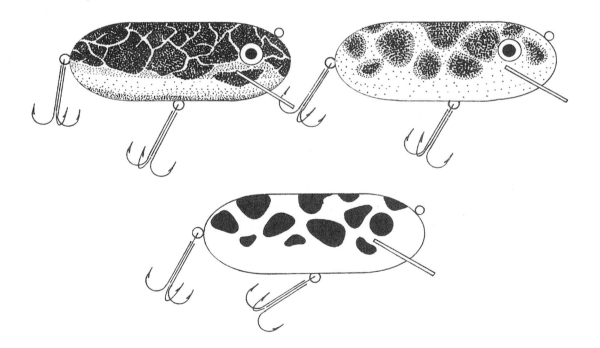

The principles of design include finishes very like the shape options available to the designer. From upper left: a realistic frogskin, a representative frogskin, and (bottom) an impressionistic frogskin.

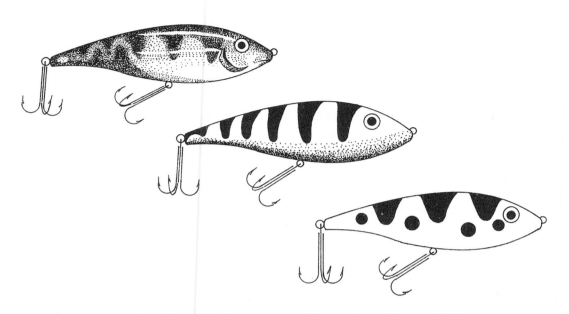

Using the principles of design finish we can create (from top) a realistic perch finish, a representative perch finish, and an impression of the perch. Each style can be accomplished by the amateur luremaker.

guides is to look in your own tacklebox at those lures that have been especially faithful over the years. You'll note that most of them have a good contrast differential and the color separations are obvious.

The tackle manufacturers have spent a lot of time and effort developing their color schemes, so their catalogs are a good place to learn about the use of color and contrast enhancement in luremaking. Pay particular attention to bass plugs, on which the contrast factor is especially important. Bass are among those fish with low color discrimination, so the patterns on bass lures are more stark and pronounced.

Color and contrast are major facets of the artificial lure, a subject that could fill a substantial volume by itself. We must comprehend the basics of color and contrast if we are building or buying really effective lures, but it isn't necessary that we become fully expert on the subject. In the finish and construction portions of this book we will deal in a practical way with the color selections for a particular lure and describe the best ways to accomplish the needed impression.

The attraction elements we've discussed so far—size, color, and contrast—are visual components that are physically a part of the lure. There are other visual aspects of the lure that are more behavioral in nature. They use physical components in their production but are aimed at specific behavioral patterns in the fish.

It is technically correct, of course, to say that all attraction components of a lure are behavioral, since the fish have no ability to make decisions about what they see. It is important to differentiate between those features that represent a food or prey source and those that elicit a purely behavioral response, triggering some primordial action.

Reflection and Refraction

Closely associated with the value of color in making a lure attractive is the use of reflection and refraction in the construction of an artificial. As we know, the fish is not able to see very clearly at a distance—at least most can't —so we use reflected rays of bright light to attract their attention through the water. The use of bright reflectors is especially important when fishing large bodies of water or in water discolored by silt, algae, or chemical impurities.

There are two ways to increase the attractive ability of a lure through reflection. We may incorporate a very light color or a reflective surface on the lure itself, or we may use a separate reflective attractor in conjunction with it. Lake trollers often drag a string of polished spinner blades ahead of the lure. In theory, the fish is attracted by the flashing lights, swims closer to investigate, and finally snaps at the trailing lure or bait. The importance of the "outside" attractor to lake and saltchuck fishermen cannot be overemphasized, but too few of us give the trolling string the attention it deserves.

Several field tests in a group of Canadian lakes indicate that success rates can be varied dramatically by choosing the proper troll for the existing conditions. Generally speaking, large lakes require large blades spaced far apart while smaller waters are best fished with small blades and relatively close spacing. This choice actually falls into the category of technique, but since it affects the attractive value of the outfit we will discuss blade combinations in detail.

It is the reflected light of the blades that does the job, and we can—either in design or in practice—put reflectors in place that will give us the maximum attraction.

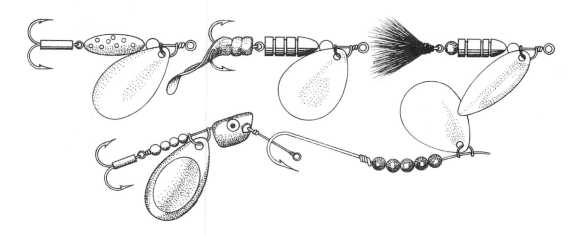

Weighted spinners, spinning jigs, and walleye worm rigs are just a few of the hundreds of spinning lures available. Spinner blades are also used for other kinds of artificials.

Our first consideration is the individual blade itself. Chrome or nickel blades reflect the most light and should be used in low light conditions. Brass blades reflect less than nickel, and copper blades have the lowest reflective ability of all. (Painted blades, by the way, have no reflective light value and are dealt with in Chapter 5.)

The second blade design factor is the shape, which determines at what angle the blade will spin. The more vertical the spin path, the brighter the reflection, but the narrower the attraction zone will be. We can see from the accompanying sketches that there is a difference in the patterns given by two different configurations.

I put together a lake troll string that combined what I believe to be the optimum balance of reflection and pattern, and I use it almost exclusively when fishing for lake trout, rainbow, or Kamloops in the northern and western lakes. I simply change from nickel to brass if the sun gets bright. The outfit seems to work better than any other combination I've ever used. No manufacturer that I know of makes this particular troll pattern, but you can easily make your own from factory-supplied components. We have devoted the final chapter of this book to using ready-made parts.

The reflective element of the lure, especially those designed for cast-and-retrieve angling, may be provided as a reflective surface painted on the lure or they may be added in the form of a spinner blade, buzzer, diving plane, or a trailed element. The invention of prismatic plastic reflecting tape has greatly enhanced our ability to put this attraction element right on the lure. The refractive value of certain patterns is especially important when fishing those waters in which visibility is a problem. When refraction occurs the light is broken into different wavelengths. Some of the refracted waves are not visible to the human eye but may be visible to fish—and that's what counts. At least a few lures can be produced that have cut-glass prisms (usually made from old costume jewelry) that will break the light into colors and sharp rays. A more common use of this refraction principle is on lures and spinners painted with everyday fluorescent paint. The very bright fluorescent paints were developed in World War II and soon became a regular part of the fishing arsenal. In technical terms, this fluorescent paint uses two or more parts of the visible-light spectrum simultaneously. The human eye can see the fluorescent quality of the color, but when photographed it cannot

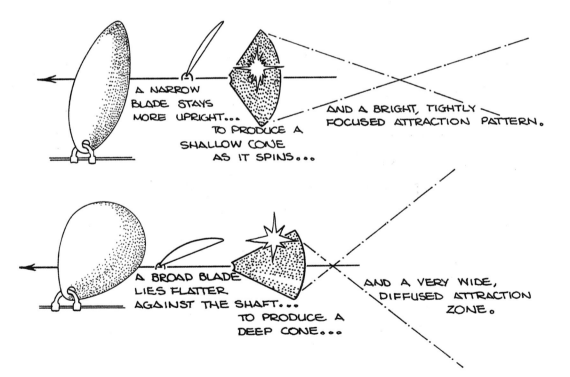

A NARROW BLADE STAYS MORE UPRIGHT... TO PRODUCE A SHALLOW CONE AS IT SPINS... AND A BRIGHT, TIGHTLY FOCUSED ATTRACTION PATTERN.

A BROAD BLADE LIES FLATTER AGAINST THE SHAFT... TO PRODUCE A DEEP CONE... AND A VERY WIDE, DIFFUSED ATTRACTION ZONE.

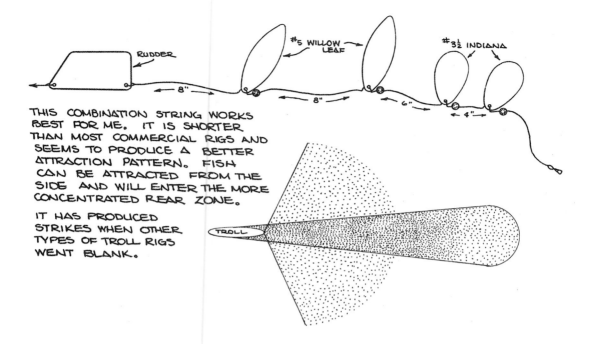

RUDDER

#5 WILLOW LEAF

#3½ INDIANA

← 8" →   ← 8" →   ← 6" →   ← 4" →

THIS COMBINATION STRING WORKS BEST FOR ME. IT IS SHORTER THAN MOST COMMERCIAL RIGS AND SEEMS TO PRODUCE A BETTER ATTRACTION PATTERN. FISH CAN BE ATTRACTED FROM THE SIDE AND WILL ENTER THE MORE CONCENTRATED REAR ZONE.

IT HAS PRODUCED STRIKES WHEN OTHER TYPES OF TROLL RIGS WENT BLANK.

TROLL

be distinguished from a similar, plain color. The color enhancement provided by this paint is outside the visible portion of the spectrum and can't really be photographed. Without getting any more technical, suffice it to say that the color will transmit better through muddy or murky water than a plain color—and so it attracts more fish. Whether the fish can actually see the fluorescence is less important to us than the fact it responds to the lure despite reduced visibility.

Motion Attraction

Motion, or action, is probably the least understood factor in the attraction value of an artificial lure. While scientists can measure the response of fish to lateral-line nerve stimuli, we aren't quite sure what frequency of motion stimulates the strike response. Certainly some lures use their action to great advantage in generating wave impulses in the water, but many are only effective when they are working properly. In recent years many anglers have discovered that the high-frequency wave generated by spinner-bar lures is more important than the flash of the spinner blade. Some manufacturers are producing very effective lures with nonreflective, flat-black finished blades, relying solely on the wave-generation of the action to attract fish. In some fishing situations, particularly when fishing low, clear trout streams, these nonreflective lures are clearly superior to reflective ones. At least a few designers believe that wave-generating motion is the only valuable effect of many spinning lures.

In the past quarter-century a number of outstanding plugs have been developed that use rhythmic, pulsating movements to generate pressure waves that are immensely powerful attractors. One spectacular example of this genre is the Luhr Jensen Hot Shot, a small wobbling lure that has changed the face of river drifting for steelhead. In appearance the Hot Shot differs very little from many similar lures. On a steelhead drift, however, the distinction is readily apparent. The plug is held against the current enough to promote the action. The lure generates a series of waves that can be felt across and downstream from the terminal for quite a distance. The waves will even flow upstream, even in riffle current. Apparently the steelhead can compensate for the "Doppler effect" of the current, as many blind strikes have been recorded from both up- and downstream. The Hot Shot is widely used by river guides throughout the Northwest, enabling many novice steelhead anglers to enjoy success in a very demanding fishing situation.

The typical wobbler spoon also generates waves that affect the lateral-line sensors of gamefish, but the effect varies widely from spoon to spoon. You can generally judge the value of a particular spoon by asking the tackle shop manager

The Luhr-Jensen Hotshot.

about sales. One cannot be certain how much of their success is derived from the wave-generation principle, but many spoons utilize the supersonic factor much more than most anglers realize. Production records from the maker of an especially effective salmon spoon indicate that demand for nickel, brass, red-and-nickel, and orange-and-brass finishes is about equal. That would lead us to believe that the wave-generation characteristic of the spoon is more important than the color or reflective value.

We cannot limit our investigation of motion and action to short pulsations designed to produce sensor waves. Another form of movement that can be incorporated into the lure is of at least as much value, but is decidedly different. A great many excellent lures owe their success to an ability to dive deeply without external weights or to remain on the surface over a wide range of towing speeds.

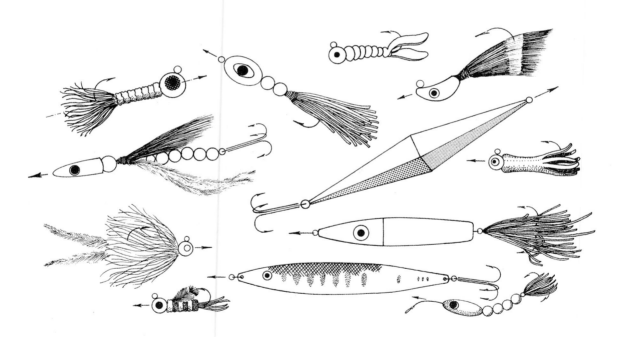

These dozen jigs represents only a fraction of the number of weighted lures used in modern angling. There are more than a thousand different brands, styles, and shapes on today's angling market!

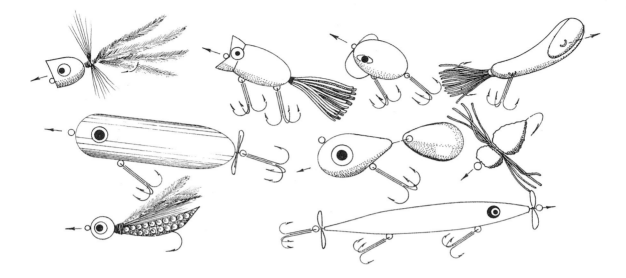

Surface lures are designed for a limited fishing application for only a few species. Some kinds of surface lures are available for almost all angling techniques.

Known as "divers," the deepwater lures include a diving plane as a part of their construction. "Popper" lures, used almost exclusively for bass, will remain at the surface during high-speed retrieves or when trolled.

Both types of lure use an angled plane and a specific towing point to produce a mathematical vector. The resultant angle of force determines the path the lure will follow. Relocating either the towing point or the diving plane will change the angle at which the lure swims. Many lures provide alternate positions for attaching the line so the angler can select either a deeper or shallower retrieve path.

The popper uses the same principle in reverse. The tow-point is below the uptilted plane to make the lure swim always upward. It cannot rise above the water surface, of course, but it stays right at the surface regardless of speed. The popper is hydrodynamically unsound, so it swims an erratic path, producing a lot of noise and bubbles as it moves. This surface agitation may be a very important aspect of attraction for some species—and it often triggers an instant strike from largemouth bass.

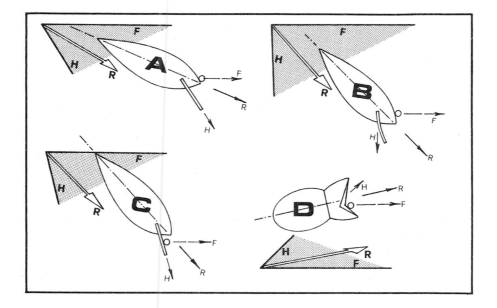

The dive angle of a lure can be changed by adjusting the point at which the lure is attached to the line, altering the size or shape of the affixed diving plane, or by using a cupped surface. The lure will dive according to a mathematical vector. In these illustrations, F equals the pulling force exerted on the line, H equals the hydrodynamic force exerted by water against the planing surface, and R equals the resulting direction of movement. The Popper, D, actually tries to climb out of the water.

Sonic Attraction

There have been a number of lures over the years that claimed the use of hydrosound as either a primary or secondary element of attraction. A few included wind-up buzzers, tiny wires stretched across holes in the lure, and even battery-operated sound generators. This horde of gimmicks is usually advertised on late-night TV as the "fishing discovery of a lifetime" or some other such nonsense. Some of these lures are among the most preposterous devices ever invented and have mercifully short lives. They were almost always touted to "drive fish crazy." They stood a better chance of driving the angler crazy!

There is no doubt that sound is an element of fish behavior, but it is a segment of our science about which we know precious little. The addition of a sonic component to a lure is risky business at best.

Pathological measurements tell us that fish can hear quite clearly in the range of 100 to 10,000 cycles per second. Some fish have a better hearing apparatus than others, but we can accept the general fact that most have quite respectable hearing senses. Unfortunately, we aren't able to use that hearing very well in designing lures.

Sonic experimentation is difficult for two basic reasons. First, tank-bound fish tend to exhibit behavior patterns that are quite different from those of their wild brethren. Open-water sonic tests are difficult to measure and very expensive to conduct. In point of fact, we as sport anglers have little reason to expend the time and money necessary for thorough tests on the effect of sound on fish. The lure designer, therefore, faces a real obstacle when attempting to incorporate sound in his lure. Lacking hard data, he might as easily generate a sound that repels fish as one that attracts them. As previously noted, it's a risky business!

There is also an environmental factor that deters the efficient use of low-level sound in our lures—the 20th-century phenomenon of induced noise. In many waters the generation of extraneous noise has reached critical proportions for many species, and it certainly reduces our chances of using specific sounds to attract fish. The level of man-made sounds in the world's oceans has reached intolerable extremes. The great blue whale, for example, is in danger of extinction primarily because individuals cannot hear one another in mating season. In decades past, naturalists estimated the distance at which one blue whale could call another at 2,000 miles. Today the sounds of ocean vessels, shoreside industry, low-level rumbles from jet aircraft and thousands of other sounds have virtually doomed some sea animals and fishes.

The greatest obstacle to sonic attraction for you and me is probably the outboard motor. While it has improved our fishing opportunities enormously, it has added a degree of sound that effectively cancels most purely sonic attraction devices. I would hate to rely on sonic attraction for my fishing in competition with a gaggle of water-skiers.

There is good evidence that sounds bordering the lower range of a fish's hearing—about 100 cycles per second—have a positive effect from short ranges. Some lures include this attraction element by design, most by accident. The sound is generated by the rapid vibration of a wobbling lure or the lopsided whirring of a spinner blade. There is even some recent evidence that the lake troller's string of flashers is generating a composite signal that could equal the reflection of the blades in attraction value.

At least one series of lures has purposely included this short-range attraction element in their design. The inventor unquestionably understood the value of low-frequency pressure waves and sound in attracting fish and designed a spinner

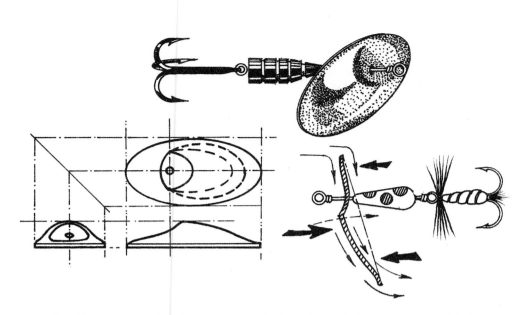

Panther Martin spinning lure. The dark arrows indicate hydraulic force around the airfoil blade, the result of accelerated currents (light arrows) along the blade surface. An enormous sonic effect results.

blade that operates in the near-100 cps range. Known as the Panther Martin blade, it is really a revolutionary concept.

The blade has both convex and concave curves to balance the pressure gradients, as well as some rather sharp lateral curves to act as a self-governor. The inventor moved the axis to the inside of the blade, thus shortening the swing radius and increasing the frequency of the sound waves produced.

The technical aspect of the lure is probably less important to us as amateur luremakers than the fact that it works very well, and we can learn to use low-frequency waves in lures we make for ourselves. For the time being, most of us will continue to rely heavily on visual aspects of the lures. A few knowledgeable experimenters may try to add sonic components to their lures. That is the history of lure development, and I hope it never changes!

Hooks

A necessary visual component of most lures is the hook. Whether it trails the lure or is built as an integral part of it, the hook will most likely be visible to the fish. The majority of fishermen consider the hook a detracting part of the lure and therefore tend to choose lures that have skirts, feathers, and other means of camouflage. That would be an understandable notion if the fish were a rational thinker—but it isn't! It cannot recognize a hook as something meant to catch it. It's just a shiny part of a curious form moving through the water…and bare-hooked lures are every bit as effective as skirted lures in some situations.

Our preoccupation with hiding the hook—almost a fetish with some anglers—probably comes from stillfishing with natural baits in calm water. In that context a hook can be a definite handicap to success. It's not because the fish understands the purpose of it, but the exposed hook can make the food look abnormal and

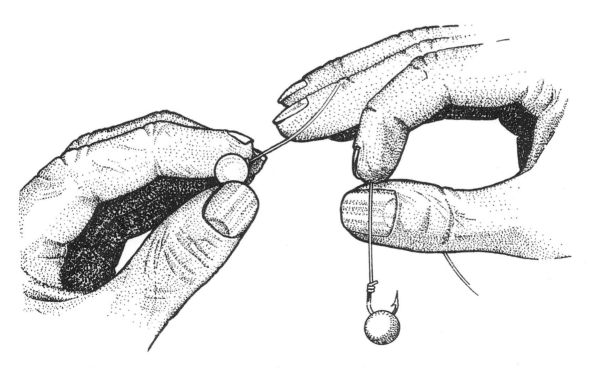

A rolled egg is at left, a hooked egg at right.

therefore probably not good to eat. In a series of field experiments conducted over two years in a swift-flowing stream, we found that trailed salmon eggs produced as many strikes as those into which the hook had been neatly rolled. The catch rate on trailed eggs was considerably lower, since many of the strikes were aimed precisely at the body of the egg. The prudent fisherman would, based on these tests, roll the hook into the eggs in traditional fashion to prevent a lot of near misses, but the tests proved the hook was not a deterrent to the strike.

The addition of a skirt, feather, or bucktail to a hook is a means of providing another attraction component to the lure. The skirt, especially on weighted jigs, provides a degree of movement and impressionistic shape that just can't be achieved in any other way. It gives the lure a secondary axis, a means of appearing to swim, like a jointed plug.

When you are building or buying a lure, think of the trailing element in this way, rather than as a device to hide the hook. If the skirt is a well-founded element of attraction it should be retained as part of the lure. If it tends to make the lure too large or contradicts the attraction scheme, you'll be better off trailing an exposed hook.

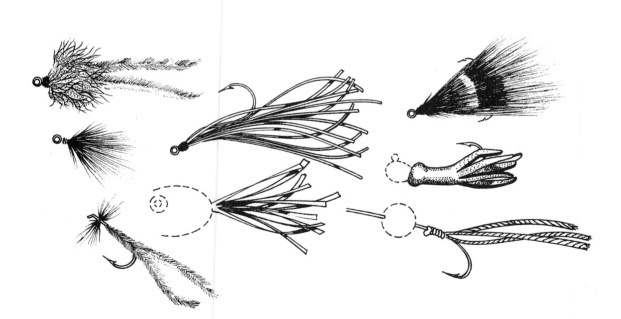

Skirts of all sorts are added to lures as either an attraction element or a device to alter the action of the lure in the water.

Response Triggers

This is the real meat of lure making, the single part of the science that separates the good lures from the near misses. A response trigger is that characteristic of a lure that makes a fish strike after being attracted. There are a lot of lures that have excellent attraction qualities but just don't catch very many fish. The reason is that the lure simply doesn't have a sufficient response trigger to cause the fish to attack.

In a few cases the trigger is a question of action, rather than a component built into the lure. In the salmon technique known as "mooching," for example, it is standard practice to strip off a few feet of line immediately following a strike at the bait. Coho salmon are notorious for first "slapping" their prey with tail or snout to disable it, then circling to pick up the fluttering herring on the next pass. The accomplished moocher can recognize the initial slap, and his quick stripping of line allows the bait to flutter helplessly downward a yard or so. It is this movement that triggers the strike response in the Coho. Unfortunately, few fish are so obliging as to give us advance warning of a strike. We have to make sure our presentation will trigger their instincts in the first place. We use what little we understand of the physical trigger elements to elicit a solid strike on the first pass by a predatory fish.

Eyespots

If we know very little of the subject of response triggers in general, there is one trigger we know very well. It is the use of "eyespots," the more-or-less impressionistic representation of the eyes of prey species. The eye is the most easily discerned physical feature of small fish and is the primary target of an attacking predator. The eye plays a part in all predator-prey relationships, aquarian or otherwise. Interestingly enough, humans refer to the center of a target as a "bull's eye."

The eyes are, in fact, the predator-prey response trigger throughout the animal world. Responses of the eye, eye contact, and avoidance of eye contact are behavioral traits in all animals—including humans—that help establish the social order and allow some animals to maintain dominance over their peers. In the case of prey fish, extreme dilation of the eye occurs in the last moments before attack. The predator appears to experience pupil contraction at the same instant. These are physiological responses, of course, but are important signals between individuals at the time of confrontation.

We, as amateur luremakers, can learn from the tests of hundreds of fish researchers who have determined quite precisely the role the eye plays in the predator-prey relationship. The eyes seem to be the single most important physical facet of the whole scenario. This is true of all game fish in either fresh or salt water.

Eyespots are important trigger components of plugs and other lures. The eye can be represented in a variety of ways.

The notable exception is among the sharks, whose eyes cannot dilate very much, and who cannot see their prey at the instant of attack. The unique position of their mouth has required them to evolve a number of specialized organs for killing, but the eyes are not a part of their scheme. In virtually all other fish, though, it is the key—and an element we can use effectively in lure design.

Nearly all behavioral tests of predator fish indicate that the eye not only triggers the strike, but dictates the speed and direction of the final attack. The predator apparently anticipates the flight path of the prey from the position of the eye relative to the axis of the body and gauges the instant of flight from the dilation pattern of the eye. In short, the eye is the key response trigger in the relationship, one that lure builders have capitalized upon in the search for efficient lures.

Several luremakers have designed plastic-prism reflective eyes that appear to change size as they are approached. The perfect eye has not yet been developed for artificial lures, but it seems inevitable that an eye will eventually come along that will appear to dilate at a specific proximation range, almost surely triggering a strike response. It will be an interesting lure to use!

The actual production of eyespots on a lure or jig may be accomplished with paint, separately built eyes, or any number of adhesive materials. We will deal with this phase of luremaking in detail in the appropriate sections of the book.

Trigger Tags

Since it is really quite impossible to incorporate features in the lure that actually change when a fish approaches, we do the next best thing: We use his unique vision and our knowledge of his behavior to produce lure components that appear to change when a fish approaches, at least from his point of view.

These trigger elements are soundly based in fish behavior and can be an effective addition to the lure. They are, simply enough, small "tags" that are added to the trailing hook or the body of the lure. They provide motion— at a different frequency than the lure itself—and a tiny bit of contrasting color at just the right moment. Let's see why they work.

The use of nervous movement, especially among prey fish, is common when they are in imminent danger of attack. We have observed herring using small, nonlocomotive twitches of their tails immediately before flight from a feeding dogfish shark. This is a protective behavior pattern meant to confuse the shark's receptors. As noted earlier, the shark cannot see his prey at the moment of attack. Instead, he relies on a set of electrical sensors set around his mouth. These pick up tiny electrical currents generated by the movement of the prey in the water. The several nervous twitches of the herring's tail probably generate such impulses and initiate the charge. An instant later, the herring begins his flight with a series of powerful thrusts of his tail, all at a definitely different frequency. This distinctive defense mechanism is a signal to the predator to make his deadly charge...and we can adapt the use of these motion-producing characteristics as a response trigger in our lure.

Our investigation of other response triggers shows that they are largely based on defensive mechanisms of the prey fish. Throughout the world of animal predation these defensive adaptations have resulted in some really bizarre coloration patterns and behavioral patterns. We are all aware of the extent to which evolution has gone to provide protection to prey species. Some animals, for example, have grown to look exactly like the twigs they live on, others have adapted intricate patterns to blend into their environment. Some fish can change their color pigments to match their surroundings, while others have learned to stay within a habitat that looks like them. Some animals display imitation eye spots to confuse predators and cause an attack away from their vital organs, and at least a few tropical butterflies have evolved eye spots that make them look like fierce predators instead of defenseless prey.

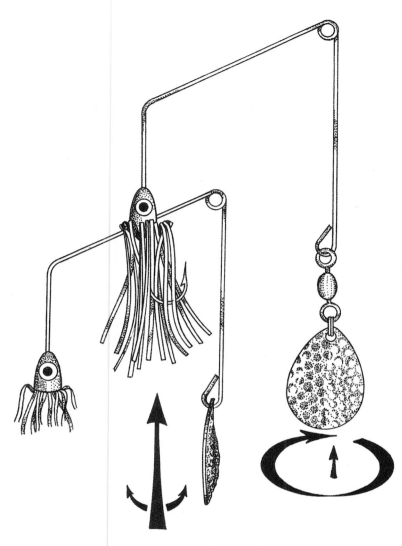

The removal of the connecting swivel prevents the blade from revolving, but causes it to "flap" and increase the attraction directly below.

In the familiar world of gamefish the defensive mechanisms are among the most innovative anywhere. Young trout and salmon display a series of elongated dots along their sides during their most vulnerable stages. Known as Parr marks, these are defensive coloration patterns that misdirect the charge of predator species.

Nature has provided such coloration techniques for many high-risk juvenile fish to insure the survival of breeding stock in most waters.

There is an interesting adaptation of this particular defensive physiology we can use in designing or choosing a lure. Among many marine species the juveniles are able to produce minor color changes when threatened. These are often exhibited as reddish spots in the tail areas. At least a few deep water marine species have taken this ability a step further, developing light-producing organs in their caudal area. At the moment of attack these organs flash, probably triggered by an abnormal hormonal flow. The bright flash serves to either confuse the predator in his strike mode or to direct the charge away from vital body organs.

Few American freshwater fish possess the ability to change caudal colors when threatened, but at least some darters, minnows, and possibly the common yellow perch can make a little color change when a predator is nearby. Whether they are able to produce defensive color changes or not, it seems evident that many large gamefish respond to minute variations in caudal coloration. Even though their normal prey doesn't exhibit color or light displays, the fish is probably responding to some primal instinct. Nearly all vertebrates harbor long-lost behavioral patterns in some cerebral cranny.

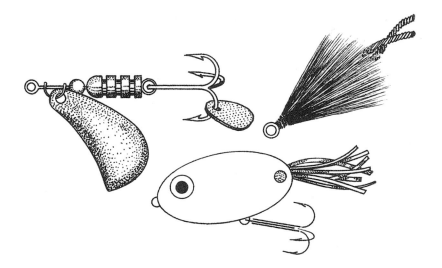

Strike triggers may include a small tab attached to a bare hook, a number of brightly colored strands trailing a bucktail or feather skirt, or a small dot of bright color at the rear of a plug.

It's pretty difficult to build a lure that flashes colored tail spots just when a trophy fish is near, so again we use the fish's visionary restrictions to accomplish our purpose. If we add a color to the lure that can only be seen at close range, we have effected a response trigger that will improve the lure. I noted with great interest the experiments of C. Boyd Pfeiffer, reported in Outdoor Life in 1983. He added a tiny red fluorescent bead to the tail of shad flies and experienced a marked increase in the strike frequency. Related species of shad in the western Pacific feed almost exclusively on a small shrimp that has an especially active luminescent tail spot. The connection seems clearly apparent to me.

The amateur luremaker can duplicate the response trigger in a number of ways. One of the easiest techniques for skirted lures is to include two or three longer strands of material in a contrasting color, so it will be seen at close proximity. Skirt material can also be tipped with a contrasting paint to get the same effect.

A tiny colored disc can be added to the trailing hook or its anchor, which will serve as both a color spot and a high-frequency generator at close ranges. This technique is employed in many good lures to produce an excellent response from the fish.

Finally, the color tag can be a simple spot of contrasting paint in the caudal area of the lure. This dot should probably be fluorescent, since the double-spectrum effect increases as the distance is reduced. At very close range the fish is acutely aware of a trigger that was virtually unseen a few yards away.

chapter
· THREE ·

TOOLS AND TECHNIQUES

There is no particular mystery in crafting a really effective artificial lure. The first effort will not be as slick as factory-made, but that's a lot less important than how well it catches fish. It really doesn't matter how you hammer it together or how rustic it looks as long as it exhibits a degree of attraction and provides a trigger to make the fish strike. It can be of the simplest materials and fashioned with the most basic of hand tools, yet it will very likely catch a fish.

Lure manufacturers have tried to keep their business and their processes as secret as possible for good reason: If everyone knew how simple it is to make lures that will take fish, not many of us would opt to pay six bucks for a gadget that could be made at home for about a dime! The fact is, most lures are easy to make and are astonishingly inexpensive. In many cases the packaging that surrounds the commercial lure costs as much—or even more—than the lure inside. So we have a choice, really; we can pay for factory production, advertising, transportation, distribution, packaging, and profit margins—or we can pay for just the materials, spend a few hours crafting a collection of good lures, and spend the difference getting out to more and better fishin' holes. It seems to be entirely up to us.

Economics aside, it is a lot of fun to sit at the bench and concoct a few nice lures, thinking all the while of the enjoyment we'll get out of using them and perhaps catching a trophy fish on one. There isn't much satisfaction in coldly laying down a few dollars at the tackle shop and carrying a colorful bauble home to add to our hoard. About the only constant in both cases is wondering if the thing will really work…and in the case of a homemade lure it becomes an exciting anticipation.

As you become more skilled at crafting lures at home, your products will begin to show the evidence of practice. The level of skill required for making even the more complex plugs and lures is probably a lot less than most people imagine, and with practice you'll soon rival the factories in polished pieces of work. My guess is that anyone capable of threading a line through the guides of a casting rod has already shown all the motor skills needed to make good lures. Some people will find the craft easier than others, but even the most hopeless of us can make some pretty darned good lures at home with some practice—and we'll add greatly to the enjoyment of fishing while we're at it!

As we begin this chapter on tools and techniques I should point out that none of the processes I describe have been chiseled in stone. The average tinkerer will probably find an easier way to accomplish a step or a different method of getting the job done. It doesn't matter just how the lure is actually built as long as it incorporates the proper elements of attraction and response triggers for that particular target fish. In short, there is no wrong way to make a lure! The methods I describe are those I have found to be most effective, but some variation might be easier for another lurecrafter. After all, making lures is quite like fishing in some respects—we rely on our own skills, strengths, and interests to do a better job.

If the tools and techniques are flexible, the dimensions are even more so. One might note in the catalogs that many lures can be found that are supplied in a range of sizes from very small to whoppers. That size differential allows for the use of a single design in many different waters for several kinds of fish. It also allows—from the manufacturer's point of view—for greater sales from one design. You need not approach luremaking with the eye or the discipline of a machinist. In practice there is little difference between a lure that is 2 inches long and an identical plug 2½ inches long. It might respond a little more slowly or have a slightly altered casting pattern, but it will take the same fish from the same water on the same day. So much for the mystery…now relax and make them the way you want.

The Toolbox

The basic tools needed for luremaking are about as simple as the materials that are used in home lure construction. One of the nice things about this hobby is that we need not spend the equivalent of a new graphite fly rod to get started. Except for those who have to call in outside help to change lightbulbs, most people already have most of the tools required. There are a few specialized tools that will make the lures more professional looking, but they will be made at home for very little cost. As a person becomes more advanced in luremaking, he will probably buy a couple of very specialized tackle tools, but that will depend on his degree of involvement.

The basic equipment for making lures—at least bass and trout plugs—is exactly what ol' James Heddon used when he started this whole thing…one serviceable pocketknife and a pair of pliers. Add to those a strip of sandpaper to make the finished product really finished and you have the essence of the tool kit. Armed with nothing more, a person can make quite a collection of plugs and other wooden or plastic lures.

Lest we kid ourselves, let's admit that we aren't going to be satisfied making one group of artificial lures any more than we would be content with one kind of fishing. To become a competent luremaker—and to make a variety of lures —a few more tools must be added to the tackle bench. The list below includes all the tools needed to make any lure in this book and perhaps a couple of thousand more.

BASIC LURE TOOLS	
Pocketknife	Hand or electric drill
Small hobby knife	Coping saw or hacksaw
Replaceable-blade cutter	Small tinsnips
Slip-joint pliers	Small ball-peen hammer
Needlenose pliers	Small vise
Small side-cutters	Assorted sandpaper or emery cloth
Heavy-duty scissors	Assorted sewing and darning needles
Assorted screwdrivers	Small half-round rasp or file

This isn't a terribly complicated list and you can do without some of the items listed, at least for a while. Another advantage of luremaking is that you don't really need the more expensive grade of tools designed for heavy work. Almost every tool on the list can be cheaper imported types if you prefer. The one place I wouldn't skimp would be on the pocketknife. It is so important to luremaking— and to fishing—that I recommend the best quality a person can afford.

I believe that an electric drill is better than a hand drill for most lure work, but having both would be pretty handy for the amateur luremaker. The hand drill should be the small, rotary type rather than the large brace-and-bit. A selection of small bits will be needed and they should be of reasonably good quality.

I won't pause here to tell how each of the tools is used, since the majority of the detailed lure instructions will cover that. None of it is difficult, and one tool will be used for many different tasks before the whole collection is complete.

Specialized Tools

There are some tools that cannot be found in the hardware store and probably won't show up in any specialty catalog. They're the gimmicks I have found to be of enormous value in making nice lures, but I had to make them myself. They aren't hard to build, but they make life—and lures—a lot nicer.

The first of these is one I consider to be absolutely essential to the making of nearly every kind of lure in the book. It's a small vise that will hold the softest of woods in every imaginable position as it is whittled, sanded, sawed, scraped, and cursed. It will secure even little odd-shaped bits of tackle during construction, pieces that would drive a person daft trying to hold and shape at once.

The vise is centered around a 4- or 5-inch C-clamp and some heavy plywood or good, dry hardwood. The jaws are drilled and carved (with the trusty old pocket

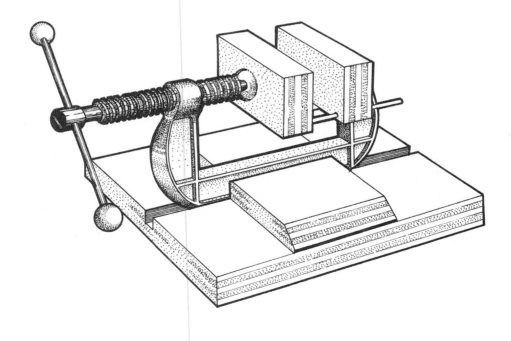

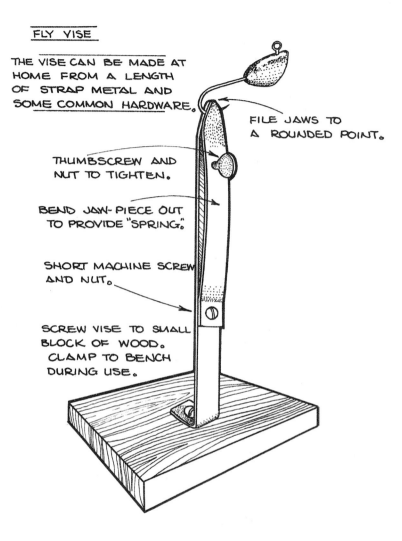

FLY VISE

THE VISE CAN BE MADE AT HOME FROM A LENGTH OF STRAP METAL AND SOME COMMON HARDWARE.

FILE JAWS TO A ROUNDED POINT.

THUMBSCREW AND NUT TO TIGHTEN.

BEND JAW-PIECE OUT TO PROVIDE "SPRING."

SHORT MACHINE SCREW AND NUT.

SCREW VISE TO SMALL BLOCK OF WOOD. CLAMP TO BENCH DURING USE.

knife) to match the jaws of the clamp and the base is sawed to accept the clamp as shown. It is assembled with a good epoxy cement—the five-minute kind—and it will hold up under a surprising amount of strain.

Another tool that can be fashioned at home is a hook vise, or fly vise. It is probably easier to buy a cheap vise of this type than to make one, but that would depend a lot on how handy the builder is and how badly he wants to save a few dollars. The hook vise is used to tie tails, skirts, streamers, salmon flies (which really aren't flies at all, but artificial lures) and other hook portions of the lures. In an emergency it is possible to put the hook in a pair of pliers and clamp the pliers in a vise, but in the end every lurecrafter will need a hook vise.

A set of really important specialized tools are what I call "pattern sanders" for want of a better name. These are four small sticks that have been shaped as a flat blade, a triangle, a small rod, and a square shaft to which has been affixed fine sandpaper. Actually, the tackle bench will require two sets of these. One should have medium (80-grit) paper and the other a fine (150-grit) paper. The cloth is attached with contact cement and when the paper or emery cloth is worn out it can be peeled off and a new layer attached. The heavier grit is used for general shaping of small configurations while the fine sander finishes the piece. These little tools allow you to put an exceptional finish on every nook and cranny of your most complicated lures.

Finally, make two larger versions of the pattern sanders in only the flat and triangular shapes and affix them with #40 or #50 emery cloth. I call these "burring tools" and use them for smoothing the edges of all the metal parts of my lures. They are great for finishing the cuts on spoons, spinners, buzzers, and other such components. They are also handy for shaping many of the plastic parts prior to final finishing.

That is essentially the list of tools needed for basic lurecrafting. There is a place for things like hand rotary punches, drill presses, lead pots and molds, rubber molding equipment and much more…but not in the kitchen of an average amateur luremaker. In this book we will deal with alternatives to punching spinner blades and melting lead. These alternatives don't do quite as good a job as the big equipment, but they make sense unless you plan to make a lot of lures or go into luremaking as a business.

Right now many home craftsmen are probably starting to think about shortcuts, using things like bandsaws, power jigsaws, scroll saws, belt sanders, and the like. I have one word of advice: DON'T!! Lures are small projects at best and they should be shaped quite carefully, even in the early stages of roughing out. I am fairly conversant with the power shop, too, and I think it's impossible to exercise the kind of control we need when the sandpaper is moving past at two-hundred miles and hour! With the techniques we will be discussing in this chapter we'll find that power tools are more of a handicap than an asset.

More importantly, I tend to think of each lure as an enjoyable project that takes shape under my hands, into which I have put feeling and care that is somehow transmitted to the action in the water. I doubt that the fish particularly cares about the love and concern I put into the lure while it is being whittled or the tender touch I choose to use on the sandpaper as I bring it into final shape. But when he strikes I am repaid many times for my effort. If you plan to manufacture lures with the cold precision of a commercial supplier, you probably aren't enjoying this book much, either.

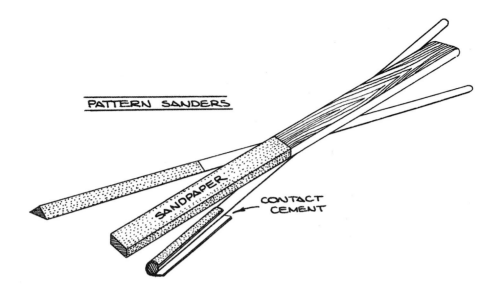

PATTERN SANDERS

SANDPAPER

CONTACT CEMENT

Basic Lurecrafting Techniques

The luremaker has both general and specialized tools at his disposal, and the techniques are likewise mostly quite basic with a few special processes added to meet the demands of the craft. Most are quite familiar to anyone who works even occasionally with his hands. Those few techniques that are peculiar to the art of luremaking are easily learned and practiced.

As we begin with the simplest of lures to build—a common plug—we must consider for a moment the instructions that will be given here and throughout this book for specific lures. The figures that are given for size, shape, and dimension are guidelines that should be followed in a practical sense, but they are not absolute. The amateur might carve the old J-plug, for example, a bit fatter or skinnier than the instructions indicate. The finished plug might turn out a bit longer or shorter than the pattern, but unless the variation is extreme it isn't going to make much difference in the actual usefulness of the lure. The new plug might run a little deeper or shallower than the original, but who's to say the change won't be an asset?

In the more technical lures we should be as accurate as possible, but there is still considerable margin for individual variations. A deep-diver might end up with a five-degree variation in the angle of the diving plane that will cause it to dive at a different rate, but not enough difference to affect the value of the lure. As you become more experienced at making and using lures, you'll be able to adjust

THE J-PLUG, IN SOME VARIATION,
HAS BEEN USED IN ALMOST ALL
KINDS OF ANGLING. IT IS ONE
OF THE EASIEST TO MAKE.

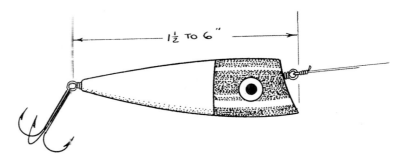

them to perform as you want them to under specific fishing conditions—and that's what is important. If you carve a plug and the unfinished blank is different from what you had expected, go ahead and modify it. If you paint the plug and then discover it doesn't quite fit your expectations, try it. You might have accidentally improved the action of the plug and discovered another great fishing tool.

With that relaxing bit of information behind us, let us start with a very basic plug—the traditional J-plug. It is nothing more than a torpedo-shaped piece of wood with a nose that has been sawed at enough of an angle that water pressure will cause it to dive erratically as it is trolled through the water. To make sure we get the hang of it, let's consider the steps necessary to make three variations of the basic design. It will be carved in a 2½-inch, 3½-inch, and 4½-inch model. Each will be about ¾ inch in diameter, since that is the thickness of most modern lumber, and we will be making these plugs from scraps of any old board.

We should begin with a stick a foot or longer in length and about ¾-inch square. With a pencil, mark off a 2½-inch section and roughly sketch the shape desired. Whittle the stick with a pocket knife until the shape has been achieved. It will be rather uneven and rustic, but that's how it should look at this stage. Put the whittled piece in a vise (or simply sit on the long end to hold the work) and use a 2-inch-wide strip of sandpaper to bring it to final shape. Using the sandpaper much the way a shoeshine rag is administered allows great control over the progress of final shaping. Turn the piece over several times as you work to insure a uniform curve all around. Once the final shape—or something reasonably close—has been achieved, rub the whole thing down with a piece of fine sandpaper to smooth it off.

The final construction step is to saw the blank free from the stick at and angle, producing the diving surface that makes it work. The exact angle should be around 15–20 degrees, but it isn't critical.

This quick exercise, which most people can complete in five or ten minutes at the most, has essentially produced a trout or salmon plug. It still needs to have the hook and eye attached and it must be painted, but the actual construction has been done.

We can pick up the original stick, mark off a 3½-inch section, and repeat the process. This will produce a somewhat longer, sleeker version of the same plug that would be used in larger water for larger fish. The process is identical and can be completed in about the same amount of time. The secret—if there is one—is in occasionally turning the stick a quarter-turn while sanding to insure a symmetrical shape.

Finally, repeat these steps with a 4½-inch blank. The result will be three plug blanks that will, after they're painted and fitted, catch their share of fish. These lures have been around for nearly a hundred years in a variety of sizes and colors. They have a proud and successful history, having taken fish from all around the world, and they've been manufactured by hundreds of firms. The lures we have just produced will fish as well as any if we have been fairly careful with our work.

In this book, as in the tackle shop, you'll find dozens of designs for wooden-bodied plugs. None are much more complicated than the ones we have just finished carving. Some will have some rather interesting contours and may include some added accessories to make them dive or swim, but they are only slightly more difficult to carve and finish. By the way, if you are holding your breath and waiting for the mysterious or complicated part to begin, you had better go ahead and exhale. I told you it was simple!

With the completed blanks on hand, we will turn our attention to drilling the holes that will allow the lure to be "rigged." This is the process by which hooks

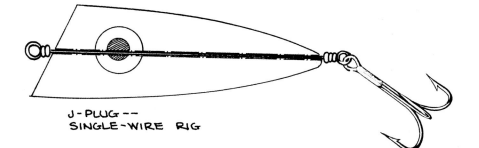

J-PLUG --
SINGLE-WIRE RIG

are attached and some device is provided that will allow the lure to be dragged through the water in search of fish. For purposes of illustration the simple plug will be rigged with one treble hook and a single strand of wire to be both anchor and towing-eye. We will get to the actual rigging in a moment; our concern just now is drilling a hole through the center of the blank.

Drilling takes a little care and some practice. The towing eye should be in the exact center of the "head," and the hook should mount right at the tail. The technique will take a steady hand and a bit of practice, but it is remarkable how often it works out perfectly. It must be easier than it looks! I recommend an electric drill for this step over a hand drill, but in either case always do the drilling with the blank held in a vise. Don't hold any lure part in your hands while drilling unless you are fond of perforated fingertips.

Before the final rigging takes place, the blank should be painted and allowed to thoroughly dry. The final finish for attraction and trigger elements is a science of its own which is covered in a separate chapter. For now the lure-bodies should be set aside as we begin working on the next construction step—bending the wires needed for rigging the plug.

Wirework for Lurecrafting

This is probably the most difficult of all techniques involved in making lures, but one that should be learned completely and practiced extensively. Almost every fishing lure will have some basic wirework that will affect the action and value of the lure. There are a couple of mechanical tools on the market that ease the job somewhat and make very professional-looking bends in stainless wires. Those who decide they are going to get involved more deeply in home lurecrafting will probably want to get one. I recommend the inexpensive models carried in the mail-order catalogs of Jann's Netcraft and Cabela's (see Chapter 13) as good, basic tools.

THE TACKLE EYE

LEARN TO BEND A COMMON EYE PROPERLY - IT IS THE MOST USEFUL OF WIREWORKS.

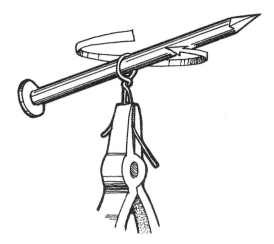

For the time being we will learn the basic technique of bending an eye onto a piece of wire with hand tools. An eye is the most common wire configuration in the business. Most lures have at least one—some have several.

To bend a simple eye onto a wire we will need two tools: a pair of pliers and a nail about the diameter of the finished eye. Wrap the wire around the nail as illustrated, leaving about a 1-inch tail. Grip the wire with the pliers and twist the nail. If you will allow the wire to slip through the pliers as the eye is being twisted you will make an excellent bend without stressing the wire. As you practice making eyes, learn to pull upward on the nail as you twist. That will keep the eye centered on the shaft and make a very neat piece of work.

You can practice this maneuver on any small piece of wire. I would strongly recommend you make dozens of practice eyes before you begin putting them on lures. It is not a difficult technique at all, but it must be done properly if the lure is to look—and work—as it should. A good choice for practice would be about 20-gauge galvanized wire. It is soft and fairly easy to bend, but it will break easily if you bend too tightly or don't allow the tail of the wire to slip through the pliers. Good practice, but the galvanized wire is no good to actually bend for lures. It will rust almost immediately upon touching the water!

For lures, use either stainless steel or hard-drawn brass wire. The most common wire sizes for lures range from .021 to .031 inches, depending on the size of the lure and the test required. Most commercial lures, by way of comparison, are bent on .026 wire. Good quality stainless wire can be ordered from almost any fishing catalog and can be found in most tackle shops.

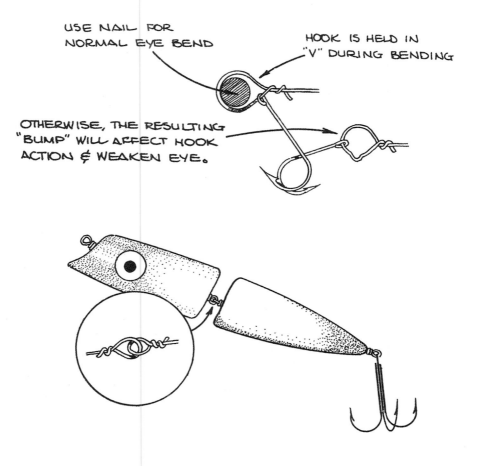

USE NAIL FOR NORMAL EYE BEND

HOOK IS HELD IN "V" DURING BENDING

OTHERWISE, THE RESULTING "BUMP" WILL AFFECT HOOK ACTION & WEAKEN EYE.

The eye is the commonest of all wire bends used in lurecrafting, but there are several others that are used in the lures in this book. Those specialized bends are relatively simple and will be discussed with the particular lure instructions. Bending a good, strong eye is critical to the amateur luremaker, but it is not the only bend that will be needed.

An associated and equally important wirework technique is bending an eye with something inside it, usually a hook. It is only slightly more difficult than bending a simple eye. The secret lies in the slight "v" that is formed in even a very tight eye where it joins the wrap. The hook should be in that "v" while the bend is being made, as we have illustrated. Practice this technique with soft wire until it has been mastered. I would urge the use of a very dull hook for the first few tries…perhaps one with the point removed. No sense in tempting fate and losing our enthusiasm for making lures!

Finally, practice bending an eye on one piece of wire and then bending it onto another eye. This is the technique used to join the parts of a jointed plug or to make long strings of trolling lures. There are few places in this book where eye-to-eye bends are used, but they are handy to know. Many saltwater anglers learn this technique to attach leaders to steel line…it is quite the same process. Many of the early-day trolling strings were made of four sections of wire thus joined, each with a blade, clevis, and beads. The old stuff was pretty effective, but not as good as today's flexible trolls.

Hook Anchors

A very different wireworking technique can be used as part of a hook-anchoring system for wooden plugs. There are several methods of attaching hooks to small plugs and many of them are admittedly superior to wire-bent anchors. But a lot of luremakers use the technique and it is a good one to know. To make a bent-wire anchor, a couple of inches of wire are looped over a nail, the ends gripped with pliers and twisted into a corkscrew shape as shown. The hook is nearly always bent onto the anchor, although some bare anchors are used with a split-ring to hold the hook. The disadvantage of bending the hook directly to the anchor is that the hook is not then replaceable.

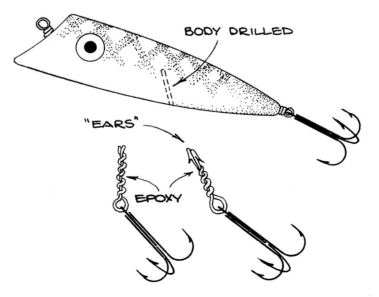

BODY DRILLED

"EARS"

EPOXY

The plug body is drilled to accept the anchor firmly and the hole is filled with epoxy before the anchor is permanently installed. I don't consider this type of anchoring system very reliable, but it will work well enough if the hole is tight enough and the epoxy is applied properly.

A better alternative is to bend two small "ears" on the anchor. These will act as barbs when the anchor is in place, adding a mechanical connection to the epoxy adhesive connection.

Whenever possible, the hook should be anchored on the same wire as the towing eye. This system leaves nothing to come apart under the strain of a fighting fish and avoids the disappointment that invariably follows such a tackle failure.

In most of the types of wood that will be chosen for lure bodies (and we will discuss this aspect of material selection in the next chapter) a tiny eye-screw is a good anchoring system. These can be purchased through most catalogs or found in some tackle and hardware shops. Some small pieces of hardware can be found in an upholstery shop, too—but make sure they are solid brass or stainless steel. Many of the little eye-screws are made of plated steel and will sooner or later rust away and break.

The one place where eye-screws will not work satisfactorily is in balsa. If you choose balsa for luremaking—and I don't recommend it for amateur

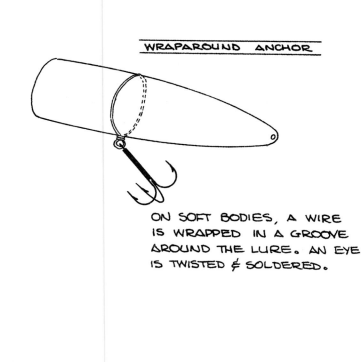

WRAPAROUND ANCHOR

ON SOFT BODIES, A WIRE
IS WRAPPED IN A GROOVE
AROUND THE LURE. AN EYE
IS TWISTED & SOLDERED.

lurecrafters—you'll need to use a combination of through-eye anchors and "wrapped" anchors in which a soldered piece of wire is laid in a groove carved around the body and then twisted into an eye. There are a variety of ways to do this and I have illustrated only one of them. Frankly, I would rather work in woods other than balsa and I don't like to trust my fishing to this kind of anchoring system. There are some commercial manufacturers who use this system very efficiently and make wonderful lures, but I don't think it's appropriate for us shade-tree luremakers.

There are some small hook-hangers available through the mail-order component suppliers that work very well and simplify hook anchoring on most wooden lures. The hook is inserted into the hanger and screwed to the lure body with a small wood screw. They are inexpensive and a good choice if you are going to make a lot of lures and don't want much fuss in mounting hooks. These are discussed along with other ready-made components in Chapter 14.

Metalwork for Lurecrafting

An important part of amateur luremaking is the fabrication of the metal parts utilized on a variety of effective lures. On many artificials a revolving metal blade—spinner, buzzer, or propeller—is the primary attraction element of the design. The lure would obviously have little effect without this critical metal component. It is something that every amateur luremaker must learn to do, but it isn't at all difficult…especially if we take a few shortcuts.

Making working spinner blades and spoons seems to many people something akin to witchcraft. The action of the blade as it revolves around the shaft or wobbles predictably during retrieve isn't magic, though. It's a simple

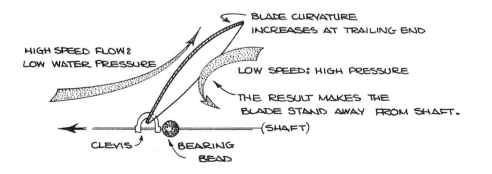

matter of physics, a basic understanding of which will help the amateur luremaker fashion more useful blades.

The action of a spinner blade is rather complex, but is simply the result of the rounded curve typical of spinners. The blade will revolve rapidly around the wire shaft when it is pulled through the water or held in moving water. The rotation, which can be in either direction, is the result of the combination of a curve and moving water. As the blade begins to move forward the water must speed up to pass the outside (convex) surface. At the same time the water pressure against the inside (concave) surface either remains constant or actually lessens through an "eddy" effect. The resultant force pushes the blade away from the shaft, where it is free to swing in a more-or-less upright position. The blade would actually remain upright if the pressures were perfectly constant. But in the fishing situation the blade is acted upon by many variables such as pressure, current, and speed changes...so it spins around the shaft, held away by the hydrodynamic function of its curves.

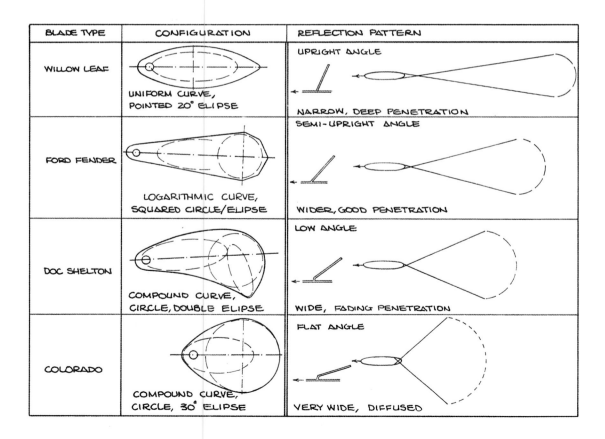

BLADE TYPE	CONFIGURATION	REFLECTION PATTERN
WILLOW LEAF	UNIFORM CURVE, POINTED 20° ELIPSE	UPRIGHT ANGLE / NARROW, DEEP PENETRATION
FORD FENDER	LOGARITHMIC CURVE, SQUARED CIRCLE/ELIPSE	SEMI-UPRIGHT ANGLE / WIDER, GOOD PENETRATION
DOC SHELTON	COMPOUND CURVE, CIRCLE, DOUBLE ELIPSE	LOW ANGLE / WIDE, FADING PENETRATION
COLORADO	COMPOUND CURVE, CIRCLE, 30° ELIPSE	FLAT ANGLE / VERY WIDE, DIFFUSED

Blades of varying shapes and curvatures will operate at varying angles from the shaft. This fact is important to the lure designer, since it allows him to direct the attracting "flash" to different parts of the water. I have illustrated four different blade types to show the various reflection patterns they provide. These are blades of standard curvature; variations in the amount of curve would also change the reflection pattern.

The importance of this principle to the amateur lurecrafter is enormous. If you want a lure that will attract fish from almost directly behind your line —trolling for example—you would choose a blade with a narrow reflection pattern.

If your intent is to attract a fish from nearly broadside of your lure—as is often the case with resting walleye—you would pick a blade with the widest pattern. The choice is also important in relation to the distance from which you hope to "call" your fish. The narrow patterns seem to penetrate farther into the water, while the broad patterns are more quickly diffused. Many successful trolling rigs use a combination of blade shape and reflection patterns.

The "buzzer" blades have become nearly standard gear for bass. They are just a modified propeller that flashes on a perpendicular line to the retrieve path. Bass, as we know, will seldom make a long charge after a lure, but rather tend to take it from short-range ambush. The broad, right-angle pattern of the buzzer blade meets this requirement perfectly.

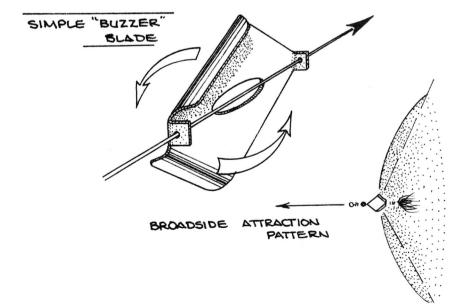

SIMPLE "BUZZER" BLADE

BROADSIDE ATTRACTION PATTERN

In home practice you can produce several styles of blades with an almost constant curvature pattern that will give you a choice of reflective patterns. In practice, the curvature—as long as it has some—is less important to the amateur than the surface area of the blade. If that weren't true, darned few of us could make spinner blades at home that would work!

Before we get to the nuts-and-bolts business of cutting spoon and spinner blades, let's think about the pros and cons of buying most of our blades from the component suppliers. It is a practice that I often follow, even though I can make pretty good blades for myself. The fact is, I can't make them as good —or as cheaply—as I can buy them. I do make quite a few, but only because I am experimenting with a design that doesn't so far exist in the size or shape I need. If the amateur is going to make a lot of lures, any of the suppliers listed in Chapter 14 have a great selection of good blades at very reasonable prices.

On the other side of that argument, there is a lot of satisfaction in having a fish fall for a blade of your own making. While I admit to having boxes of blades from several sources, I still really enjoy cutting and pounding a few blades for use on my fishing vacations. I get a genuine thrill from taking a nice fish on a wholly homemade rig…that's probably the most important reason for making any of your own tackle!

Start making spinner blades by cutting a variety of blade shapes and sizes from aluminum. It isn't a particularly satisfactory material for lure blades, but it's great for practice. Aluminum is too light in relation to its mass to function well as either a spinner or spoon. To make a really good blade, the amateur can take some castoff metal article that already has the kind of curve needed and cut the blade from it. I have made some excellent blades from the cover of a steam iron, others from the base of a tossed-out slow cooker, and several fine ones from the metal reflector of an automobile headlight. It is kind of fun to find bits of shiny junk and turn them into professional-looking lure components.

If you have access to some sheet brass or other flat stock that will make spinner blades, cut a few pieces into the proper shape and drill them to accept the clevis. Using a small ball-peen hammer, slowly shape the flat blade into the desired shape over the anvil portion of a vise. If you don't have such a tool, use a sturdy old teaspoon or serving spoon. Just lay the flat piece over the back of the "bowl" of the spoon and pound lightly to achieve the desired curve.

Spoons are somewhat modified versions of spinners that produce their attraction by "wobbling" rather than revolving. The reflection pattern cannot be so easily varied on a spoon, but the effect can still attract fish from the broadside position. The line is fixed to one end of the spoon and the hook to the other, so the axis required for a full spin is absent.

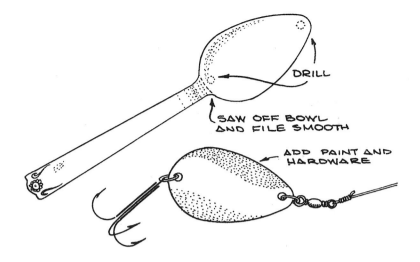

DRILL

SAW OFF BOWL
AND FILE SMOOTH

ADD PAINT AND
HARDWARE

The blades are much thicker than on spinners in order to achieve the weight necessary for casting. They are, therefore, harder to cut out of the basic metal, but can be made with a hacksaw rather easily. The rough spoon will then be filed or ground to final shape. For the first handful of spoon-type lures you might make, use a few castoff teaspoons. Just saw off the handles and file the resultant cut smooth. This is how the spoon originated (thus the name, I suppose) and they work quite well.

The buzzer blade has only recently regained popularity with bass anglers, but it began a long time ago with the British minnow harness. There are several variations in this book and they are deadly under certain conditions. You may cut the blades from thin aluminum—it's the preferred material for this kind of blade—following any of the various patterns. The blade tips can be rounded over a dowel or screwdriver shaft, or may be bent at a sharp angle with pliers. The buzzer will be off-center because the tabs are both on the same side, but it will still spin quite easily. The eccentric motion also generates plenty of sound waves in the water, adding to the attraction of the lure.

In both the spoon and buzzer blades, you'll need to smooth the edges with a burnishing board to remove any burrs or rough spots. Be especially careful with this process, since even the smallest of burrs will damage line and leader, weakening it significantly.

Many of the components for home-crafted lures are cut from common household plastic items. They're easy to cut with heavy-duty scissors and can be smoothed along the edges with sandpaper. To give the component—such as a diving plane—a very smooth edge, hold it in a small flame for a few seconds. I have a disposable butane cigarette lighter on my tackle bench for just that purpose. You'll need to experiment a little to keep from scorching or melting the plastic, but it's really easy to make these components with just a little practice.

Adhesives for Lurecrafting

There has always been an argument surrounding the right choice of adhesives for lures, rods, ferrules, and every other fishing purpose. I guess it's the nature of fishermen to argue about the little things while they agree on the importance of fishing in a modern world. The fact is, the science of glues and adhesives has changed enormously in the past few years and new discoveries are cropping up almost every day. The amateur luremaker is one of the prime beneficiaries of this research.

I can't adequately discuss the field of adhesives, since I haven't had an opportunity to try them all—but I can tell which have been best for me. The hands-down winner as an all-around glue product is five-minute epoxy. The kind you have to mix from tube A and tube B—the messy kind!

I particularly like epoxy because it can be mixed in small quantities without much waste, is totally waterproof, and is odor-free once it has completely cured. It holds small pieces with incredible strength and I recommend it for about 80% of all luremaking jobs. One thing epoxy won't do is secure the plastic pieces that are used on many of our designs.

Many of the components we will make are cut from plastic coffee can lids, fruit drinks containers, and margarine tubs. Epoxy will not bond with this kind of plastic with any reliability, so we will have to use some kind of household glue. It helps to "rough up" the part of the plastic that will be , cemented. When joining plastic on plastic on lures like the Parker Drifter, it's possible to use the tubes of cement designed for assembling plastic models. Nearly all of the plastic we will use responds well to the styrene-based model adhesive.

When all else fails,-I use a stick of ferrule cement to glue my components together. It is a little more brittle than I would like, but I have some lures that have survived my frustrated flailings for many years! The old-fashioned sticks of ferrule cement (the kind you set on fire to melt) are getting harder to find, but they are available through most mail-order suppliers.

On almost every trip to the hardware store I find some new adhesive that is touted as the "world's strongest" and that may be true. I have not yet discovered one of those superglue formulas that work at all for lures, but there are bound to be adhesives that are well-suited to our craft. I'd like to find something better than five-minute epoxy for holding twisted anchors in wooden lure bodies, but so far nothing better has appeared.

Snells and Knots

There are no fishing knots that are exclusive to lurecrafting, but a couple are used more often than most others. The first is the jam knot, or clinch knot, that is used to tie snaps, swivels, and lures to a line. The other is the common snell that wraps a hook to a monofilament leader. Both are fairly easy but must be tied properly to insure a reliable rig.

The jam knot is used for practically every kind of fishing. It's as useful for ultralight tackle as for shark rigs and will hold dependably under incredible strain.

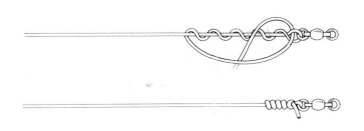

The snell is rather more difficult to tie properly by hand, but is a snap if you make the little tool I have illustrated here. It is the neatest gadget I've found for making good quality snells either in the field or at the bench. Several of the lures in this book are based on a snelled outfit, and this tool —with just a little practice— will enable the amateur to make very professional snells almost immediately.

One important step in constructing this tool is in the burnishing and smoothing of the cut edges. Any aberrations on the edges are apt to nick the leader being tied and leave a badly weakened terminal as a result. Take the time to deburr the edges before you fold the hook tool, then rub the edges thoroughly with fine sandpaper or steel wool. When you can run a fingernail along the cut edges without feeling any roughness the tool is ready to be folded and used. Just follow the instructions for making the snell.

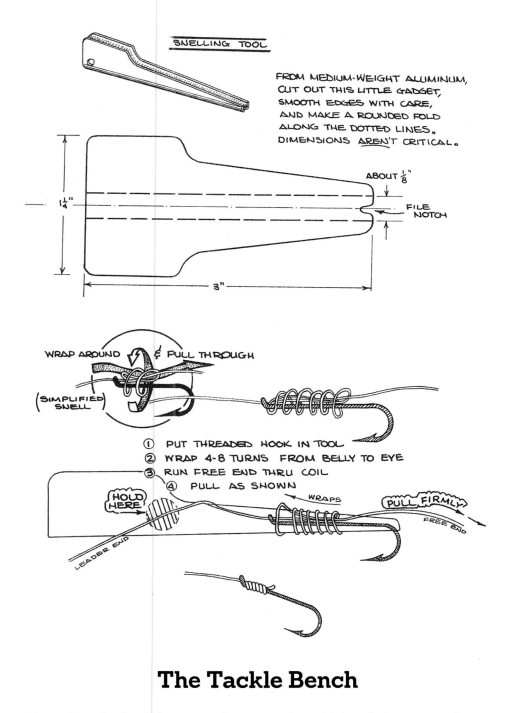

SNELLING TOOL

FROM MEDIUM-WEIGHT ALUMINUM, CUT OUT THIS LITTLE GADGET, SMOOTH EDGES WITH CARE, AND MAKE A ROUNDED FOLD ALONG THE DOTTED LINES. DIMENSIONS AREN'T CRITICAL.

ABOUT $\frac{1}{8}$"

FILE NOTCH

$1\frac{1}{4}$"

3"

WRAP AROUND & PULL THROUGH

(SIMPLIFIED) SNELL

① PUT THREADED HOOK IN TOOL
② WRAP 4-8 TURNS FROM BELLY TO EYE
③ RUN FREE END THRU COIL
④ PULL AS SHOWN

HOLD HERE

WRAPS

PULL FIRMLY

FREE END

LEADER END

The Tackle Bench

Throughout this book there are references to the tackle bench. It is a general term that refers to any place we might work on our lures, but it can be a facility designed for that specific job. Any amateur luremaker who finds sufficient fascination with this do-it-yourself aspect of fishing should seriously consider making one. Everyone has different needs and space limitations, so I've illustrated two types of efficient tackle benches. I have both and use them often. The larger, free-standing bench is particularly valuable to the dedicated angler-craftsman since it can also

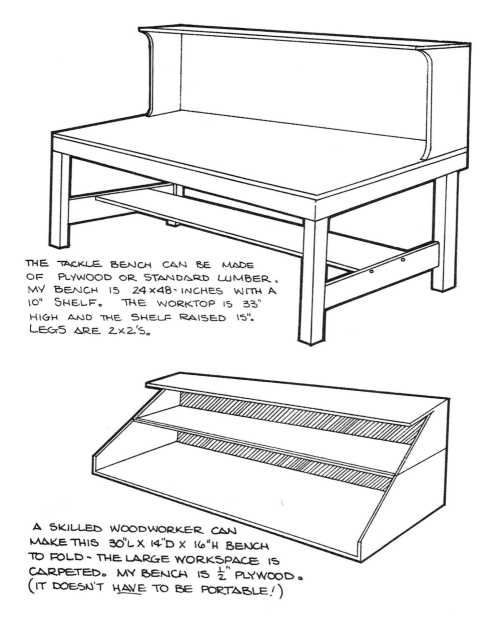

THE TACKLE BENCH CAN BE MADE OF PLYWOOD OR STANDARD LUMBER. MY BENCH IS 24×48-INCHES WITH A 10" SHELF. THE WORKTOP IS 33" HIGH AND THE SHELF RAISED 15". LEGS ARE 2×2'S.

A SKILLED WOODWORKER CAN MAKE THIS 30"L × 14"D × 16"H BENCH TO FOLD - THE LARGE WORKSPACE IS CARPETED. MY BENCH IS ½" PLYWOOD. (IT DOESN'T HAVE TO BE PORTABLE!)

be used for winding rods, shaping fly-rod handles, fixing reels, and all the other tasks that are needed to keep our gear in shape.

The smaller bench is more-or-less portable and I've used it in the field during tackle-testing outings. It gives me an opportunity to make fine adjustments to my lures, change components, and even build new lures to meet unexpected fishing conditions. Most people won't carry their affair with artificials to such an extreme, but you might—and this item is pretty handy. As the amateur works his way through the techniques outlined here it is easy to see just how simple they really are. The tool inventory is not painful to accumulate and the skills can be learned in a short time. Luremaking is similar to many crafts in that it gets easier as we practice. With just a little care and patience, any home lurecrafter can be making some very professional lures that are at least as effective as any you might buy.

The Sketchbook

As we move along to another stage of lurecrafting, let me insert an important word of advice. Every time you make a totally new lure or design an artificial you think might work in your favorite fishing hole, make detailed sketches and notes before you leave the tackle bench. I have several notebooks filled with sketches of lures I have concocted over the years, most of which I will never need. This habit of keeping accurate notes is the result of one of the most painful lessons I've ever learned.

I made up a couple of dozen lures in preparation for an outing up to the Canadian northwoods. Many of these were whimsical little novelties, but all of them incorporated solid attraction and trigger elements. One lure proved to be dynamite in the cold, overcast conditions we found after a two-day drive into the backwoods. Nothing else worked worth a hoot except this one...and it was catching 90% of the fish landed by our party. On the third day of fishing I snagged bottom and lost the little gem despite frantic efforts to free it.

For the rest of the trip we caught virtually nothing, yet when we got home I couldn't for the life of me remember how that red-hot little lure had been made. I don't even remember what it looked like except that it was red and white and sort of small.

Today I keep copious notes and sketches of every new lure I make. I would suggest every home luremaker do the same!

chapter
· FOUR ·

MATERIALS FOR LURECRAFTING

Making lures at home is a pretty innovative activity from the very start, but gathering the materials for lurecrafting is great fun and an opportunity for absolutely unsurpassed creativity. A word of warning, though—once you begin picking up the odds and ends needed for making lures at home you'll never look at a garage sale in quite the same way!

Instead of sorting out the frayed fishing rods, balky reels, and repairable hip boots—all the normal stuff—we paw through boxes of costume jewelry, fur neckpieces, castoff leather purses, and feather dusters with pathological passion. I have actually broken into a cold sweat while waiting for some lady at the Goodwill store to decide against a cheap rhinestone-and-red-bead necklace. I wanted that gaudy bauble so badly I could have screamed. I was already envisioning the quarter-ton of trophy trout that would succumb to the lures I would fashion from that bit of tasteless rubble!

Prowling around surplus outlets and yard sales is the indelible mark of the dedicated home lurecrafter, since the vast majority of his raw materials will be found in such places. Many of his greatest inspirations occur after finding an otherwise useless piece of junk at such an outlet for the indescribable.

Much of our best material will come from such reliable everyday sources as lumberyards, hardware stores, thrift shops, and the city dump. (In those places where the city dump is not open to the public we can try the garage sales—it's almost the same!) There are a few components that the amateur normally won't try to make at home, most notably his hooks, clevises, swivels, and other small hardware pieces. For the most part, though, our basic materials will come from ordinary retail outlets and throwaways.

Wood Selection

Nearly all the plugs and poppers begin with a wooden body which we can whittle and sand into very effective artificial lures. About a quarter of the designs in this book feature a wooden body, so we should discuss in some detail the kinds of woods that have proven most useful for the various needs of our plugs.

There is no single variety of wood that is applicable to all lures, nor is any particular design limited to only one wood species. We must consider the weight, buoyancy, strength, and workability of the wood used for a given design. In most cases we will find several kinds of wood that will work. The decision should be made in large part on how the lure will be fished. If the plug is designed only for casting, it must have enough weight to allow it to be easily tossed toward productive water. A trolled lure may be of less dense material but must be fairly durable. A surface lure must be made of a more buoyant material than a diving lure, but must still have enough weight to make it function properly.

From a practical standpoint we will have to choose woods that can be worked with hand tools, but we find some restrictions within this group of materials. Balsa is easy to carve and sand but is very difficult to rig reliably. It is so soft that normal anchors won't hold under the slightest strain. Seasoned oak, on the other hand, is enormously strong but is nearly impossible to carve and sand with regular hand tools. Most kinds of wood mercifully fall somewhere between these extremes and provide a good compromise between strength and workability.

The softest woods that are practical for the amateur luremaker are cedar and white pine. Both can be worked easily and still retain the cellular strength needed for dependable anchors and tow-points. The hardest woods practical are kiln-dried fir and hemlock. These can be worked with just a little difficulty but are very solid. Mahogany—technically classified as a hardwood—is relatively easy to shape and has excellent strength. Mahogany is surprisingly buoyant but it takes a lot of very fine sandpaper to get the smooth finish required of a good lure. Pine is very easy to smooth out, but must be chosen with care. Individual pieces of pine have an excess of turpentine and oil that prevents paint from sticking very well.

There are literally hundreds of kinds of wood that will make good lures. I tend to stick with pine and cedar for buoyant lures and fir, hemlock, or mahogany for heavier casting plugs. It would be easier to list those species that aren't suitable, since most woods will work just fine. I do not use oak, maple, hickory, alder, or any other wood that is too hard to whittle and shape easily.

It will not take long to decide which woods work better for you—and you'll make the majority of your products from the handful of species that are comfortable to work with and readily available. The one constant factor in any wood choice is that the material must be bone-dry. It is a little disappointing to take the time and patience to carve a nice lure only to have it crack and check as it dries. Any variety of wood will shrink as it cures, causing anchor holes to draw away from the anchor. The result of using green wood —even if it doesn't crack and split—is loose rigging and an unreliable lure.

The eventual choice of wood will be a compromise between strength and ease of working, but the choice is much like the techniques for lurecrafting; there isn't any wrong wood, but some are a great deal better than others.

There is one further note about choosing wood that allows a lot of individuality, and that is the natural shape of the piece. If we are going to produce a plug with a curved body, for example, it is possible to find a stick —often near a knot—that has almost exactly the grain desired. It is a good practice to set such pieces aside, keeping a supply of odd curves around to meet specific lure requirements. When the luremaker decides to tackle a new project or fool with a brand-new design a particular piece of wood may suggest an interesting course to take. Experience will give the amateur a better feeling for which bits of wood hold greater promise. As for me, I can't even chop a box of kindling without setting a few pieces aside for a future flatfish or a wounded minnow!

Choosing and Using Metals

As a home lurecrafter, you don't have to be an accomplished metalsmith, but you will develop something more than a nodding acquaintance with some metals. You will learn the basic techniques required to incorporate them into your lures as a matter of absolute necessity. Almost every artificial lure in the fishing inventory requires at least a few metal components, so the ability to fabricate common metal parts is essential to the craft.

Making the proper choice of material for a given component will have a profound effect on the value of the lure. If a blade is fashioned that turns out to be too light to spin properly we will have lost the attraction element of that lure. If we choose a wire that is either too brittle or too soft we will have altered the mechanical reliability of the lure. Components that are too heavy will seriously affect the desired action of our offering when we finally try it in the field. It is quite important to pick the right materials if our finished lure is going to get out there and catch fish. We needn't take a clinical approach to our investigation of metallic materials, but we must look at them from the practical standpoints of workability, suitability to the marine environment, and ready availability. These three considerations fortunately narrow the field of potential choices to a handful.

Virtually all luremaking tasks can be accomplished with four metals. Wires, shafts, and anchors will usually be of brass or stainless steel. Spoon and spinner blades will most often be brass amalgams or aluminum. Buzzers and diving planes will nearly always be aluminum, while jig bodies, sinkers, and other heavy components will be fashioned from lead. I will confess to making a lot of spinner blades from a castoff piece of chrome-plated steel, but I do it with the knowledge that they are going to be short-lived. Rust and corrosion will quickly take their toll of such components, but I operate on the theory that if they catch fish for just one afternoon they have served me pretty well!

Let us first consider the proper material for the wire we will use for spinner shafts, hook anchors, and plug rigging. The wire has three requirements with regard to material structure. It must be soft enough to bend into tight eyes, strong enough to meet the demands of fishing (including the occasional rock or submerged snag!) and it must not corrode or weaken when exposed to fresh or salt water. Given these restrictions, our practical choices become limited to stainless steel or hard-drawn brass. Of the two, stainless is somewhat harder to bend with hand tools but produces a dependable lure for both salt water and fresh. Brass is considerably easier to bend but has less breaking strength for a given diameter. Brass is the usual early choice for amateur luremakers, but most will eventually use stainless almost exclusively as they become more skilled at wire-bending.

Spoon blades are quite thick and are nearly always cut from brass or a brass compound. Spoons must be much heavier than spinner blades in order to provide the weight needed for long-distance casting—and brass provides the density while remaining fairly easy to cut and shape. Brass compounds are really the only practical choice for the luremaker. A few of the cheaper factory-made spoons are made of plated or heavily painted steel, but they are quite unsatisfactory in the long run. The slightest chip or scratch will cause them to rust or discolor quickly.

Spinner blades constitute the vast majority of the sheet-metal work done by the home lurecrafter. These components can be cut from almost any substance that is thin, fairly dense, and nonferrous. Aluminum will not work for all blades but is a reasonable choice if weight isn't a factor in the design. More often than not these components will be cut from either brass or a junked piece of chrome-plated steel. The latter material—as pointed out earlier—will rust along the edges after a single use. Brass doesn't provide the high degree of reflection that chrome or nickel plate does, but is a great choice for blades that will be used in bright sunlight. Brass is quite easy to form into the curves that spinner blades require.

I know a couple of home lurecrafters that make all their blades out of castoff pieces of chromed steel, but they coat the blades with a heavy coat of varnish or fiberglass resin. The treatment allows the blade to retain a good degree of reflection while preventing immediate rust or corrosion. To be perfectly honest, I buy most of the blades I use in lurecrafting. I can't make blades quite as good as those from the component catalog and the ready mades are relatively cheap.

The other metal with which we will become intimately familiar is lead. It is very heavy, extremely soft, and doesn't corrode much when exposed to water. Unpainted lead will oxidize a little, producing a light gray powder at the surface. It can be a minor problem when it occurs on lead jig-heads, but the oxide can usually be wiped off easily before the lure is fished. An important property of lead is that it has a low melting point—and that's very beneficial to the advanced amateur luremaker. It can be melted easily to a liquid state, from which it can be poured into molds to produce all sorts of tackle items. Most home lurecrafters will eventually make their own sinkers, jig-heads, bodies, and other lead pieces.

The designs in this book can be made without melting lead, but some readers may want to adapt some of the designs to poured lead processes. We have list some of the lead equipment available and take a basic look at the techniques in Chapter 13. Instructions come with all the necessary equipment when it is purchased—and you'll find using lead quite easy and a means of greatly expanding your options in some luremaking. It's a very important skill to the saltwater angler who experiments with jigs and other deepwater lures…but the freshwater angler will also find a lot of uses for poured lead.

Using Plastic

A person would be hard-pressed to list the most significant events in all the history of mankind. He would probably include the time Moses came down with the tablets, the deep rumble in the Nevada desert proclaiming the secret of the atom had been unlocked, and the day man first broke the shackles of earth in a NASA capsule. Heady stuff, but only baby-steps when compared with the day the fishing tackle industry discovered plastic! This versatile family of synthetics soon found its way into every facet of angling, especially to the terminal end of our lines.

With plastic, a manufacturer can mass-produce lures to precise tolerances in unthinkable numbers in a twinkling. He can exactly duplicate food sources, prey species, and natural forage of every known game fish. Some plastics are as hard as metal but are reliant. Some are softer than skein-eggs but will last for many fishing seasons. The big luremakers are able to impart natural scents, chemical stimulants, and enticing consistencies to their products. Using the incredible arsenal of plastic they have done everything except design the foolproof lure.

The amateur doesn't have the luxury of pressure-molding or chemical scent-bonds as he fashions his lures, but he is nonetheless a beneficiary of the high-tech plastics race. This miraculous material is in such abundance that tons of it are discarded every day—almost all of which is perfectly suited to the art of luremaking. It would be reasonable to suggest that every household in North America has enough suitable plastic at any given moment to supply the amateur with material enough for several seasons of lurecrafting.

I like to think of household plastic for fishing lures as the ultimate recycling scheme. It is conceivable to use a pat of margarine to fry a mess of trout that were caught with lures made from the last margarine tub. With this plastic container we could make a few lures, catch a couple of bass, and fry them in the next tub of margarine, ad infinitum. If we add to this plan such staples as coffee-can covers, fruit drink containers, half-gallon milk jugs, and detergent bottles we should soon have enough fish to feed all the underdeveloped nations of Asia and have enough left over to keep Africa knee-deep in organic fertilizer. (You may notice that I have trouble controlling my enthusiasm for plastic as a medium for lures!)

Actually, there are many components that can be made from these low-cost plastics that are probably better than from any other material. It is easy to work with, completely impervious to water, and can be painted easily to match other lure parts. Many of the lures in this book have been designed specifically to incorporate these milk-jug components. The designs would probably be less efficient if metal parts were substituted.

A few of the lures and accessories will utilize plastics that are heavier and a bit more difficult to shape than the disposable types, but specific instructions are given with those projects. A few of the heavier plastics are unpredictable during the heating and bending process. That may mean several tries to get precisely the component we need, but the material is either free or so cheap that we can afford to toss out a few attempts before we get the final piece.

There are some components that demand plastics of a better grade, thickness, or quality than the disposable pieces will provide. Having polished your prowess as a second-hand sorcerer, you will find an ample supply of these better items at the Salvation Army or the neighborhood thrift shop. (While prowling the garage sales for such high-grade plastic I once found a rather gauche stainless breadbox that produced dozens of wonderful spinner blades. The hardwood knob was used to replace the handle of an old Penn Jigmaster that had barely survived one of my infamous docking maneuvers. It was kind of an object lesson in imaginative resourcing!)

Wherever the instructions in this book call for components made from household plastics, they are meant—as usual—as general guidelines. There is usually plenty of latitude in deciding which kind of plastic to use and how to handle it. As often as possible the instructions will explain the precise function of the part, allowing the home lurecrafter to be as innovative as necessary and as flexible as his supply of plastic will permit. There are so many plastics available that exact specifications would be pure folly.

You will have to spend some time experimenting with the adhesives you will use. The various cements, glues, and epoxies have a widely varying effect on different plastic materials. As you tinker with various plastics, you'll find some that work and some that don't. It is probably a lot more practical to find a couple of types that work well and stick with them than to spend a lot of money trying to find more alternative adhesives.

The amateur is seldom equipped to handle plastics in a liquid form or to mold them into intricate shapes. The exception will be the "rubber" lure plastics supplied by lurecrafting specialists. Those products are designed specifically for the home craftsman and will be discussed later. The hard plastics and household items just aren't mean to be melted and restructured by the amateur. Our major activity regarding this huge group of materials will be cutting blades, control planes, and fins. In some cases we will heat and bend (but never melt) common plastics to meet specific component needs. Heating will be accomplished with hot water or heated sand as indicated in the particular project instructions.

A word on heating plastics for lurecrafting: if a piece of plastic that is being softened begins to melt into a liquid form, DISCARD IT AT ONCE! Get it outdoors and away from the heat source. Most plastics are perfectly safe while solid but will release harmful vapors when melted. Never breathe the fumes from melting plastics of any kind.

Regarding the one kind of plastic we can handle in a liquid form, the soft material for rubber worms, crawdad tails, minnows, and other familiar lures is a great medium for the amateur. It can be purchased from a variety of mail-order suppliers and is relatively simple to use. It requires a little heating in an old pan before it is poured into factory or homemade molds to produce a wide array of components.

Live-rubber plastics can be colored to suit any lure and is reusable if the design just doesn't work out. I know of no sources other than the mail-order houses, but most amateurs will only need to purchase a supply on rare occasions. A gallon of the basic mix will make plenty of lures for several seasons and any leftover tackle can be remelted into other components. This versatile material allows the amateur a lot of chance for invention and innovation and is fun to use.

Hard-Bodied Lures

You cannot successfully pour hard-bodied plastic lures with the equipment commonly available to the small shop, but there are other materials that can be utilized to make some fine lure bodies. It's important to be able to mold several identical bodies or duplicate an existing shape so you can field-test different color combinations or trigger elements. Any system that will allow the molding of hard plug bodies is an asset.

The primary material for this technique is fiberglass resin. It is available almost anywhere, fairly easy to use in the small shop, and is well suited to the casting of plug bodies, jigs, and other components. The amateur who keeps alert to possible material sources will find other suitable liquids for plugcasting, often in the most unlikely places. The do-it-yourself ads in some of the popular handicraft magazines will suggest a few potential materials. I know one luremaker who bought five gallons of some stuff that was touted to make him rich by producing birdbaths, front-yard flamingoes, and those statues of a nude woman with a clock where her stomach ought to be. He neither got rich nor made any birdbaths, but he has five gallons of great stuff for pouring heavy lure bodies and jigs. I'm constantly amazed at the imagination some home luremakers exercise in this area of lurecrafting. I met one hobbyist who poured some very interesting little trout lures from nothing but several layers of paint. He had made plaster molds resembling a popular fly-rod lure and then carefully filled them with colored layers of old-fashioned enamel. He hardened his lures by baking the molds in an oven for a couple of hours and they turned out quite nice…and a lot tougher than I would have imagined.

The basic process of pouring lures is very simple. We need only a liquid that will harden to a useful consistency and a mold that has been shaped to produce the desired lure. The liquid is poured into the matrix, allowed to harden, and rigged for fishing.

Making a mold can be one of the more challenging aspects of lurecrafting. It can be either a one-piece (flat) mold or the more typical two-piece (enclosed) style.

Most of us will make our home-fashioned molds from either concrete mortar or from plaster of paris. To produce a flat mold for objects like a deepwater jig, we need only mix up a batch of mold material, put it in a sturdy containers, and press the original (pattern) into the top of the mold When the mold hardens we remove the original, leaving the matrix into which the new lure material is poured. We will arrange some system for placing the rigging wire inside the body cavity before it is poured The accompanying illustration shows the easy process. The flat mold is effective for any number of simple lure shapes.

A first-time project is often a disaster for the amateur, usually for one of two reasons. First, the cavity may have been made in such a way that the hardened lure physically couldn't be removed from the mold. Any mold feature that encloses the poured material-even slightly-prevents removal of the final product. A second problem occurs when the material sticks to the mold and cannot be removed. This is a common experience, but one that can be overcome quite easily. It's just a matter of coating the mold with some substance that prevents the material from adhering as it hardens. We call this nonstick coating a "release agent." There are

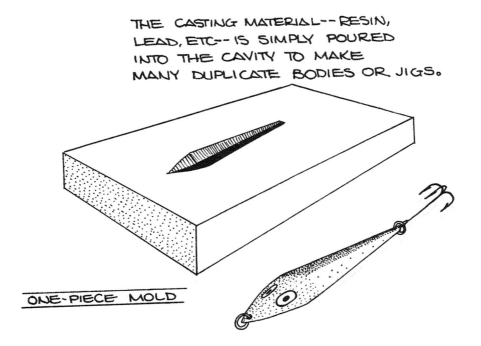

THE CASTING MATERIAL--RESIN, LEAD, ETC--IS SIMPLY POURED INTO THE CAVITY TO MAKE MANY DUPLICATE BODIES OR JIGS.

ONE-PIECE MOLD

some commercial compounds available in large quantities—usually 55-gallon drums—that aren't practical for the homecrafter. As an alternative we can use vegetable oil or one of those spray-cans of nonstick cooking aids. Any similar oil will usually work, but don't use machine or motor oil. It will allow the pattern to be released but will often give the lure a permanent odor of petroleum…and the fish will avoid your offering like the plague!

The two-piece mold is constructed in much the same manner as the flat mold. After the lower section has hardened—and without removing the pattern—we simply spray the pattern and the hard section with a release agent and pour a second section over the top. The two sections are separated and the pattern removed to expose the cavity into which our liquid will be poured. In the illustration we have used a whittled cone of wood to provide a funnel-shaped channel so the final material can be easily poured. This mold-making system is remarkably easy and efficient as long as the exact position of the pattern allows easy removal of the finished product.

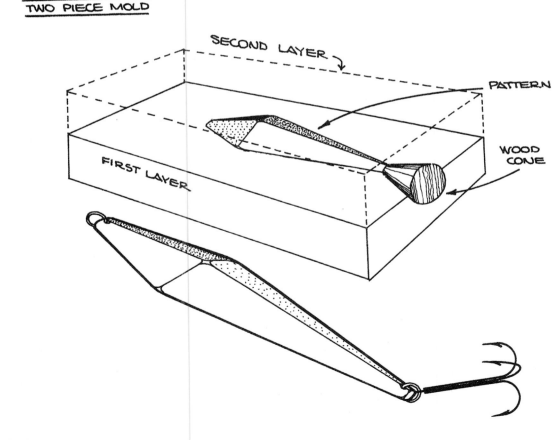

TWO PIECE MOLD

SECOND LAYER

PATTERN

WOOD CONE

FIRST LAYER

Hooks and Hardware

I am not going to suggest that you should start making you own terminal hardware. We cannot fashion hooks, swivels, snaps, or other tiny mechanical pieces with anything like the precision or the economy of factory components. I would hate to think how long it would take me to build a number-12 swivel that I can buy for about a nickel—and I'm sure mine wouldn't work nearly as well as theirs. Our discussion of hardware in this chapter is to detail which bits should be used on various lures.

We will begin by looking at the single most important terminal item—the hook. Hooks are manufactured in many materials and designs, at least one of which is appropriate for every lure we will make at home.

Most hooks are made of bronzed steel, galvanized steel, brass, or stainless steel. The non-stainless types are usually made from varying grades of spring steel that keeps them from bending easily, but we will find some imported hooks that are made of very poor steel that will break rather easily. Some designs can be interchanged on certain lures but many hooks won't work well on a particular design. Regardless of the design involved I always recommend the best quality you can afford. It seems silly to risk our fishing success on a soft-iron import when a top-quality hook costs only a few pennies more.

Plated or galvanized hooks are all right for saltwater bait fishing, but I would never use anything but stainless steel for a saltwater lure. All other hook materials will eventually corrode after exposure to saltwater and it's a lot of bother to change hooks after every use.

There are a couple of hundred different hook designs on the market. Many were conceived expressly to improve the odds for bait anglers. We will limit our investigation of hooks to those more suited to our noble purposes.

Plain shank or Siwash. The most common single hook for lures. This will be chosen for spoons, small trolled lures, and in most waters that prohibit the use of multiple hooks. The straight eye allows the hook to trail neatly behind the lure and offer a very little reverse drag.

Aberdeen hook. Similar to the common long shank, the Aberdeen is made of soft brass. It will bend easily when snagged, allowing the angler to recover his lure when it is hung up. It can be bent back into original shape with the fingers but is obviously suitable only for smaller fish.

Worm hook. Designed for use with artificial worms and other rubber-bodies used by bass and pike anglers. A kink in the shaft prevents the worm from slipping back as it is fished. There are several variations of this design available.

HOOK STYLES

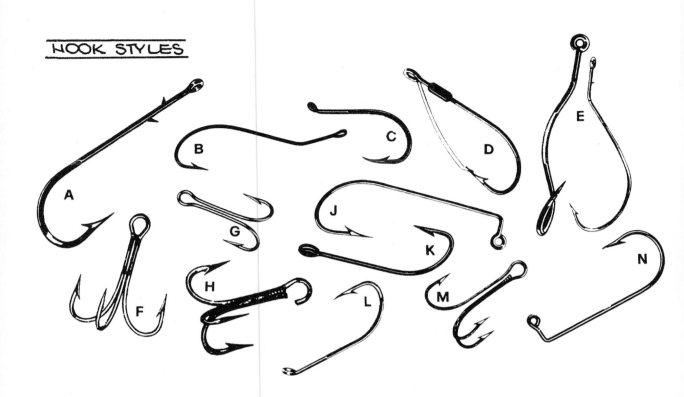

These are the most common hook styles used in luremaking. They include: (A) Worm, (B) Draught, (C) Beak, (D) Weedless, (E) Messler, (F) Common Treble, (G) Double, (H) Open-eye Treble, (J) O'Shaughnessy Jig, (K) Plain Shank or Siwash, (L) Plain shank, turned-down eye, (M) Slip-on Treble, (N) Aberdeen.

O'Shaughnessy jig hook. Made for lead-heads and other jigs and useful for cork "poppers." The right-angle shaft gives us the option of putting the eye above the center of gravity. This keeps the lure swimming in an "upright" position.

Weedless hooks. Especially useful for bass lures and other artificials that will be cast in or near floating or submerged beds of aquatic plants.

Messler hooks. A fairly recent innovation for soft-bodied lures, this hook is made to force a half turn sideways under the pressure of a strike. It is sometimes helpful for fishing kokanee, ocean perch, and other fish that tend to nibble very softly at soft lures. The "turn" keeps the point aimed at the upper or lower jaw instead of the open side of the mouth. There are many new tradename variations of this design.

Draught hooks. These are modifications of the common plain or long shanks with a deeply bowed belly for rigging plastic worms and minnows. The long curve allows the barb to be stuck directly into the plastic lure. This technique (Texas-style rig) makes the lure practically weedless but keeps the point involved in the strike.

Beak hooks. Available with either turned-up or turned-down eye, these hooks are designed for snelling. They are used on many of our salmon, trout, and steelhead lures that are based on a nylon leader rather than a steel shaft.

Plain shank, turned-down eye. This specialized hook is used to tie several walleye and other lake lures that are based around a nylon core.

Double hooks. An excellent choice for many plugs and poppers. The double can be rigged with the points either up or down to reduce snagging and to put the points in line with the strike. The double can be removed from an anchor easily without a split-ring.

Treble hooks. By far the most popular choice for most plugs and artificials. The treble literally bristles with active points and will hook a strike from almost any position. The treble tends to snag more easily than other types, but that same characteristic makes it the deadliest of hooks on most fish.

Open-eye treble hooks. Designed to be attached to permanent anchors without a split-ring. Not as strong as a standard treble but tough enough for all but the largest fish.

Slip-on treble hooks. Another hook that is designed to be quickly changed on a lure with permanent anchors. The slip-on treble gives us the flexibility of an open-eye without sacrificing any of the strength of a standard. These hooks are relatively expensive as compared to standard trebles.

These few designs—only a fraction of what's available—represent the majority of hooks needed by the home lurecrafter. There are others that could be used on almost any design but the experience of thousands of anglers have proven these to be the best for the jobs at hand. If you don't have a particular style in your tacklebox, go ahead and use something different. It might not work quite as well as the style recommended, but it will usually work.

The rest of the hardware inventory is small and somewhat intricate stuff that is better bought than built at home. There are a couple of tackle tools that allow us to bend some nice snaps and it is possible to fashion a rather rustic clevis if we are caught afield without one. By and large, the hardware is not a practical aspect of do-it-yourself fishing tackle. Our time will be better spent making plugs and lures.

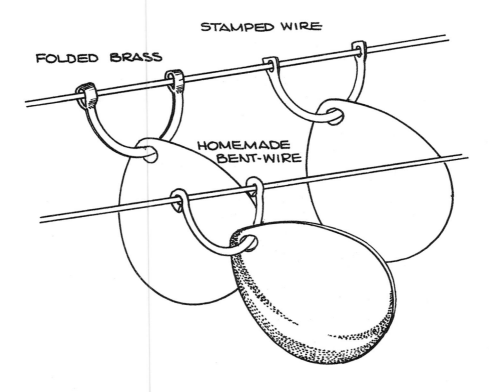

STAMPED WIRE

FOLDED BRASS

HOMEMADE BENT-WIRE

Fur, Feathers, and Fabrics

Many of our jigs and lures require some kind of fabric wrap for bodies, feathers, and bucktails as an attractor on hooks, and other common material as a part of the works. It would be futile to tell anyone where to get these components since they are so commonly available in so many places. The amateur who prowls the garage sales and thrift shops will soon find sources for every conceivable kind of soft material. It is also readily available at fly shops and tackle centers, but the prices are pretty stiff when compared with the same materials in a recycling atmosphere.

It is possible to buy a small packet of hackle feathers at the fly shop for around a dime a feather. You might, on the other hand, find an imported feather duster at the dime store that contains thousands of similar feathers. It will cost less than a couple of commercial packets and will most likely meet the hackle requirements at your house well into the next generation.

Bucktail and deer hair are hard to find outside the specialty shops, but there are all sorts of furs—real and artificial—in the thrift shops. If you know a successful deer hunter you can usually clip the tail and a few chunks of raw fur from his harvest without much argument, but almost any fur will work for the bucktails and skirts among the designs in the project sections of this book. I recently bought, by way of illustration, a bunch of imported Chinese paintbrushes that each make several wonderful skirts and salmon lures. Common fabric dye can be used to color the hair when necessary. Such dye is easy to find and use, is inexpensive, and doesn't give the fur an odor that will chase the fish away.

For heaven's sake, don't look to the family dog or the neighbor's pedigreed Siamese as a source of lure material. It might seem innocent enough at first, but a bald cocker spaniel eventually becomes a source of embarrassment. If you live in the country you'll be tempted to stop and pick up the usable remains of road-kills. They are an interesting source of supply and I've gotten a lot of pheasant feathers and otherwise unavailable fur in that way, but it requires a bit of caution. It would be such a waste to get hit by an transcontinental semi while trying to excise the tail-section of an imprudent roadside raccoon!

The chenille material for jig bodies, fuzzy yarns for salmon and trout lures, and various other threads and yarns will be found in any fabric department or sewing-goods shop. In the individual project instructions there are tips on locating fabric components that aren't so common.

An angler who wishes to add porkrind tags to his bass lures has the option of buying the ready-mades at exorbitant prices or making his own for practically nothing. They are made from old pieces of leather and impregnated with a scent that will make them more effective. Once again, the thrift shop becomes the primary source of supply for the old purses, suede gloves, or other castoff leather that will be used. To make these valuable trigger components just cut the leather into the appropriate shape and soak it for several days in a mixture of commercial angling scent and water. I use old salmon-egg jars to soak the rinds until they are needed. The soak should be in scented water rather than in oil, since a water-based scent will remain suspended in the lake or stream, leaving a scented trail for the fish to follow. Oil-based scent will rise to the surface and lead the fish off-course.

The Goodie-Box

Eventually you'll accumulate a box (or several!) of odds and ends of material that you'll find some way to use. The goodie-box will likely contain a jar of costume jewelry, some hacked-up pots and pans, a fur muff or neckpiece, strands of chenille, Christmas decorations, rolls of wire, ballpoint pens, bundles of yarn, and feathers liberally mixed throughout. As an exercise while putting these thoughts together I dug into my own goodie-box and picked out enough parts to make a cho fly.

Some evening, you'll rummage through the box and randomly set aside a piece here and there from which you'll fashion a plug, jig, or spoon. The next weekend, you'll realize one of the cherished dreams of our craft: you'll catch a shining trophy on your homemade lure.

chapter
· FIVE ·

FINISHING AND DETAILING

Adding the finish and detail to a plug or popper is probably the most satisfying part of making lures. It is the stage at which our science turns to art, where we add the magic touch that transforms a common chunk of wood into a real lure. There may not actually be any mystery involved, but there is still a degree of astonishment when a fish actually strikes our homecrafted offering.

Choosing the Finish

There are three distinctly different ways to produce an effective attraction surface on a lure. We have discussed them briefly, but it seems appropriate to investigate them more thoroughly as we consider finishing our lures.

The first finishing scheme is realism—in which the lure is prepared to look exactly like a natural element of the food chain. The commercial manufacturers have access to some amazingly complex machines and processes in order to build the very lifelike lures that are in vogue today. They are effective enough in some angling situations, but they are prohibitively expensive and time-consuming for the amateur workshop. There are other limitations to the realistic lure that will be examined later.

The other two finishing techniques, are perfectly suited to the amateur. These include the representative lure, in which we produce a lure that approximates the size, shape, and color pattern of the prey species. We can add a number of attraction components that aren't found on the real thing but will draw greater attention to our lure without scaring the target fish away. In practice, most of our lures fall into this category.

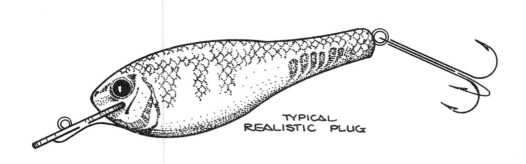

TYPICAL
REALISTIC PLUG

The third finishing option is the impressionistic lure. In this case we have chosen a shape and finish that incorporates many attraction elements but gives only a suggestion of the actual prey—if it resembles anything at all! It isn't any easier to produce than a representative lure, but often has the advantage of attracting fish under quite difficult circumstances.

Before we get to the actual process of painting a lure, let's examine the three finishing schemes carefully. An understanding of the theory and practice of each can help us to be better luremakers…and better anglers.

Realistic Lures

The first truly realistic lures didn't appear until the 1970s. There were some very good handpainted lures before that, but they were painstakingly finished and terribly expensive. They were much better suited to display in an angler's den than on the end of a line. The development of photo-offset processes and some very flexible printing machines opened the door to the production of perfectly realistic lures. There are now some rubber or plastic worms and minnows that look good enough to eat—and that's apparently what the fish think. The ultra-realistic plugs and soft baits are unquestionably effective in some circumstances, but their limitations seem to outweigh their advantages in most fishing situations.

First of all, the realistic lure generally attracts only a fish that is feeding, and then only a target species which includes that particular item in his normal menu. A rubber herring, for example, might attract a feeding cod at the bottom of a bay, but will likely be completely ignored by a passing rockfish. A white-painted leadhead jig, by contrast, will attract virtually every kind of game fish in the same water.

MANY SOFT & HARD-BODY LURES HAVE ACHIEVED EVEN GREATER REALISM FROM MOLDS CAST FROM THE ACTUAL ANIMALS THEY REPRESENT.

The second disadvantage of a realistic presentation—at least for the home luremaker—is more practical than theoretical. It is simply too difficult for us to duplicate the scales, fins, parr marks, and other intricate physiological details of a living fish or frog. If we were to spend the hours necessary to thus paint a lure, we wouldn't want to subject it to the danger of actually fishing with it. More likely, such a lure would be reserved for show-and-tell at the local fishing club.

It has been my experience that the production of a totally realistic lure doesn't justify the time and effort when measured against the angling success it provides. You may get a big kick out of producing a realistic lure, and that's fine. It is, after all, one of the reasons for making your own tackle. For most of us, the impressionistic and representative lures will be the bulk of our activity.

Representative Lures

I would call this category of lure the most practical compromise for the amateur lurecrafter. In fishing terms, of course, it really isn't a compromise. The representative lure is probably the most effective artificial we—or anyone else—can make. If we were to review the most popular and productive lures of the past fifty years we would find they were all of the representative persuasion. The reason for this imbalance is simple—representative lures just work better!

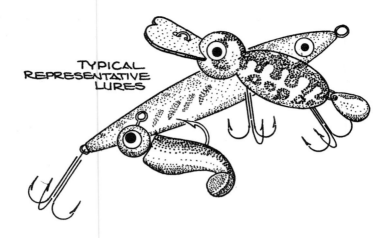

TYPICAL REPRESENTATIVE LURES

From a production point of view, representative lures are perfectly suited to amateur lurecrafting. They can be produced without an excess of skill in a reasonably short time with the simplest of material and tools. That's a very satisfying formula for the home tacklemaker.

In effect, a representative lure approximates the size and shape of the prey species and has the same general coloration. If we can make the lure mechanically fishable and give it some natural action we will have produced a good representative lure. We cannot give our lure scales, for example, but we can give it the effect of having scales through simple painting techniques. This type of lure doesn't have the detail of the real thing, but it gives the effect of lifelike detail. If it then actually catches fish, we can consider it a smashing success.

Impressionistic Lures

The true impressionistic lures—and there are a lot of them—are less detailed than any other type yet are very effective across a wide spectrum of fishing situations. A couple of familiar examples are the famous torpedo lake plug and the common pipe jig. Neither looks even remotely like something a fish might eat, but they catch a lot of fish. In a given situation they might give the target fish the impression they are something to eat, or they might appeal to some other instinct to make him bite. Whatever the reason, these pure impressionistic lures are very effective.

Most spoon and spinner lures are also impressions, created through movement rather than shape. Throughout our chapters on specific lure projects we will see any number of artificials that really don't resemble anything familiar, but are deadly attractors of game fish. Very often the finish and detailing add response elements that help complete the illusion.

Within those three groups of lure techniques will be found all of our finishing and detailing concerns. The majority of our work will be with plugs and poppers that have been carved and sanded to a particular shape but have no real means of attracting fish until they have been finished. It is the painting and detailing that make them work—and we will look carefully at each of the steps in that transformation.

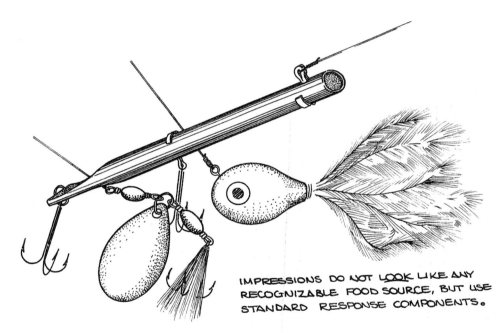

IMPRESSIONS DO NOT LOOK LIKE ANY RECOGNIZABLE FOOD SOURCE, BUT USE STANDARD RESPONSE COMPONENTS.

The Painting Process

The paints that we choose for lurecrafting must be bright, waterproof, and very hardy. We need to stay with one basic formula so that we can paint one color over another without a chemical reaction to spoil our finish. The medium we will invariably use is enamel. There are a lot of other paints around, but none is so well suited to luremaking as good old-fashioned enamel. As you buy paint for your creations, avoid any (even enamels) that contain latex. These paints have greatly eased the burden of homeowners and interior decorators, but they don't work for lures. Latex has a characteristic odor that never seems to disappear from your plug and tends to put fish off. Plain enamel, airplane dope, or any standard enamel should work well. Some luremakers use lacquer—which is just fine—but then you must use all lacquers and no enamels. The two don't work well together at all.

One of the problems confronting the amateur lurecrafter is finding a place to do his painting. Ideally, the paint area should be fairly free of dust, warm enough to allow the paint to fully harden in a short while, and should not be right in the middle of family traffic patterns. It's nice to keep your wet lures away from curious fingers that cannot resist "testing" to see how dry the paint really is. Having a paint

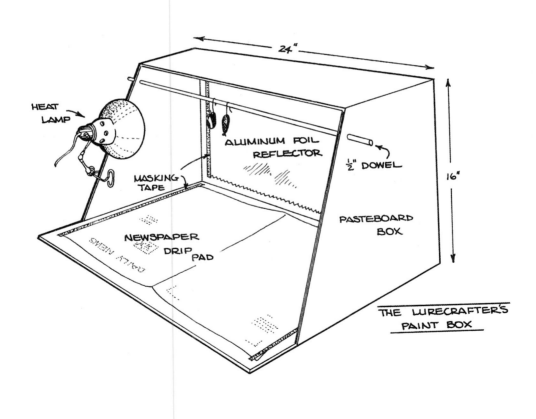

THE LURECRAFTER'S PAINT BOX

area well away from other activities seems an important tactical decision as well. It's sometimes hard to convince your spouse that all those speckles and tints on the wallpaper are really quite avant-garde and add a lot to the decor!

I managed to solve that problem by building a cardboard "paint box" that keeps the overspray contained and keeps wet lures out of sight during the drying process. The illustration shows how to construct one quite easily. They cost virtually nothing and do the trick quite nicely. The reflective rear panel is important to insure even drying if you use a heat lamp. If your artworks are to air-dry, you can omit the foil.

Step One—Dipping Heads and Bodies

Many small lures, jig-heads, and other components are best painted by dipping them in a container of paint. There are no brush marks, the coat is quite even and tough, and a large number of pieces can be painted in a short time. The single drawback is that the piece—particularly a plug body—tends to pick up an excess of paint and then runs at the bottom as it hangs to dry. This can be avoided by either thinning the paint slightly or by removing the excess with a small paintbrush.

In most cases the body will have already been drilled for rigging. I just run a wire through the hole, make a small bend at the bottom to keep it on, and a bend at the top to hang the body during drying. Any drippage will fall on the newspaper drip pad.

The solid color dip of the basic body is almost a universal first step in most plugs and poppers. To this base color you will eventually add the representative color masses, details, and eye spots. The base color chosen is usually a very light one, often white or yellow.

Dipping lead jig-heads, sinkers, and other metal or plastic pieces often begins with a dip in a gray metal primer. Enamel doesn't cover or stick very well to lead until it has been primed.

Double dipping is a process for painting two-color plugs that has been used almost since plugs first appeared on the angling scene. It is just a case of dipping a one-color lure partway into a contrasting color of paint. It gives the head a bright, smooth coating with a sharply defined line between it and the body. Many of our plugs can be handled in this way, giving us a professional quality paint job on a broad selection of lures.

Another technique calls for a dipped body to be oversprayed and then dipped to provide the contrasting section. The torpedo lures, for example, are sometimes dipped in white, sprayed with chrome, and then dipped to make a bright red or yellow head. The result is a familiar big-lake lure that has been around for years.

The double-dip finish process is used on a lot of plugs and poppers, but is a viable finishing technique for spoons and spinner blades. Many lures can be modified by changing the plated spoon or blade into a painted component. The process is the same as for dipping and double-dipping any part. Nickel-plated blades usually will not require priming; the paint seems to stick to the plating quite readily.

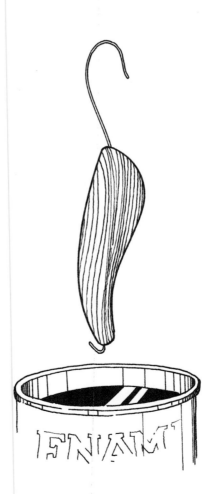

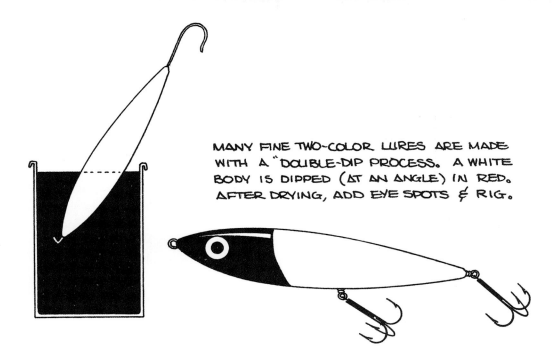

MANY FINE TWO-COLOR LURES ARE MADE WITH A "DOUBLE-DIP PROCESS. A WHITE BODY IS DIPPED (AT AN ANGLE) IN RED. AFTER DRYING, ADD EYE SPOTS & RIG.

Brush Coatings

A body or jig-head can be brushed instead of dipped, but the process is slower and the result less uniform. If you are going to brush the basic body coat be certain to use plenty of paint and give the piece two or more coatings. It is nearly impossible to give as nice a first coat by brushing as by dipping but it can be done with some patience. Get plenty of paint on the piece with each coat, remove the excess, and allow it to dry thoroughly between coats.

Brushing is not a good means of getting the delicate belly, side, and back colors on a plug or lure. It is possible, of course, but there is no practical way of brushing the special effects as well as they can be sprayed. There really isn't any good reason to brush on tint colors when spraying can be done so easily with a minimum of equipment.

Step Two—Spraying and Overspraying

Once the base color has been applied and the project thoroughly dried, we can begin the actual finishing process. This generally consists of a medium color applied to either side, a faint tint sprayed along part of the belly, and a dark back color added.

If a very faint, suggestive tint is to be applied along the belly or the sides, the process is called "overspraying." It takes only a couple of seconds and provides a very powerful visual effect.

The greatest problem most of us have with the overspray process is that we usually use too much paint. A couple of passes with the spray from a distance of around a foot is plenty! When we are putting a faint tint along a belly or a silver shade along the side, a single pass at perhaps 18 inches will often be enough. I find myself (and you will, too!) looking at the tint and thinking, "that looks nice…maybe just one more little shot." By then you will have put on more color than you needed or wanted. It really takes a lot of self-discipline to keep your finger off the trigger.

Overpainting isn't as much of a problem with the back, where we are usually trying to get a more solid, vivid color in blue or green. We are still better advised to spray a little at a time, adding several thin layers until we achieve the proper effect.

Most amateur luremakers will do their spraying and overspraying with aerosol cans of spray paint. It is relatively cheap—one can will paint a lot of lures—and

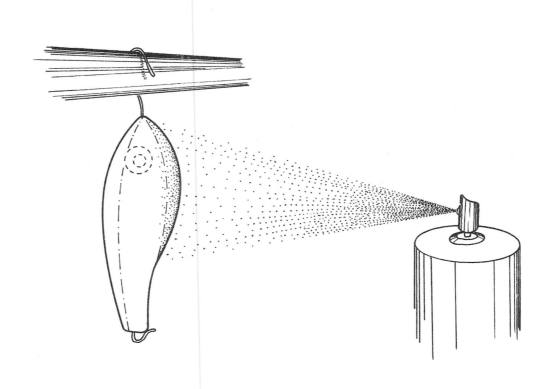

comes in virtually every color you might want, including the very glossy chromes, "wet look" paints, and fluorescents. Spray cans are a lot easier and cheaper than a spray gun and there is no tank to clean after spraying a quarter-ounce of paint.

In a typical finishing scheme—and without getting fancy—we will dip the body with white, spray both sides with silver, and overspray the belly with a red tint and the back with dark green. We have used no special effects, but the addition of an eye spot and the rigging will make a darned effective lure for a variety of game fish. It really is that simple!

Step Three—Masks and Screens

The most important special effects we will need are accomplished with a simple overspray using masks and screens. A mask is nothing more than a piece of thin cardboard on which we have drawn the desired design and then cut it out. The card is held about a half inch from the plug and we overspray through the holes, leaving a splotch of color in a fairly precise pattern. A screen is just a piece of mesh gauze or window screen that is held against the plug while we spray the back or sides. When removed we will have left the screen pattern, giving the effect of a scaled fish skin. The screen can be held in place with a couple of spring clothespins during the overspraying operations.

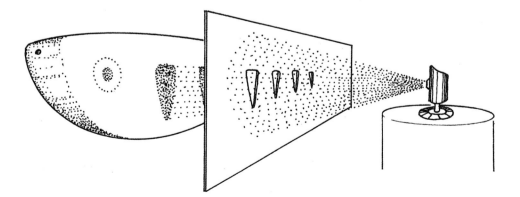

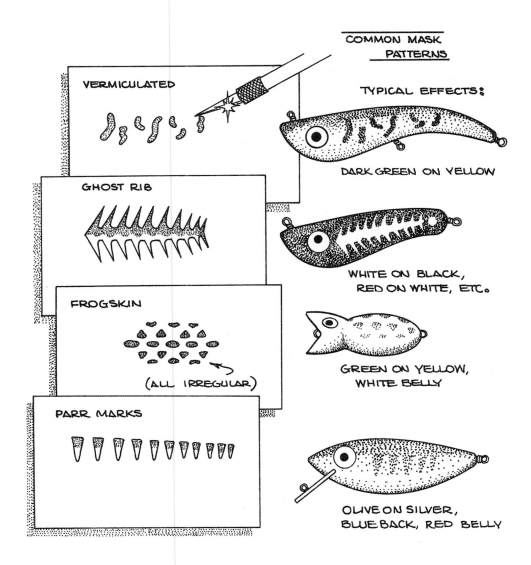

COMMON MASK PATTERNS

VERMICULATED

TYPICAL EFFECTS:

DARK GREEN ON YELLOW

GHOST RIB

WHITE ON BLACK,
RED ON WHITE, ETC.

FROGSKIN

(ALL IRREGULAR)

GREEN ON YELLOW,
WHITE BELLY

PARR MARKS

OLIVE ON SILVER,
BLUE BACK, RED BELLY

To make the mask you just trace the outline of the plug on cardboard, draw the desired pattern, and cut it out with a sharp hobby knife. The accompanying drawings show how the mask effects are achieved. There are several masking effects that are used on common plugs. These have been illustrated along with the effects they create.

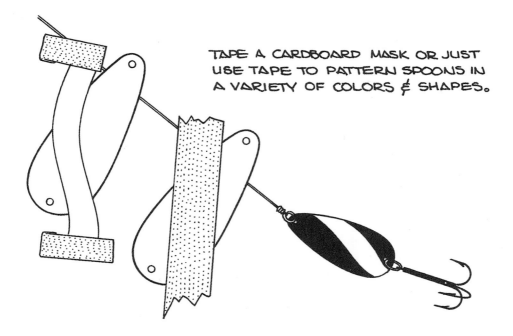

TAPE A CARDBOARD MASK OR JUST USE TAPE TO PATTERN SPOONS IN A VARIETY OF COLORS & SHAPES.

The same processes can be applied to spoons and spinner blades…or any lure component you want to finish. A more common practice with spoons is to use adhesive masking tape to cover that portion that is to remain chrome. An overall spray can be applied and the tape removed after the paint has dried. There are hundreds of effects that can be achieved on blades in this manner.

Mask and Brush Effects

It is possible to create some excellent representative lures by combining a masked pattern with a more deliberate brushed-on finish. In the example shown we have oversprayed a masked pattern of large, separated spots. Inside each we have painted an irregular spot of a darker shade. If we spray an olive pattern over a yellow or gold body and then paint in splotches of darker green we have created a fairly effective "frogskin" that is applicable to a lot of plugs and poppers. You can practice these combination techniques on a piece of dowel until you feel comfortable with them. Mask and brush combinations are limited only by your imagination and the effect you intend to achieve.

MASK-AND-BRUSH EFFECTS

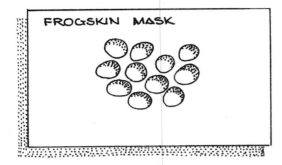

FROGSKIN MASK

CUT A NUMBER OF ROUND AND OVAL HOLES IN A MASKING CARD. SPRAY FROM THE BACK OF THE PLUG WELL DOWN THE SIDES.

USE A SMALL BRUSH TO ADD SOLID, IRREGULAR BLOBS OF DARK COLOR INSIDE EACH SPRAY PATCH. THE EFFECT CAN BE VARIED BY SPRAYING LIGHT ON DARK OR DARK ON LIGHT, FINISHING EITHER WITH A DARKER BRUSHED CENTER.

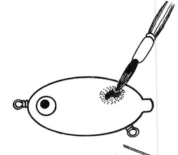

Step Four—Eyespots and Triggers

One of the critical details of any artificial lure is the eyespot. We discussed the importance of this device in behavioral terms and concluded that it is probably the most significant single detail component in coaxing the strike. The be fully effective the eyespot must be cleanly contrasted, perfectly round, and carefully painted. Fortunately, the eyespot is very easy to produce...unless we try to use a brush!

Creating a good eyespot uses a simple law of physics instead of the variable skill of the luremaker. It takes a special set of tools to produce eyespots, but they are easy to fashion at home. In fact, each is nothing more than a small nail. Each different sized spot requires a nail with a head about the size of the spot desired. If you dip the nailhead in fresh paint and hold it in a head-down position, you will see a drop of paint hanging from the head. Simply bring the head down to the exact place you want the eye and just let the paint touch the surface of the lure. Don't let the nail actually touch the surface, only the drop of paint. The paint will flow down onto the lure, spreading out in a perfect circle. Let the drop dry and then add a smaller black pupil with a tiny nail head. Once dried, it is a really fine eye.

To make the process easier I have made a set of eyespot tools by driving a number of various nails into old paintbrush handles, sometimes binding the

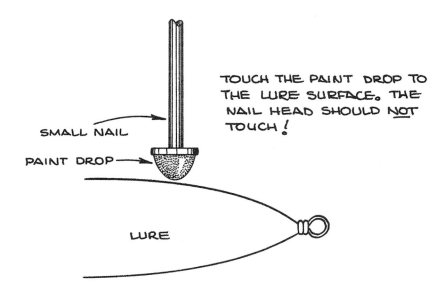

SMALL NAIL

PAINT DROP

TOUCH THE PAINT DROP TO THE LURE SURFACE. THE NAIL HEAD SHOULD NOT TOUCH!

LURE

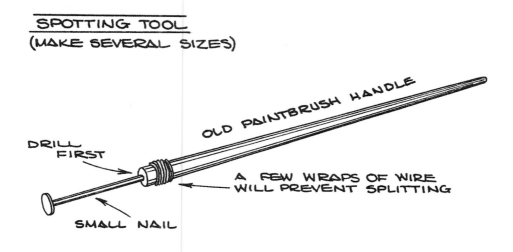

SPOTTING TOOL
(MAKE SEVERAL SIZES)

OLD PAINTBRUSH HANDLE

DRILL FIRST

A FEW WRAPS OF WIRE WILL PREVENT SPLITTING

SMALL NAIL

handle with a few wraps of fine wire. After painting a batch of eyespots, I need only wipe the nails clean and set them aside for the next time.

Trigger spots at the tail or elsewhere are produced in exactly the same manner. You might choose to put a red or silver spot at the tail or elsewhere by just picking a small spotting tool, dipping it in paint, and letting the spot form as desired. It's only slightly easier than falling off a log!

Step Five—Brushed Effects

Once in a while you may want to produce some unusual effect by putting rib lines, fins, or some other addition to the painted surface of the lure. This is the only part of the detailing process that requires a measure of artistic skill. Use a small brush and thinned paint to carefully draw in the lines or effects you desire. When adding such devices to a lure, take a clue from the overspray process—less is usually better!

We have outlined some of the special brushing effects you might want to add to a particular lure. It appears that a universal tendency among novice lurecrafters is to try and cram all the effects onto a single lure. We need to calculate what attraction components are necessary for a given lure and then finish with the best possible effects to achieve effectiveness. During this planning stage it is best to proceed with some restraint. If a brushed or sprayed detail doesn't contribute directly to the lure it will probably be a deterrent to the strike!

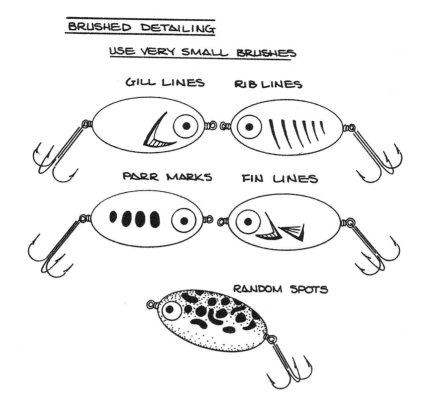

BRUSHED DETAILING

USE VERY SMALL BRUSHES

GILL LINES   RIB LINES

PARR MARKS   FIN LINES

RANDOM SPOTS

Adhesive Surfaces

Some useful attraction components can be added after the painting is complete. One of the best of these is reflective tape or sheets to provide a highlighted surface on the sides or back. Many tackle shops and gear catalogs have this product in a variety of colors, often at a rather high price. It's just as easy to drop by the local auto parts store or a discount outlet and find the same reflective material sold for auto trim.

If the design calls for a reflective surface we need only cut out the proper shape and size, peel off the protective paper, and apply the self-adhering reflector to the lure. The adhesives used on the automotive products are waterproof and surprisingly reliable. If they do come off, just cut and add a new piece.

There has recently appeared a group of high-visibility fluorescent tapes that were made for adding a daylight safety element to bikes, cars, tractors, etc. These tapes are colored with dyes that effectively break down light into very bright refractive elements. This tape can be applied to lures in the same way as the prism tapes discussed above and will add a fine attraction element to deepwater rigs.

Looking through the tackle catalog you will see hundreds of spoons and spinner blades that have these reflective tapes applied at the factory. You can achieve a great many enhanced effects by thus modifying your own home products.

Accessory Detailing

The completion of a lure sometimes requires the addition of an accessory device that puts another attraction component in play. It could be a skirted hook, a tiny colored tag, or even a shiny spinner blade. The components are included in the specific instructions for the individual lures. Before you add such a component be sure it adds to the effectiveness of the lure. It might be a neat little bauble to look at, but unless it has a designed function it would be best left in the goodie-box for another time.

A little practice and a dash of imagination will make the finishing techniques easy and lots of fun. There is no end to the effects an experienced lurecrafter can produce. There are a great many quite attractive lures lying in the bottom of our tackleboxes because they just don't work. Even the most judicious of us will sometimes succumb to art and bad taste and produce the kind of lure that might catch fishermen but have no effect on fish. Don't feel too badly about it—a lot of tackle manufacturers do the same thing on purpose!

The Finishing Touch

As we end our discussion of finishing techniques, let me reemphasize the most important single consideration of all. The finish of any lure should be a calculated design, based on the known characteristics of the target fish and the conditions under which it will be used. The finishing scheme should be fully planned before the first drop of paint is spilled! Once we begin the actual process of putting on paint and detail it is too late to start thinking of the finished product. If you design the finish as you go, you will almost invariably end up with some sort of nondescript brown gadget that is neither a credit to your skill nor an asset to the grand art of angling.

It is alright to carve a lure at whim, letting the grain and the "feel" of the wood dictate the direction you might go. Once carved, however, the entire finish should be committed to paper and tacked over the workbench. Any modifications that suggest themselves during finishing might be tried out on paper but will seldom be incorporated into the lure. If the new idea proves to be an interesting experiment, go ahead and make it a part of the lure…but it seldom will work out that way.

The truly experimental lure will be made just like one of the standard designs. You will consider what you intend to catch, where you intend to fish with the new creation, and how to incorporate the attraction components that are in your mind. Luremaking—and especially lure finishing—is not an extemporaneous exercise.

chapter
·SIX·

CONSTRUCTING
FRESHWATER PLUGS

There is evidence that the first artificial lure to be widely used was a metal spoon, but the wooden plug followed shortly and soon became the lure of choice for most anglers. Early bass anglers in particular embraced the plug, it being more practical and reliable than bait. James Heddon's first plug was probably designed for smallmouth bass (although we cannot be perfectly sure), but it was almost immediately adapted for largemouth, and the plug remains the traditional standby for Stillwater bass angling.

There have been more design departures among the plugs than any other kind of artificial lure, and over the years literally thousands of creations have been tried and marketed. On closer examination, we find that the arsenal of freshwater plugs can actually be reduced to about two dozen specific forms, the remainder being adaptations of those originals. An examination of a modern tackle catalog reveals an astonishing assortment of plugs, but a close inspection will still show only a couple of dozen different designs. The selection is made so large because of differences in size, material, and finish or color. Any given design can be produced in fifty individual models or more, the color and finish pattern being the chief distinction.

Luremakers have tried to wrap their creations in a cloak of mystery and intrigue that borders on voodoo, but the facts are actually somewhat different. The production of an effective plug is only slightly more difficult than falling off a shoreside log, and anyone with sufficient coordination to spincast while maintaining a standing position can build them with no trouble. There simply are no secrets to fashioning a decent plug, despite the claims of the commercial lure manufacturers.

The designs we've included in this chapter can all be made with a pocket-knife, some sandpaper, a drill, and some patience. The finishing process, during which we add the paint and other attraction elements becomes something of a science, but there is certainly nothing mysterious about it. These designs are quite general, of course, and allow for a lot of construction latitude —either considered or accidental! In short, the design is meant to be a guideline, and some individual change in size or shape—within reason—will not significantly detract from the usefulness of the lure.

Constructing the Basic Plug

Let's begin by theoretically building a handy-dandy, all-purpose single wire bass plug. To make this exercise truly educational, we'll add a diving plane and some weight to make it a better diver. In fact, we'll add loose shot as the weighting element to make the plug rattle, giving it an added attraction component for low-visibility waters. Please refer to illustration 6-1 as we move through this armchair exercise.

First, choose a stick of wood from which to whittle the lure. Since this plug is rather thin, we'll choose a material that is sturdy but soft enough to shape easily. You might pick fir, hemlock, mahogany, cedar, or almost any other common softwood. I realize that mahogany is technically classified as a hardwood, but it works easily and is a pretty decent choice for many lures. Avoid using oak, hickory, maple, or other true hardwoods…they're just too difficult to carve and shape properly.

The plug designs have been transferred to our drawings by means of a grid system. If you have any difficulty getting a good reproduction of the design on the raw wood, you can draw a larger grid on the wood and use it for reference. Simply mark the point on each grid line where the outline crosses and connect the points. It is possible to use a french curve or a ruler to join the dots (and thus complete the outline), but it probably isn't necessary. Anyone with sufficient skill to open a pocketknife can whittle the design close enough to be useful. As we've noted elsewhere, these drawings are just essential guides; small variations in shape or size are not only tolerated, they're encouraged.

Having chosen the piece of wood, roughly pencil the outline of the lure on the side and top so you have something to guide your first few moments of carving. As the lure begins to take shape, you might adjust the whittling operation to take successively smaller cuts, but don't try to achieve the final dimensions with your knife. The sandpaper will be used to reach the ultimate shape. It's important not to detach the plug from the stick of wood until after the sanding operation is complete. The waste part of the wood gives us something to hang onto while we sand it to shape.

MAKING SINGLE-WIRE RIGS

WHITTLE AND SAND TO ABOUT THE
SIZE & SHAPE SHOWN. THE BODY
DOESN'T NEED MUCH TAPER ON
THE SIDES. A VERY THIN PLUG
WOULD BE TOO WEAK.

USING SCISSORS, CUT
A PIECE OF WASTE
PLASTIC INTO A LONG
DIVING PLANE.

SAW THE PLUG BODY AT ABOUT
45° FROM THE LINE IT WILL SWIM.
MAKE THE CUT JUST UNDER
½-INCH DEEP.

CAREFULLY DRILL A SMALL
HOLE THROUGH THE BODY.
KEEP THE DRILL AS NEAR
THE CENTER LINE AS POSSIBLE.

THE LURE WILL BE PAINTED AND DETAILED
BEFORE THE DIVING FIN IS CEMENTED
OR THE RIGGING ADDED.

THIS LURE CAN BE MODIFIED BY CAREFULLY DRILLING A ¼" HOLE
UP INTO THE BODY AS SHOWN: DROP A FEW
B-B'S OR BIRDSHOT INTO THE HOLE AND EPOXY
A ¼" DOWEL TO SEAL. THE SHOT WILL MAKE THE
LURE RUN DEEPER AND WILL "RATTLE" FOR BASS OR TROUT!

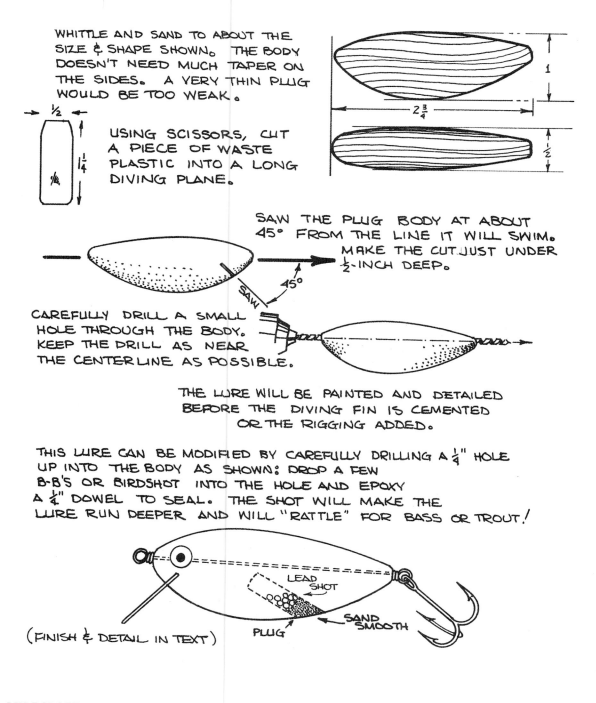

(FINISH & DETAIL IN TEXT)

LEAD
SHOT

SAND
SMOOTH

PLUG

Once the blank has been sanded to shape, cut it off the stick and finish sanding and shaping the nose or tail, depending on which part you left attached to the stick. The shaped and sanded blank is now ready for drilling and rigging.

At this point the tackle vise outlined earlier becomes an indispensable part of the operation. It is virtually impossible to saw the slot for a diving plane or to drill the blank for rigging without the aid of a vise. Any attempt to hand-hold the blank for these operations will usually result in a botched lure and perhaps a perforated pinky. I would discourage the asking of a friend or spouse to hold the blank during the sawing or drilling operation, too. I realize that relationships need occasional testing, but this may be carrying things a bit far.

The diving plane, which has been cut from a waste piece of plastic or metal, will be cemented in place before the finishing if it is to be painted along with the body. If it is to be left clear—which is the normal approach—it will be added after the paint job. Likewise, the single-wire harness is generally added after the lure has been finished. Adding the belly-weights, as we've done in this case, is done before the finishing operation.

Again, the blank must be placed in the vise if weights are to be added, and the hole drilled carefully. Note that the weight cavity comes very close to the small lateral hole that has been drilled for the rigging wire. You will need to measure quite carefully to prevent those holes from intersecting. Once the belly hole is drilled you may add the weight, in this case a few pieces of shot. Some designs call for a solid piece of pencil lead to be added and it's best to drill the cavity to precisely fit the lead. That's easy, since the lead comes in uniform $\frac{3}{16}$, $\frac{1}{4}$, or $\frac{3}{8}$-inch diameters. Just choose an appropriate drill bit for the lead on hand and make it fit. With shot, it will be necessary to whittle a tight-fitting plug and cement it in place. Sand the plug smooth and go on to the finishing process outlined earlier.

The finish for this plug can range widely, depending on the specific use you have in mind for it. Chapter 5 outlines the actual techniques, and each of the designs included here has suggestions for colors, patterns, and contrast elements that will help make the lure more effective.

Rigging the Plug

The rigging operation for our all-purpose exercise was the simplest type we can make. It consists of a single wire running through the plug, to which we attach the hook on the rear and twist (bend) an eye at the head, from which the plug is

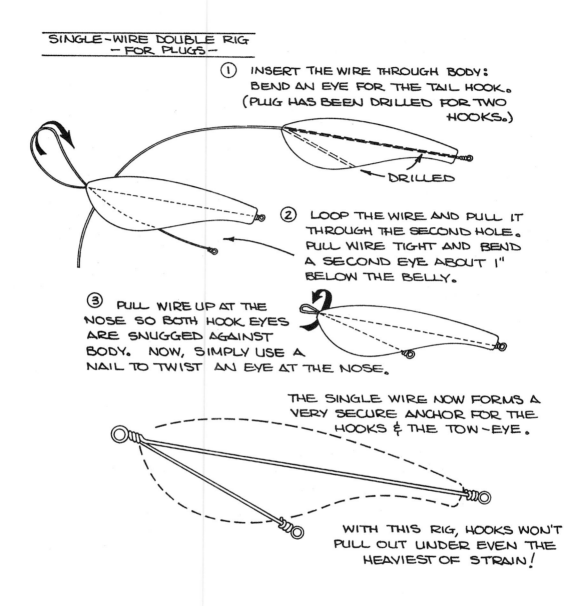

SINGLE-WIRE DOUBLE RIG
— FOR PLUGS —

① INSERT THE WIRE THROUGH BODY: BEND AN EYE FOR THE TAIL HOOK. (PLUG HAS BEEN DRILLED FOR TWO HOOKS.)

← DRILLED

② LOOP THE WIRE AND PULL IT THROUGH THE SECOND HOLE. PULL WIRE TIGHT AND BEND A SECOND EYE ABOUT 1" BELOW THE BELLY.

③ PULL WIRE UP AT THE NOSE SO BOTH HOOK EYES ARE SNUGGED AGAINST BODY. NOW, SIMPLY USE A NAIL TO TWIST AN EYE AT THE NOSE.

THE SINGLE WIRE NOW FORMS A VERY SECURE ANCHOR FOR THE HOOKS & THE TOW-EYE.

WITH THIS RIG, HOOKS WON'T PULL OUT UNDER EVEN THE HEAVIEST OF STRAIN!

trolled or cast. It's the best possible type of rigging, since the single wire provides the most possible strength. As our lures get more involved, though, we have to seek alternative methods of achieving the maximum mechanical strength for the hook attachment.

MAKING CURVED-BODY PLUGS

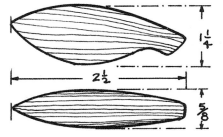

1¼

2½

⅝

THIS PLUG MAY RANGE FROM 2" TO 4½". LARGER SIZES SHOULD BE PROPORTIONATELY THINNER. DON'T WORRY IF THE SANDED BLANK IS SOMEWHAT IRREGULAR—AN ERRATIC MOTION IS PART OF MINNIE'S ATTRACTION.

DRILL SEPARATE HOLES FOR THE ANCHOR AND EYE. THIS BODY DESIGN WON'T ALLOW A SINGLE-WIRE RIG, SINCE THE HOLE COMES TOO CLOSE TO THE EDGE!

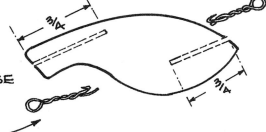

¾

¼

BEND TWO EYES & EPOXY IN PLACE.

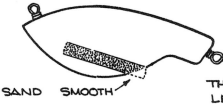

SAND SMOOTH

THIS PLUG SHOULD BE KEEL-WEIGHTED WITH A PIECE OF 3/16 OR ¼ PENCIL-LEAD. DRILL THE HOLE CAREFULLY, GLUE LEAD IN PLACE, THEN FILE OR SAND SMOOTH.

THIS PLUG MAY BE MODIFIED TO A VERY DEEP-RUNNING LURE BY ADDING A #2 OR #3 COLORADO SPINNER BLADE AS A DIVING PLATE. MAKE THE CUT ABOUT ½" DEEP, TAKING CARE NOT TO CUT THE EYE ANCHOR.

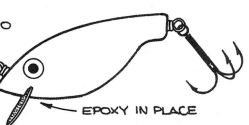

EPOXY IN PLACE

When the plug demands a two-hook configuration, it's possible to provide a very solid foundation by fastening both hooks to a single wire. The accompanying illustration shows how this is accomplished. The towing eye is the last part of the rig to be bent, allowing the hooks to be snugged up against the body. The hooks can be bent directly onto the anchor wires or the resultant loops can be fitted with split-rings to allow frequent changes of hook sizes or styles. It is a simple but very reliable means of fitting the lure with multiple hooks.

If the body of the plug is quite curved it will be difficult or impossible to drill a single hole from end to end for a conventional single-wire rig. In those cases, we'll need to bend separate anchors for the eye and the hook. In some curved application we can run a wire from the tow-eye to the belly hook, but the tail hook will need to be anchored. Note that the end of each anchor features the tips bent back into a barb that helps keep a strong mechanical connection to the body. In addition, each anchor is coated with epoxy as it is secured. The cement hardens within the twists of the wire, strengthening the bond.

In this illustration we have also shown the method of drilling and inserting a solid lead keel-weight to change the diving characteristic of the lure. The soft lead can be carved and sanded smooth, allowing an invisible finish to the drilled area after the plug is painted. The diving pattern can be further changed by inserting a convex or concave diving plate at the nose. Some of the patterns that follow will include specific suggestions for changing the dive characteristic by using a particular type of spinner blade.

Building Basic Freshwater Plugs

From these few examples you can see that it is fairly easy to make a polished, effective lure. Carving and sanding the body, drilling for rigging and weights, and adding a variety of diving or control surfaces are really very simple. The two dozen designs that follow represent almost everything any angler will need in the way of plugs. The amateur will alter the size or length of a plug to suit his particular needs and may even want to experiment with some differences in shape. Every one of these popular plugs evolved as a result of individual experimentation—and I thoroughly encourage such hacking and chopping whenever the spirit moves you. I am convinced that there is a lot of improvement waiting in all artificial lurecraft, and I know that the occasional departure from the basic designs is going to produce some very successful fishing. Most important, it's great fun to catch a nice fish on a lure you've fiddled with, fine tuning it to your own needs.

These designs, then, form the basis of nearly all the plug inventory—but the real excitement lies in wait for the knowledgeable amateur who tinkers in the right direction. Please use the designs as they are intended…simply as a point of departure from which you can experiment.

Shad

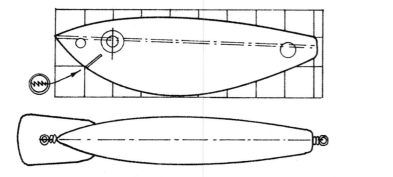

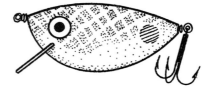

Minnie

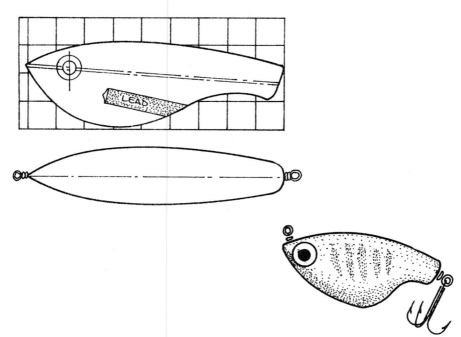

Shad

First developed in the late 1940s as a saltwater lure, the Shad apparently occurred simultaneously on both the East and West coasts of the United States, perhaps carried from one to the other by a globetrotting fisherman. It was very quickly adapted to freshwater fishing and was an established lure for bass and lake trout by the early 1950s. It has been since modified for virtually every game fish and is particularly popular in the smaller sizes.

Carve and shape the body, drill for a single rig, and add the diving plane. Lure may be 1½–3 inches long. You'll note that the plane is set at about 45 degrees from the long axis, which both keeps the lure running fairly deep and keeps it on a free-running course. For bass, it seems to be better if the diving plane points more forward (25°-35°) so it swims shallower with a more erratic retrieve pattern.

Finish with a silver color overall, a blue or green light spray along the back, and a yellow or light red spray under the belly. Eye spots should be high-contrast, preferably black on white, and a bright red trigger spot is added in the caudal area just ahead of the trailing hook. Use smaller sizes for trout and other deep water species, larger sizes for bass.

Minnie

A latecomer to the ranks of freshwater plugs, the Minnie appeared in the late 1970s. The rather unstable shape requires the use of a keelweight, but the plug is effective for almost any freshwater game fish. I have not seen this lure in large sizes, although a bigger version might prove effective for saltwater.

Carve and sand the body to shape and drill for a single wire rigging. Lure is 2–3 inches long. There is no need to add a dive plane, since the weight-formed configuration and the lighter tail allows the lure to dive moderately well without one. The nose needs to be quite pointed when viewed from the top to prevent a very erratic swim pattern. The lure works best when trolled or retrieved at a fairly rapid rate of speed.

Almost any high-contrast finish will be effective for this lure. I like to use a silver or white body and overspray with a blue or dark-green back. I've often put a sprayed set of parr marks or rib markings on the side. Make the eyespot quite large.

Skyler

Nugget

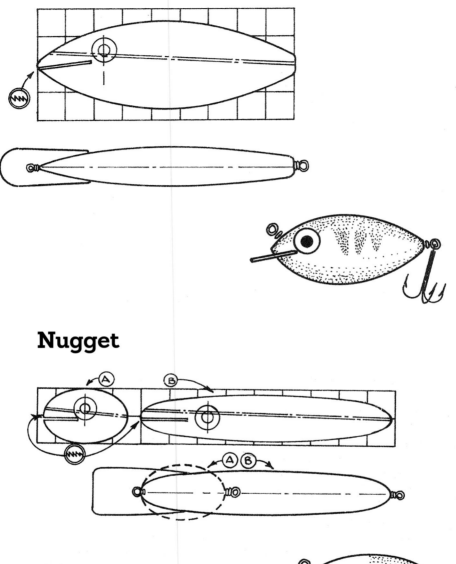

Skyler

Skyler is an extremely thin plug that compensates for an unpredictable trolling pattern with a stabilizing dive plate inserted at a very slight upward angle. I designed this particular plug for warm-weather lake-trout fishing. I found that the deep but thin shape attracted large predators that prowled the warmer shallows in search of pumpkinseed or other sunfish. It's been very successful in some of the mid-Canadian lakes and seems to be just the thing for warm evenings.

Lure is 1½–3 inches long. Use a well-cured softwood for greater strength. I use clear fir almost exclusively for this lure. Drill for a single rig with the rigging hole well above the centerline so the plug is retrieved in a nose-down attitude. Cut the dive plane from clear or soft plastic and epoxy in place.

Although this lure is generally fished morning or evening in dim light, I give the light body a distinctive dark back and a rosy belly. A few sprayed rib marks will add considerable attraction to the lure. Make the eye quite large and very definite.

Skyler is a valuable lure on almost any kind of lake or slow-moving stream. I usually have several different sizes and finishes of this pattern in my tacklebox and rely on them when other plugs just aren't getting any action.

Nugget

Nugget is almost a surface plug, designed to run at the top of the water or just a few inches below. As you can see from the drawings, it can be made in anything from a 1-inch stubby little ball to a 4-inch elongated cigar—and there is an appropriate application for either. Nugget answered a special need for a lure that could be fished in the foot or so of clear water that is often found above a submerged bed of waterweed.

The construction is ridiculously simple. Rough out the body with a knife and sand to final shape with a strip of sandpaper manipulated like a shoeshine rag. It's remarkably easy to get a smooth, regular shape…or at least close enough to fish easily. Drill for a single-wire rig.

Cut the slot for the squared diving plane as carefully as possible, making sure there is only the slightest angle to the plane. It is almost a horizontal plane and may take some adjustment after the lure is completed to keep it from diving too deeply. Ideally, the Nugget lures should run barely below the surface when retrieved at a medium rate.

I have had the most success when fishing a very high-contrast color scheme with a front and back division.

Finback

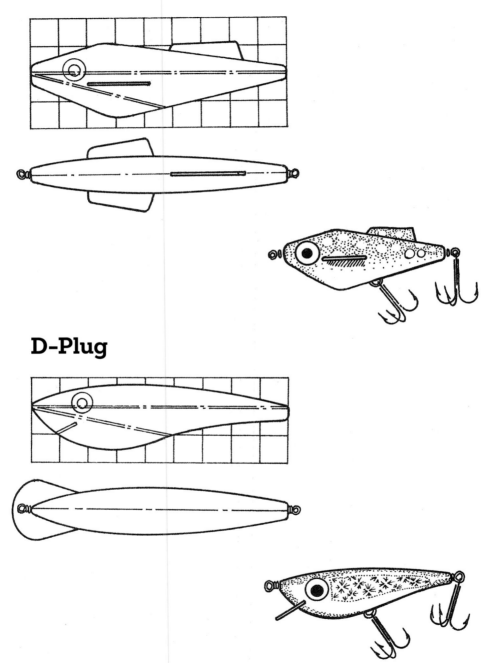

D-Plug

Finback

Finback is a hydrodynamically neutral lure that is designed to be trolled behind a string of flashers and some considerable weight. It will swim in a rather lazy side-to-side motion even at faster troll speeds in a very deep troll pattern. It is thus excellent for the big lakers and char. The smaller versions, when trolled shallow behind a single flash string or a dodger, offer the kind of gentle movement that characterizes a fine musky lure.

This is a larger lure, 3–5 inches long, and generally requires two sets of hooks, so drill for a single-wire double rig. The belly hook also helps maintain the even stability of the lure under troll.

The most successful color scheme for this lure is a pale green body, dark green back, and a slight yellow overspray on the belly. The dark green back is randomly dotted with white spots to provide the stark contrast typical of deepwater lures. I add two red "trigger" spots in the caudal area to help elicit the strike of a following predator. The eye is small and unremarkable, usually a black pupil on a yellow eyespot.

D-Plug

The D-Plug is a variation of one of the better all-around lake rigs for trout, char, and almost all other coldwater game fish. It has taken bass in some multi-species impounds but those were incidental to a trout fishery. It doesn't have the action that bass plugs generally exhibit, but it can be finished with a good attraction scheme that will coax a strike from nearly any fish. D-Plug is a good free-diver and is especially effective when using medium-light tackle in deep water. The configuration includes a very light tail, midpoint towing angle, and a wide, scooping dive plane. The result is a lure that dives deeply at reasonably slow trolling or retrieve speeds and maintains a fairly rapid "wobble" as it swims. The larger sizes (4 to 5 inches) are universally trolled, while the smaller sizes (2½–3 inches) can be trolled or cast.

Drill for a single-wire double rig. Note that the rear hook is mounted above the center of the tail and the belly hook well behind the center of gravity. These placements allow the angler to fine-tune the lure by moving the rear hook to one side or the other to change the wobble while the lure swims.

The finish should be a light-colored, medium-contrast combination, since the lure will be fished in deeper, darker conditions. I've found a white body to be very effective when oversprayed with a faintly darkened back of black or blue and a faintly colored belly of yellow or pink. The eye should be small but a markedly high-contrast effect. In general, apply a white eyespot over the darker back color and put a sharp, black pupil at center.

Grunt

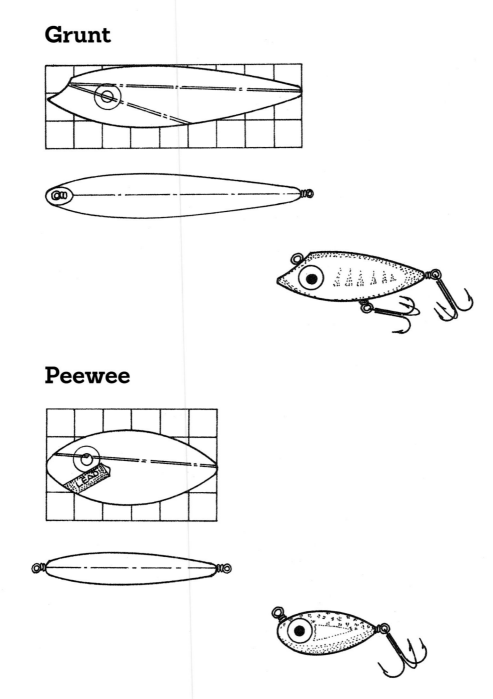

Peewee

Grunt

Grunt is a wonderful small-to-large bass plug for winter fishing the deep structures. Winter fishing is a matter of prospecting as a rule, and this plug produces an erratic pattern within easily controlled bounds. Actually, Grunt swims in a very predictable, controlled line on the retrieve or troll, but does a lot of dancing and twisting as it moves along.

Carve and sand the plug as shown, making certain it is thickest at a point just behind the eyespot of the drawing. Drill for a standard single-wire double rigging, and use hooks that are smaller than average for this size plug. Grunt is 3–6 inches long.

Finish with a very high-contrast effect for maximum attraction during the cold, lethargic winter season. I prefer a light body, very dark blue or green back, and a fluorescent yellow or orange belly. I almost always include a panel of reflective tape or "scalelight" to each side to increase the visible attraction in the low-angle light conditions of winter.

Peewee

Peewee is a small, thin, fragile little plug, 1¼–3 inches long. Drill for a single-wire rig. The ¾-inch pencil-lead chin weight will help the lure dive (if that's what you need for a particular application) and will keep it swimming upright even on a slow retrieve. The lure could be built without that weight, but it would have a tendency to flop over on one side when it slows down. Even with the weight, this lure will roll over and play dead at rest, but that can be a positive attraction as well. There are a number of skilled anglers who fish this for bass, working it sort of like a horizontal jig. They move the lure quickly for a few feet, allow it to roll over on its side for an instant, and crank it back upright for a few feet. This technique approximates the action of a badly wounded prey fish—and the bass usually responds with a vicious strike!

The finish for this lure will depend entirely for the application for which it is built. Among the more popular are perch finishes, parr-marked finish, and frogskin. Just look through any tackle shop and you'll see an endless combination of patterns…and most of them work.

Lumpjaw

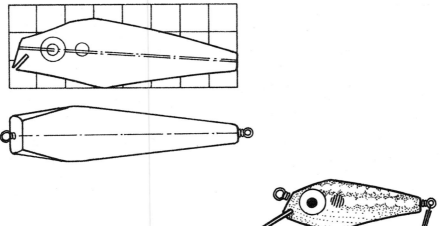

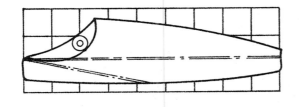

Runt

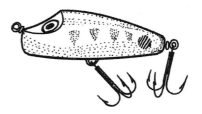

Lumpjaw

Lumpjaw is a multipurpose plug that can be adapted for trout, char, pike, musky, bass, and almost any other fish by varying the size and finish. A generally small lure, it has a lot of mass to allow casting control, a steep diving plane to allow it to run deep and erratically, and an odd shape that produces a lot of water disturbance when it moves.

To be most effective, this plug should be carved from a very light, buoyant wood—preferably cedar or pine. (Pine is harder to finish unless it is thoroughly dry before working.) It should be 2½–3 inches long. The more buoyant the plug, the easier it is to control for spincasting or cranking. Drill for a single-wire rig. I recommend metal for the dive plane as a means of adding some weight forward on the plug and improving the dive characteristic.

The finish should be another high-contrast effect, but it need not be very involved. I prefer a pale green or yellow body, a very dark blue or green back, and a white or fluorescent yellow belly. The eye is small and vivid with a trigger spot—usually red—added directly behind the eye.

When trolled, this lure tends to keep diving until it hits the bottom and starts kicking up mud. Some fish that almost never take plugs—burbot and catfish, for example—have been taken on a trolled Lumpjaw…but those are extremely rare.

Runt

This plug came along very early in the history of artificial lures. It was among the first commercially produced lures, manufactured by James Heddon's Sons. It appeared in various disguises all over the United States, only the size and finish altered to suit local fishing prejudices. It was enormously successful both from a commercial and a sporting standpoint.

The Runt is really quite easy to carve and shape. It looks difficult because of the distinctive nose, but it's only a matter of a couple of knife strokes to produce it. It is 1½–5 inches long. The amateur may have to practice on a few sticks before he gets it perfect, but it isn't at all tough. Otherwise, it's just a flat-bottomed, round-backed plug! Drill it for either a single-wire or a single-wire double rig, depending on the size and finish.

Again, there are no restrictions on finish. This plug has probably been produced in every possible combination from red-and-white to snakeskin—and I would be surprised if all of 'em didn't catch something!

Nurdle

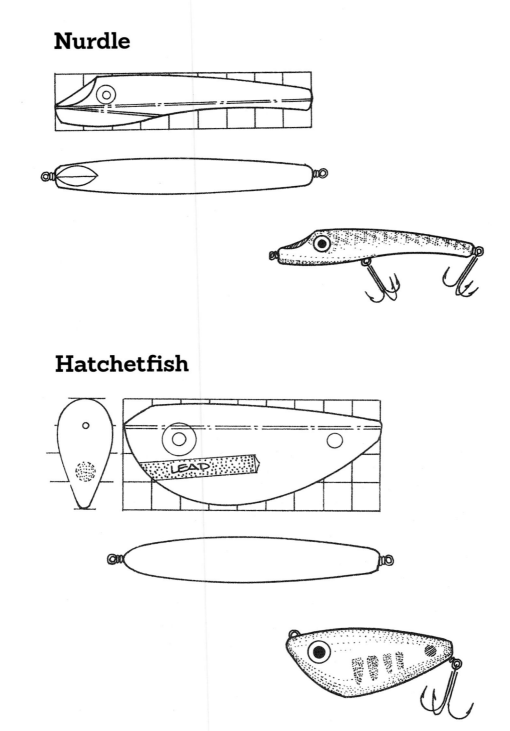

Hatchetfish

Nurdle

This elongated plug, 5–7 inches in length, is effective only in the northern lakes—as far as I know—but has taken it's share of muskies, pike, trout, and char for a great many years. It has a straightforward swim pattern with very little jitter or wobble when trolled. It is often pulled behind a flasher string, usually with enough weight to keep it quite deep, and it necessarily follows the heavy trolling tackle cleanly.

As is true with most pure trolling plugs, Nurdle depends entirely on shape and color for attraction. To some extent, this is a proximity lure; put something the right shape and the right color in a specific predator habitat. . . and something will try to eat it. That's how Nurdle works.

Drill for a single-wire double rig, being sure to make the tow-point well below the centerline.

Finish with a silver body, a dark blue or green back that is screened, scaled, or cross-hatched, and add a blush of red at the belly. The eye should be large.

Hatchetfish

Hatchetfish is a plug I designed to provide a little more action in waters where the popular Shad wasn't getting enough strikes.

Notice that the cross-section of this plug resembles an airfoil; it's thick across the back but tapers sharply down to the belly. When trolled or retrieved in a nose-down position, the currents slide past the back and create a partial vacuum around the trailing belly. This causes the plug to "jiggle" rapidly on the retrieve. If the finish includes a reflective side color, the lure will flash wildly and produce a very wide attraction element.

The design calls for a plug about 3 inches long. I've had good success with trout and bass with a smaller lure about 2 inches long. On smaller or larger models, keep the keel weight in proportion.

In carving and sanding the body, take care to taper it downward quite sharply. Drill for a single-wire rig and insert about 1½-inches of lead in the lower half of the body. Note that the rigging hole is drilled well up on the body so the tow-point stands very high on the body.

Finish with a silver or imitation chrome body, a fairly dark back in green, blue, or black (a masked screen or scale effect is preferable), and add just a touch of yellow or pink to the belly. Because of the rapid action, a bright red or fluorescent orange trigger spot is added at the tail.

J-Bomb

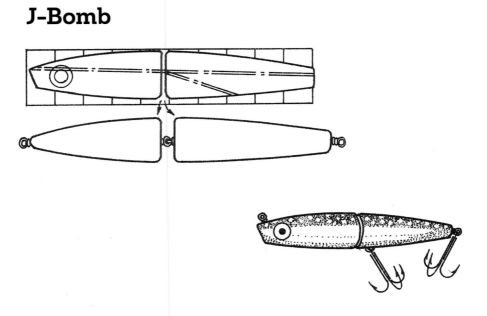

Screemer

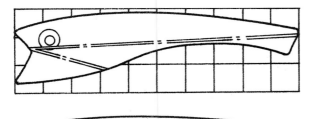

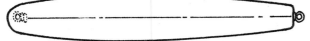

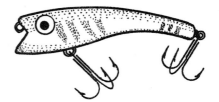

J-Bomb

This a standard jointed plug that is very active and adaptable to many different situations. Designed primarily as a bass surface plug, the J-Bomb— in a silver finish— has become a standby for sockeye salmon in many western lakes. The larger versions in dark, mottled finishes have been very effective for muskies, char, and large rainbow. A slight modification of this jointed lure has proven good for huge cutthroat trout in Nevada and Utah. More recently, a blue-and-white series of J-Bombs have been used on the Great Lakes and in western saltwater for coho and chinook salmon.

The J-Bomb is 3–5 inches long. Carve and shape the body in a single piece. After sanding, cut the body in half and drill the forward half for a single-wire rig and the rear section for a single-wire double rig. Rig the rear section first, then bend the forward shaft onto the established rigging. Insert the forward wire into the body and bend the tow-eye onto it. Once the plug has been assembled, "tune" the plug by bending the eyes at the center until the rear section trails directly behind the front.

This lure gives you ample opportunity to experiment with color and finish. It can be as simple as a red head over a white body, a plain silver lure with simple eyespots, or even a solid green…or it might be a frogskin, perch, or vermiculated paint job.

Screemer

Screemer is another plug that will attract almost any game fish. It is a simple double-hooked plug that has a good, active swim pattern and adds a sonic element on even a moderate retrieve. The inverted "V" shape of the mouth generates a sound wave ahead of the lure.

Screemer has a good side-to-side wobble—sort of a partial roll—that is a result of its basic design. For that reason, it's important not to overdo the vertical curve of the tail section. If the tail hooks downward too deeply the plug will roll over on the retrieve. The addition of the belly hook tends to stabilize the pattern; it's required on even the smaller versions. I prefer to use a fairly large treble at the belly for stability.

The plug is 2½–4½ inches long. Use your burnishing stick or a flat pattern file to smooth the surfaces of the mouth. These need to be quite flat and very smooth to generate the forward sonic waves on the troll or retrieve. Drill for a single-wire double rig with the belly hook forward.

Finish with a bright body—silver, chrome, or white—and spray over a dark back in green or blue. The back should be masked for a scale or screen patterns. The inside of the jaws can be red and the belly lightly sprayed for a red blush. The eye can be quite large and definite.

Sundown

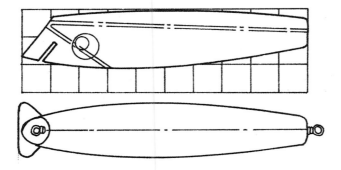

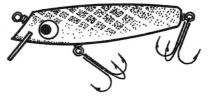

Shoehorn

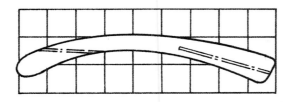

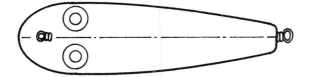

Sundown

Sundown is a squared-body plug that attracts a variety of fish but is not particularly well-known as a bass lure. That's really a shame, because this plug attracts bass in open water.

Carve and shape the body to a length of 2–6 inches. Drill for a single-wire double rig and saw a very steep diving slot in the lower jaw. Note that the diving plane is parallel to the nose plane. The dive plane is a wide triangle that is cemented in place before finishing so it can be the same color scheme as the body.

The finish will depend on the specific application, but the deep lures almost universally require high-contrast patterns. The back can be vermiculated or scaled in a dark color and the belly should have a blush of fluorescence or bright color. The eye is set low on the head and should be very definite.

Shoehorn

Shoehorn is a plug I designed to provide a totally different action from the commercially produced flat-type of lure. This plug has a more moderate wobble and can be trolled rather slowly without losing its action. It is most effective for lake trout, char, and large rainbow when trolled bare. It is not a particularly deep river, but manages to maintain a nose-down position even when following weights or flashers. The thickened tail adds an element of buoyancy that is missing in the manufactured lures.

The lure is 2½–3½ inches long. Note that the nose—unlike the commercial lures—is not concave. Drill for a single-wire belly hook and a separate hook anchor at the tail. Leave a fairly long tow-eye so the lure can be tuned while fishing. Bending the eye upward will deepen the dive pattern; bending the eye down against the body will shallow the pattern.

Finish with either a solid color overall or almost any high-contrast pattern. My best success with this lure has been in a candy-apple red with a silver bottom and a bright orange with random red spots. I've also caught fish with a green/yellow frogskin and a blue-and-silver vermiculated finish.

Viggler

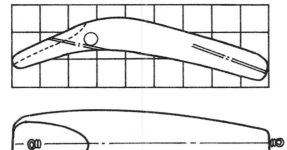

Twinktail

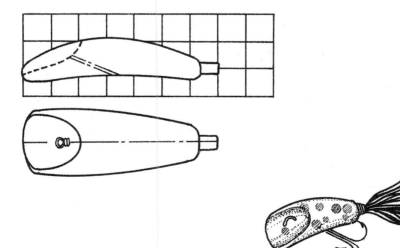

Viggler

Viggler is a variation of the famous Flatfish, one of the most successful trout and freshwater salmon lures of all time. This is a hot-weather version, designed to dive deeply without added weights or a troll string. The body is widest at the point of the sharp bend, acting as a built-in dive plane, the nose area is hollowed out, giving the nose an added downward turn when trolled or retrieved. This lure is especially effective when cast for trout or steelhead in a fast-moving stream. The dive pattern takes it down to the rocks when it is merely held against the current. It is equally effective in lakes when retrieve rapidly or trolled at moderate speeds.

Carve and sand the body, which is 3–6 inches long, using a rasp or sanding board to produce a concave curve at the nose area. Drill for a single-wire belly hook and a separate tail hook as shown. It is fine-tuned in the same manner as the Shoehorn.

Finish in bright solid colors, contrasting dots, or in a basic frog or scale pattern. The eyespots are small and inconspicuous, acting as a proximity trigger for the following fish.

You might want to build several models with varying degrees of body curve for a variety of diving effects.

Twinktail

Twinktail is another variation on the flattie styles, but designed for trophy fish. While the plug is fairly small, the added mylar or rubber skirt makes it appear considerable larger. Since there is no tail hook, the fish must strike directly at the body before it is hooked.

This is a small lure, 1½–2½ inches long. Make the concave nose cavity rather deep. Drill for a single-wire rig as shown, the tow-point quite high in the nose depression. Leave a ¼-inch tail stub, to which you'll tie the skirt or tail.

Because the body must be the focus of the strike, finish it carefully to incorporate the most effective trigger elements. Choose a dark body color and spray the belly white or silver. Add a few rib-stripes or vermiculations of gray or green to the belly and place a bright trigger spot immediately behind the hook. There are no distracting eyespots in this scheme.

Winchester

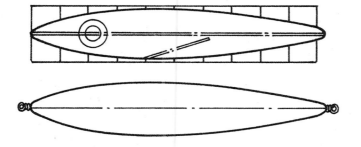

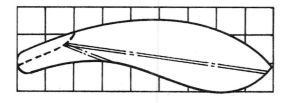

Queenbug

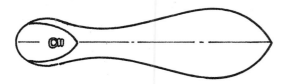

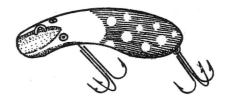

Winchester

Winchester is about as classic a lake plug as can be found. It's a simple torpedo-shaped body that swims straight forward with little more than a rolling motion. It's the kind of plug that is retrieved through a school of similar-sized baitfish for char, lakers, muskie, or almost any other large game fish. It's one of the few plugs than can be effective when trolled for bass. Obviously, you won't always find a school of prey fish, but the plug represents that food source—and the fish often respond with a blind strike anyway.

Carve and sand the plug to a length of 4–7½ inches. Most of the shaping is done with a strip of sandpaper used shoeshine fashion. Even some asymmetry is acceptable in this lure because it still follows rather calmly even if lopsided. The plug doesn't dive at all and must rely on outside weights or trolling gear to get down very deep. At rest, the plug will surface and will stay near the surface on a slow retrieve. It's especially good for weed-bound pike and musky when dragged over the tops of the weedbeds.

Drill for a single-wire rig through the body and a reversed separate anchor for the belly hook. Winchester is designed for very large fish and the reverse angle of the belly anchor adds considerable integral strength during the fight.

This is a plain-swimming lure and the finish matches its character. It is almost always has a solid white or silver body with a dipped red or deep gold head. The eyespots should be very large and prominent.

Queenbug

This is an original design that I developed strictly for bass, but that has been adapted by other anglers to a variety of fish. I wanted a lure that could be cast long distances, would dive and rise quickly in short, jerky retrieves, and would provide a maximum of strike attraction through its shape. Queenbug was the result. The line can also be trolled.

Carve the odd-shaped body to a length of 2–5 inches and bring it to a final form with a lot of sanding. Drill for a single-wire double rig with the belly hook set at the rather narrow neck. The tail hook exist just below the pointed tail.

Finish with a very high-contrast effect. I generally use a white body with a dark red head and red rib-stripes both on the upper and lower body.

Queenbug is a pleasure to use along rough, rocky shorelines and around partially submerged cover. It is an easily controlled crankbait and that allows for a very skillful presentation in difficult waters.

Piker

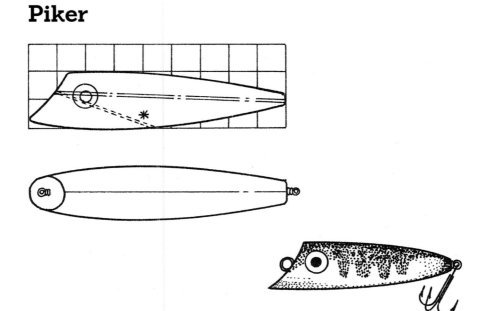

Devon Minnow

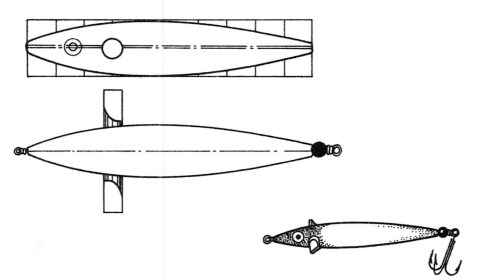

Piker

Another all-around lake lure that can also be fished in most slower rivers with grand success. It is patterned after the old red-and-white salmon plugs of the 1930s. The single distinction is the flattened tail that gives the plug greater stability when fished as a bass or trout lure.

The lure is 2½–3½ inches long. Make the flat face slightly concave. Drill for a single-wire double rig with the tow-point just above center. The belly hook is placed about midway on the body. (Smaller plugs may omit the belly hook and go with a single-wire rig.)

Finish with a white or silver body, dark overspread back—patterned if you wish—and a tinted red or yellow belly. The eyespot is prominent, high-contrast, and centered at the head.

Devon Minnow

Just for fun I've included one of the oldest known plugs, the classic Devon Minnow. It was designed to take Atlantic Salmon from the ancient redds of Great Britain. I built a few of these plugs prior to a trip to Canada's fabled Campbell River, a wonderful place where the atmosphere nearly approximates angling in Britain. To my astonishment, I quickly hooked a gigantic Tyee salmon, a chinook subspecies unique to the eastern side of Vancouver Island. After perhaps fifteen minutes, the fish—in the 50-pound class—threw the hook and got off, but for a few moments I was transported to another time in another place…fishing the legendary rivers of the English midlands.

Carve and sand the thin, regular body to a length of 4–5 inches. Drill for the ¼—inch dowel that will become the "wings," insert the dowel and cement in place. Then, drill the body carefully for the center shaft, which should be stiff stainless wire. Put a bend behind the body so it can rotate around the shaft. Bend a treble hook at the tail and a tow-eye forward. The dowel is carved into a "propeller" to cause the lure to spin on the retrieve or when held against the current.

Finish with a yellow body, red head, and a black-and-white eye. No point in fighting tradition!

Scat

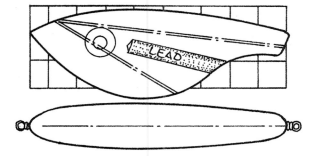

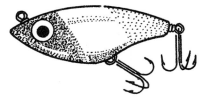

Bluefish

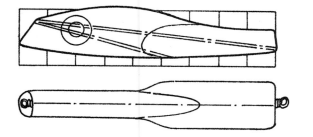

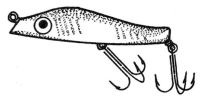

Scat

Scat is another all-purpose freshwater lure that can take almost all game fish. It is somewhat similar to the traditional Minnie but is double-hooked and includes a belly weight to stabilize the swim pattern. Scat is effective for slow retrieves in cold water when the bass or char are somewhat dormant.

The lure is 2½–4½ as inches long. Drill for a single-wire double rig and insert a lead weight forward from the tail section. Note that the tow-point is well back on the head.

Finish with perch, frogskin, or other pattern. The lure is effective with nearly all finishing schemes but seems most effective in a high-contrast pattern.

Bluefish

Bluefish is a modification of a classic saltwater plug that was originally known as a "Tin Squid."

It is—despite the odd appearance—a pretty standard freshwater plug that can attract a variety of game fish. It is a little difficult to carve, but offers a steady swim pattern, a stabilizing tail for fishing heavy current, and a shape that seems attractive to trout, char, and muskies.

Carve and sand the body with a distinctive "knee" midway back. The lure may be 2–5 inches long. The forward half of the plug is sort of a vertical block, the rear half a horizontal block. Drill larger models for a single-wire double rig and the smaller for a single-wire tail hook.

Finish in silver with a blue back and faint red belly. The eye should be large and prominent.

Variety—the Spice of Plugs

These two-dozen plugs represent only a small fraction of the final effects the home lurecrafter can achieve with a little imagination and some patience. Most are easy to make and offer plenty of opportunity for experimentation.

Plugging is only one of many fishing techniques, and the avid angler will utilize it when it fits. In the chapters that follow we'll show how to build lures for almost every kind of fishing situation.

Our next group of lures, however, is limited to a single species—the large mouth bass—and a single technique. Surface fishing for bass, however limited it might seem, is one of the most exciting of all fishing experiences.

STEP-BY-STEP LURECRAFTING AND GALLERY OF LURES

In the original edition of this book, Russ Mohney included some brief step-by-step photography for carving and painting lures, as well as a small gallery of handmade lures based on his designs. In this updated edition of the book, a new section with fresh photography and more detailed steps for carving and finishing lures has been included. I have been a lurecrafter for over 25 years, and I have greatly enjoyed the process of recreating Russ's step-by-step instructions and hand-carving his interesting lures.

First follow along as I sketch, carve and sand a basic lure body by following simple but effective steps. Next, learn different techniques for painting and adding texture and detail to your lure to make it catch a fish's eye. Then, enjoy the gallery of 29 handmade lures that I based entirely on Russ's designs. Finally, included are two paint charts of recommended paints for lurecrafting that are safe and easy to work with and available in a wide variety of colors.

While recreating Russ's lures for this gallery, it occurred to me that there have been major improvements in paints and parts in the past 25 years. I made these lures to Russ's original specifications and tried to be faithful to both the original designs and the spirit of each lure. These lures vary from the originals only in the type of paint used and some accessory items; otherwise, they are fair likenesses of the original designs. The original lures were painted with solvent based enamel paints, and these lures were painted with a new water-based paint from Component Systems Coatings (*CSIPaint.com,* see color chart), which has all of the characteristics of enamel, but has a more user-friendly odor and cleanup and is safer to your health. Furthermore, the original lures were designed as wire-through only, and Russ mentioned eye screws in passing because they were not readily available and/or not made of the proper material. Today there are stainless steel eye-screws made specifically for lure making which are very inexpensive to use and easier to incorporate than the wire-trough types. For the making of the lures in this gallery, these types of materials were graciously donated by *lurecraft.com.*

I sincerely hope you like the fresh new lures that I crafted in Russ's individual style.

—*Rich Rousseau*

Carving a Lure

1

Prep your wood. Nearly all the plug patterns in this book are made to be carved from ¾" square pieces of lumber. You can see here that I have cut 8 pieces of wood ¾" x ¾" x 12" long from a piece of standard 2' x 4' construction lumber.

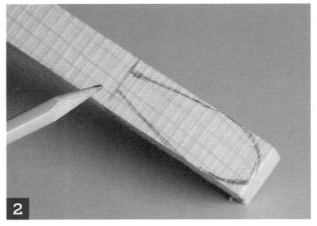

2

Sketch one side. Draw one side of your lure pattern at the end of a ¾" square, 12" long stick of wood. The length will act as a helpful handle during the carving process.

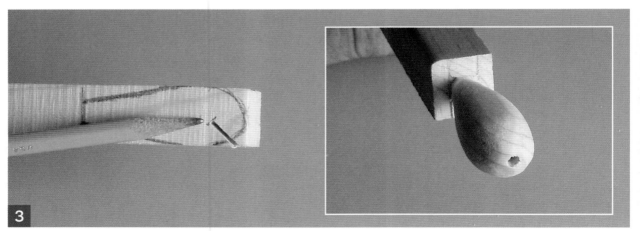

3

Make necessary cuts and holes. The lure you are carving may need to have certain cuts or holes made. You will find it very easy to make these accurately by clamping the wooden handle into a vise and working your saw or drill with both hands free. The cuts can be made into a square blank as show, but you may find it easier to make them after your lure has been carved and rounded.

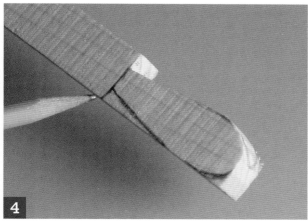

4

Carve one section. Either saw or whittle out a single section of the pattern you drew. You can carve the top, bottom, or side; it doesn't matter.

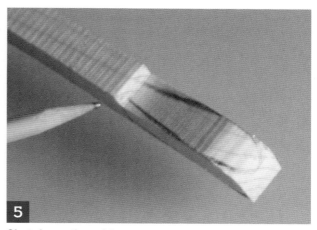

5

Sketch another side. Rotate the handle and draw the other half of the pattern onto the area you already carved away.

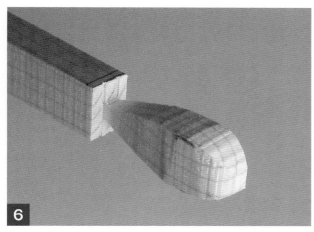

6

Carve the rest. Cut or whittle the rest of the lure until you have a squared-off basic shape.

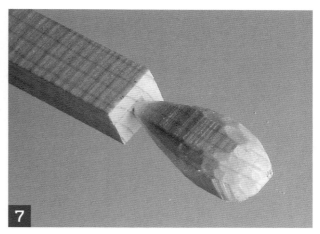

7

Round roughly. Now take off the corners and edges until you have a roughly rounded lure shape.

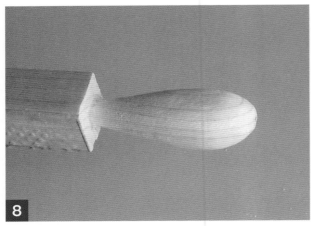

8

Finish and sand. Refine the rough rounding. You may clamp the handle in a vise and use sandpaper to finish the shaping. At this point you can also drill your holes or make any necessary cuts if you haven't already.

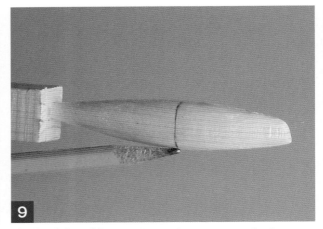

9

Making jointed lures. If your lure is jointed, clamp the handle into a vise, saw the rounded body in half, cut the rear half loose from the handle, and sand the raw end smooth. Cutting the lure free from the handle is always the last cut to make. You are now ready for painting and rigging.

Painting and Finishing

Note: I attempt to show many techniques in this example, but please keep in mind that simple two-color lures are very effective, and the entire process could be done with a dip of white followed by a partial dip of another color. Sometimes simple is better, sometimes not.

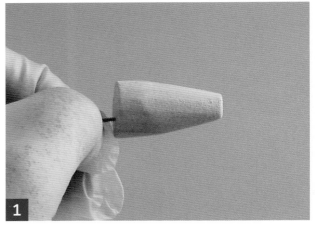

1

Add wire. When you have finish-sanded your lure and drilled your wire hole (or pilot holes for small stainless steel eye screws), insert a wire long enough to "hang" the lure with the head upward. This will prepare your lure for dipping in paint.

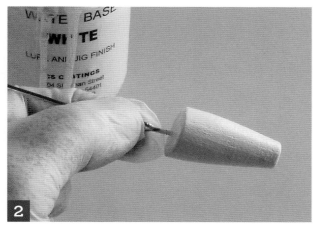

2

Prep the wood. You will want to prime and base coat the wood. White makes a good base because it allows all subsequent coats of paint to show good color value.

3

Dip in the base color. Once the primer/base coat has dried, re-dip the lure into your chosen color base coat. This photo shows silver pearl, but it could be yellow, red, gold, green, etc.

4

Dip the head. When the base color is dry, move the wire or screw to the tail (back) of the lure so that just the head may be dipped. By inverting the lure, you can dip the head without the paint running all over the lure.

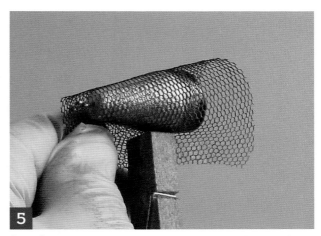

5

Attach a screen. Once the head color is dry, apply a screen around the lure in order to spray scales onto its back (top).

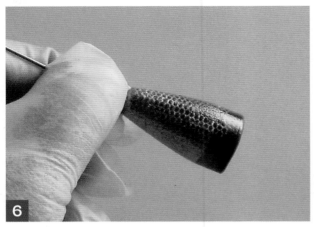

Spray on the scales. Spray the scales onto the lure's back. After spraying, take the screen off right away.

Spray the belly. Turn the lure and spray the belly the color of your choice. This photo shows white, but red, yellow, etc. could be used. Belly colors are not generally screened. Hang the lure to dry.

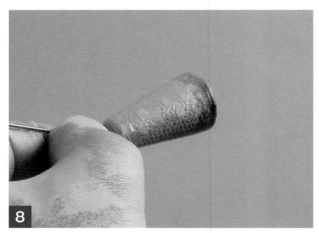

Begin painting details. This lure has a pattern of attractors on both sides, between the back scales and the belly edge. Use a small paintbrush to apply a series of random yellow spots. Paint different size spots randomly, without a regular pattern.

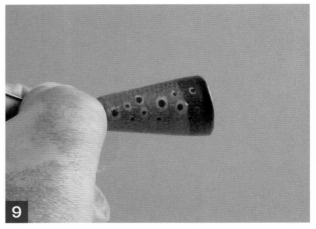

Add to details. When the yellow spots are dry or nearly dry, go back with a smaller brush and paint a red dot in the center of each yellow spot.

10

Detail the back. After the spots dry, vermiculate the back of the lure over top of the scales. Use black paint and a very fine brush to paint random "worm" marks. Paint enough marks to darken the back, but not so many as to hide the sprayed scales.

11

Add eyespots. You may paint eyespots, or use stick-on eyes if you want a holographic/prismatic eye that is difficult to imitate with paint.

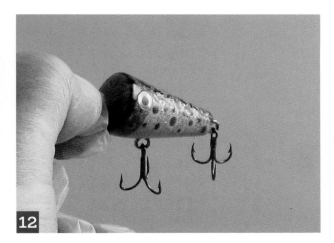

12

Clear coat. Once the eyes are placed and all paint is dry, dip the entire lure in clear coat. This protects the hand-painted details and sets the eyes. Try a clear coat with an ultraviolet reflector in it, so the lure flashes even in the lowest light. Here's the finished lure after being rigged with hardware.

GALLERY

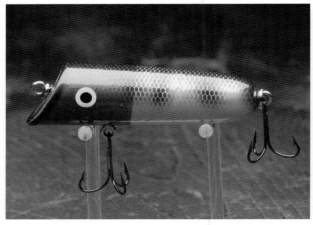

J-Plug. This basic lure has been used in almost all kinds of angling, in one variation or another. *See page 46.*

Shad. Developed in the 1940s, Shad is good for bass and lake trout. Though it is made in many sizes, it is especially popular when small. *See page 106.*

Minnie. Minnie appeared in the 1970s. The lure needs a keelweight, but is effective for many types of fish. *See page 106.*

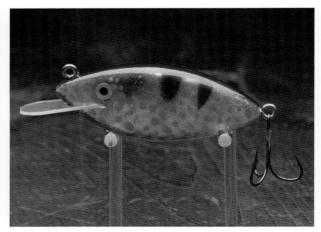

Skyler. Good for warm-weather lake trout fishing, the deep but thin shape of this lure attracts large predators that prowl the warmer shallows. *See page 108.*

Nugget. Nugget answered a special need for a lure that could be fished in the foot or so of clear water that is often found above a submerged bed of waterweed. *See page 108.*

Finback. Designed to be trolled behind a string of flashers and some considerable weight, this lure is excellent for big lakers and char. *See page 110.*

D-Plug. As this lure will be fished in deeper, darker conditions, try painting it with a white body with a contrasting back and belly. *See page 110.*

Grunt. Grunt is a wonderful small-to-large bass plug for winter fishing. It does a lot of dancing and twisting as it moves along. *See page 112.*

Peewee. Among the more popular finishes for this lure are perch finishes, parr-marked finish, and frogskin. *See page 112.*

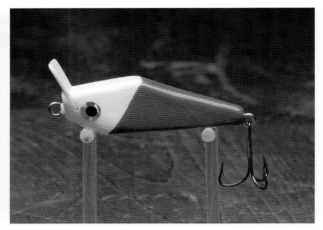

Lumpjaw. This multipurpose plug can be adapted for trout, char, pike, musky, bass, and almost any other fish by varying the size and finish. *See page 114.*

Runt. This versatile lure was among the first commercially produced lures, manufactured by James Heddon's Sons. *See page 114.*

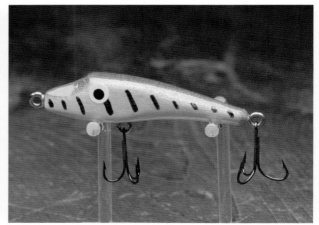

Nurdle. As is true with most pure trolling plugs, Nurdle depends entirely on shape and color for attraction. *See page 116.*

Hatchetfish. This lure is a good alternative option in waters where the popular Shad lure isn't getting enough strikes. *See page 116.*

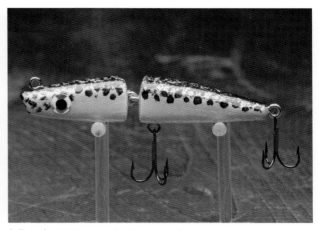

J-Bomb. This standard jointed plug gives you ample opportunity to experiment with color and finish. *See page 118.*

Screemer. Screemer has a good side-to-side wobble, and the inverted "V" shape of the mouth generates a sound wave ahead of the lure. *See page 118.*

Sundown. This square-bodied plug is not known as a bass lure but it does attract them in open water. *See page 120.*

Shoehorn. The lure provides a totally different action from the commercially produced flat-type of lure; it has a more moderate wobble. *See page 120.*

Viggler. This is the hot-weather version of the famous Flatfish, one of the most successful trout and freshwater salmon lures of all time. *See page 122.*

Twinktail. Because the body of this lure must be the focus of the strike, finish it carefully to incorporate the most effective trigger elements. *See page 122.*

Winchester. This classic lake plug has a simple torpedo-shaped body that swims straight forward with little more than a rolling motion. *See page 124.*

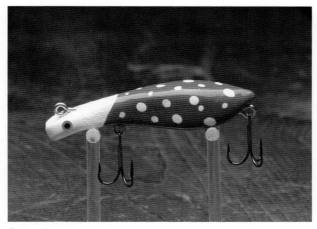

Queenbug. Queenbug is a pleasure to use along rough, rocky shorelines and around partially submerged cover. *See page 124.*

Piker. This lake and slow river lure is patterned after the old red-and-white salmon plugs of the 1930s. *See page 126.*

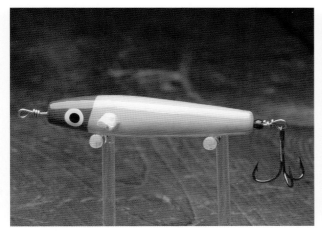

Devon Minnow. This is one of the oldest known plugs. It was designed to take Atlantic Salmon from the ancient redds of Great Britain. *See page 126.*

Scat. Scat is most effective for slow retrieves in cold water when the bass or char are somewhat dormant. *See page 128.*

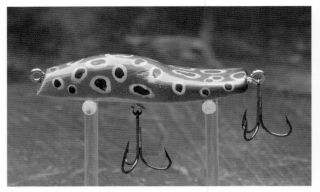

Bluefish. Though more difficult to carve, this is a standard freshwater plug that can attract a variety of game fish like trout, char, and muskies. *See page 128.*

Hatchethead. Why this lure attracts so many fish is a bit of a mystery, but it works in diverse waters all over the country. *See page 134.*

Hambone. This river plug is excellent when fished from a drift boat or cast downstream into a flowing pool. *See page 214.*

Squamish. This bigwater lure is specifically designed to be towed behind a weight or flasher string. *See page 242.*

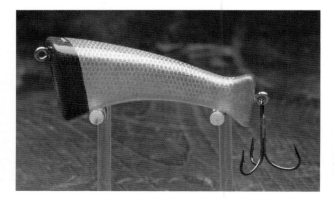

Kokanee. This popular lure works well in both fresh and salt water, including large inland lakes. *See page 246.*

Polytranspar Airbrush Paints

OPAQUE & SEMI-OPAQUE SERIES (non-bleeding)

Lacquer Based (FP) / Water Based (WA)

FP10/WA10	Superhide White
FP11/WA11	Whitetail Ear Light
FP12/WA12	Whitetail Ear Medium
FP13/WA13	Whitetail Ear Dark
FP15/WA15	Bass Belly White
FP29/WA29	Black Umber
FP30/WA30	Black
FP31/WA31	Payne's Gray
FP32/WA32	Diver Gray
FP33/WA33	Pintail Gray
FP34/WA34	Yox Nose Pad Gray
FP60/WA60	Light Bass and Trout Green
FP61/WA61	Medium Bass and Trout Green
FP62/WA62	Dark Bass and Trout Green
FP63/WA63	Hooker's Green
FP64/WA64	Scale Detail Green
FP65/WA65	Scale Detail Black
FP70/WA70	Chocolate Brown
FP71/WA71	Burnt Umber
FP72/WA72	Sahara Tan
FP75/WA75	Blending Brown
FP90/WA90	Bright Orange
FP105/WA105	Phthalo Blue
FP106/WA106	Wigeon Blue
FP139/WA139	Tooth Yellow
FP140/WA140	Cadmium Yellow
FP141/WA141	Yellow Ochre
FP142/WA142	Teal Yellow
FP143/WA143	Waterfowl Base Yellow
FP144/WA144	Mallard Yellow-Green
FP160/WA160	Gill Red (Cadmium)
FP161/WA161	Snow Goose Red
FP162/WA162	Mars Red
FP165/WA165	Flesh
FP166/WA166	Mohr Flesh
FP167/WA167	Lavender Flesh
FP180/WA180	Turquoise
FP185/WA185	Deep Blue-Green
FP200/WA200	Sienna
FP201/WA201	Musky Green

TRANSPARENT SERIES (blending/bleeding)

Lacquer Based (FP) / Water Based (WA)

FP50/WA50	Light Bass and Trout Green
FP51/WA51	Medium Bass and Trout Green
FP52/WA52	Dark Bass and Trout Green
FP350/WA350	Transpar Green
FP260/WA260	Bright Yellow
FP380/WA380	Transpar Orange
FP270/WA270	Blood Red
FP280/WA280	Intense Red
FP300/WA300	Sailfish Blue
FP320/WA320	Transpar Violet
FP340/WA340	Transpar Brown
FP360/WA360	Gold Transparent Toner

PEARL ESSENCE

Lacquer Based (FP) / Water Based (WA)

FP400/WA400	Sparkling White Pearl Essence
FP401/WA401	Satin White Pearl Essence
FP402/WA402	Silver Pearl Essence
FP411/WA411	Trout Red
FP412/WA412	Bronze Orange
FP413/WA413	Walleye Yellow
FP414/WA414	Emerald Green
FP415/WA415	Steel Blue
FP416/WA416	Chrome Violet
FP422/WA422	Warm Gold Pearl Essence
FP423/WA423	Sparking Gold Pearl Essence
FP424/WA424	Softest Gold Look Pearl Essence
FP425/WA425	Yellow Gold Pearl Essence
FP426/WA426	Metallic Red Pearl Essence
FP427/WA427	Metallic Yellow Pearl Essence
FP428/WA428	Metallic Blue Pearl Essence
FP429/WA429	Metallic Green Pearl Essence

LIGHT REFLECTORS

Lacquer Based (FP) / Water Based (WA)

FP100/WA100	Burnished Silver
FP110/WA110	Bright Silver
FP120/WA120	Bronze Gold
FP121/WA121	Copper Gold

IRIDESCENTS

Lacquer Based (FP) / Water Based (WA)

FP440/WA440	Shimmering Blue Iridescent
FP441/WA441	Shimmering Green Iridescent
FP442/WA442	Shimmering Gold Iridescent
FP443/WA443	Shimmering Red Iridescent
FP444/WA444	Shimmering Violet Iridescent
FP445/WA445	Shimmering Blue-Green Iridescent

Manufactured in the USA by WASCO | A McKenzie Company
PO Box 480, Granite Quarry, NC 28072
To Order Call: 1-800-279-7985   www.mckenzietaxidermy.com

Component Systems Lure and Jig Finishes

	01 White
	02 Yellow Chartreuse
	03 Green Chartreuse
	04 Blaze Orange
	05 Black
	06 Hot Pink
	07 Flame Red
	08 White Pearl
	11 Bright Green
	12 Hot Yellow**
	13 Yellow
	14 Red
	15 Purple
	17 Glow**/Overcoat
	18 Brown
	19 Blue
	24 Silver*/Silver Pearl**
	27 Pumpkin Orange**
	28 Gold
	29 Grape**
	31 Glow White*
	32 Glow Yellow Chartreuse
	33 Glow Green Chartreuse
	34 Glow Blaze Orange
	35 Glow Bright Green*
	36 Glow Hot Pink
	37 Glow Flame Red
	38 Watermelon Pepper*

	40 Watermelon
	41 Candy Green
	42 Candy Yellow
	43 Candy Orange
	44 Candy Red
	45 Candy Purple
	46 Candy Pink
	47 Candy Raspberry
	48 Transparent Gold
	49 Candy Blue
	51 Pumpkin Brown
	52 Super Glow Yellow
	53 Super Glow Green
	54 Super Glow Orange
	55 Chartreuse Glitter Coat
	56 Super Glow White
	57 Super Glow Red
	58 Candy Lime*
	59 Super Glow Blue
	60 Gold Glitter
	61 Transparent Copper*
	62 Gold Holographic Glitter*
	63 Smoke*
	64 Green Pumpkin
	65 Green Glitter
	66 Dark Watermelon*
	67 June Bug*
	68 Root Beer Flake*

	69 Watermelon Flake*
	70 Silver Glitter Coat*
	71 Copper Head*
	72 Silver Holographic Glitter*
	73 Firecracker Glitter Coat
	74 Red Bug*
	75 Orange Glitter
	76 Ruby Slipper*
	77 Baby Bass Green
	78 Dragonfly*
	79 Pearl Pepper*
	80 Red Glitter Coat
	81 Sapphire Blue*
	82 Black-Blue Flake*
	85 Black Glitter
	90 Blue Glitter
	92 Purple Glitter*
	95 Fuchsia Glitter*
	28 Gold
	26 Magenta
	21 Green Pearl
	22 Pink Pearl
	23 Yellow Pearl

 * Available in Powder only
** Available in Liquid only

Note: Due to the limitations of the printing process, actual colors may vary from those shown. Please visit *www.CSIPaint.com* for additional color reference.

CS Coatings, Inc.
5004 Sherman Street, Wausau, WI 54401
To Order Call: (715) 845-3009   www.CSIPaint.com

chapter
· SEVEN ·

CONSTRUCTING SURFACE LURES AND POPPERS

A highly specialized fishing technique has grown up around the tendency of largemouth bass to cruise for food just below the surface of warm-water lakes and ponds. A subsurface lure is often viewed with suspicion by the bass, but a noisy surface lure will represent a food source struggling to escape.

Many bass anglers have helped develop this set of plugs by modifying lures intended for subsurface or cranking duties. The luremakers eventually realized the need for a specific set of such plugs and began to manufacture lures that were highly buoyant, incorporated mechanical or hydraulic components that produced bubbles and noise, and were finished with highly detailed color schemes that reflected well on the undersurface of the water at close range. Fortunately, all of these lures are fairly easy to reproduce.

With one exception, the dozen plugs included in this section are based on a standard wooden body, but all have been significantly modified to meet the demands of surface fishing. The components include propellers, reversed dive planes, or integral design components that keep them at the surface and produce a lot of confusion on the retrieve. Poppers and surface plugs are almost never trolled, although a few anglers achieve a measure of success in a handful of natural lakes by dragging them along the shoreline weedbeds.

The poppers are usually made of highly buoyant materials. Moreover, each lure has some means of directing itself upward during an accelerated retrieve. Usually this component is an uplifted dive plane or a flat lifting surface as a part of the body. The hydrodynamics of the plug make it want to rise out of the water, but gravity keeps it wet.

A good example of the principles at work can be seen in our first design. It is a simple body fitted with a concave blade pointed back and down, forcing the plug upward on the retrieve. Let's move directly into construction and note the physical control features as we go.

Betty Bloop

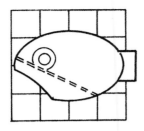

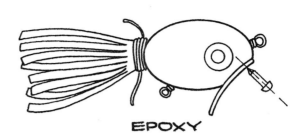

EPOXY

Kalua

REMOVE

CEMENTED

Betty Bloop

This is an egg-shaped sphere of softwood, 1–1¾ inches long. I prefer well-seasoned spruce for this lure, but cedar, pine, and very dry fir are quite acceptable. It is carved with a small plug at the rear to which a skirt is tied. The plug is hollowed out at the chin to accept a medium-sized Indiana spinner blade. The blade is epoxied in place and a brass brad added for mechanical strength. A tail skirt of mylar, rubber, plastic, or any other sheet material is cut and added. It's best to cement the skirt in place and then secure it with a few turns of nylon thread tied tightly and sealed with paint or nail polish.

Note that the body has been drilled for a short single-wire rig with the hook hanging from the bottom of the lure. Many anglers fit the plug with a single weedless hook, but a treble will work fine in most circumstances.

The body is finished before the rigging, blade, and skirt are added. One of the most effective color schemes is a white body and a dipped red head. It is pretty simple, but quite attractive.

Kalua

A chunky little popper, about 1 inch long, Kalua stays at the surface and is not as noisy as many top water lures. I designed this particular lure for use in warm, murky waters where visibility can become a problem. The stiff tail-skirt generates a steady stream of tiny bubbles, effectively giving the fish a trail to follow in the water.

Kalua takes a little patience to construct, but it isn't at all hard. Carve and sand the body, making certain the upper jaw is considerably longer than the lower. You can drill a ring of holes at the back of the lure, remove, the wood between with a knife, and epoxy stiff bristles in place. I found it possible just to make the holes in the end-grain of the wood with an awl (an ice-pick will work) and glue four or five bristles in each hole. It actually makes a bushier tail and creates more little bubbles behind the lure.

The body should be finished in white and oversprayed along the back with a dark color or vermiculated with a medium dark color. The bristles from an old plastic-bristle brush can be almost any color. The eye should be prominent and of high contrast. Note that the hook is hung at the midpoint of the belly.

Torpo

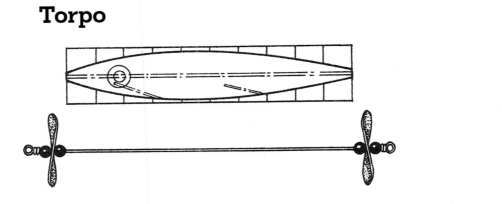

Hatchethead

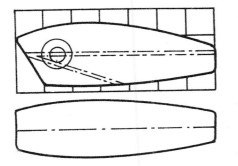

Torpo

This large lure was designed for surface-fishing for bass, but has been used successfully on several other game fish. You'll see this lure touted as a topwater attractor for trout, pike, muskies, and others. In fact, it's best for bass and makes the kind of noise and bubbles that bass respond to better than any other fish.

Carve and sand the body to a length of 4–6 inches. Drill for a center shaft and add two belly hook anchors as separates. The tiny propellers are cut from aluminum or other light metal and placed between beads at each end of the plug. The propellers need not be reflective or otherwise finished. It is the churning of the water—not the flash or movement—that makes them effective.

Finish the lure with a silver body and dark green vermiculation on the back. You might overspray the back in blue, green, or black, screened to give a scale or cross-hatch effect. The belly could be tinted with red or yellow. The eye spot is prominent.

Hatchethead

There is no reason for this dumb little plug to catch fish, but it does. In fact, it catches lots of fish year after year in waters all over the country. There is some mystery to the attraction and I suspect it involves the body shape, perhaps an impressionistic trigger that suggests a lot of different food sources.

It's a very easy lure to cast and retrieve and is fairly stable on the run. The lure, while small (1½–2½ inches), requires both a tail and belly hook to maintain stability. The elimination of the belly hook—even though it might be a single, weedless variety—causes the lure to begin spinning over during retrieve. Therefore, drill for a single-wire double rig. Be certain that the nose slopes back generously as indicated in the design sketch. Rig with a bare single or treble at the belly, but add a bucktail or feathered jig at the tail. The added dynamic "drag" of the skirting makes the lure swim with a "porpoising" up-and-down motion that adds to its attraction.

A typical finish for Hatchethead would include a pale green body with deep green parr marks on the sides and random, irregular splotches on the back. The belly is oversprayed with silver, yellow, or pink. The eye is typically white with a stark black pupil. Frogskin and perch finishes are also quite effective.

Tinbelly

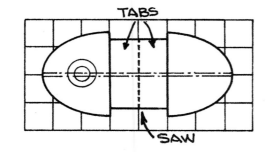

TABS

SAW

Oskar

SAW

WINGS

Tinbelly

I was intrigued by an early machined metal plug I once saw at a tackle collector's show—and I decided to make a modern equivalent to see if it would work. I was pleasantly surprised by how well this lure will attract largemouth when fished in a foot or so of clear water over some weeds.

Tinbelly doesn't do much except float like a cork and rattle like a snake on the retrieve, owing to several brass B-Bs inside. The dimensions of the lure will be determined by the size of chrome tubing you can find. Mine came from a rather large bathroom tissue holder and was around an inch in diameter which turned out to be quite reasonable. The lure should be 1½–3½ inches long. I make the wooden end plugs on my lathe out in the woodshop, but they can easily be carved by hand. Cement the ends on a inch or two of tubing inside which you've deposited a dozen or so B-Bs or lead shot. Then drill for the single-wire rig. A bare treble hook completes the lure.

The wooden end plugs should be painted solid blue, green, or red before assembly. Any bright color gives a high degree of contrast and makes the lure extra attractive…although I think the rattle is more important than the color. The eye is black on white and very prominent.

Oskar

This lure has been adapted from a popular West Coast salmon/steelhead lure that is traditionally fished in deep, swift water. The wooden body makes Oskar heavy enough to cast and to spin in the water, but light enough to remain on the surface during the retrieve. It whirrs and struggles through the water for a few feet, flops over with wings spread at rest, then suddenly starts whirring and frothing again when the retrieve is resumed.

Carve and sand the rounded head and elongated body and sand them smooth. Oskar is 2–3 inches long. Drill both for a center shaft and set the body into the vise so the opposite diagonal slots may be sawed. Cut the wings from milk-jug plastic and cement them in place before finishing. Be sure to rig with a bead behind the body to act as a bearing, allowing the body to spin freely on the retrieve.

Finish Oskar in a high-contrast scheme such as a white body, red wings, and a red head. You might use a mottled overall finish, a frogskin effect, or divide the body horizontally with a light and dark color. It's the action as much as the finish—so long as high contrast is achieved—that makes Oskar such an effective lure.

Snapper

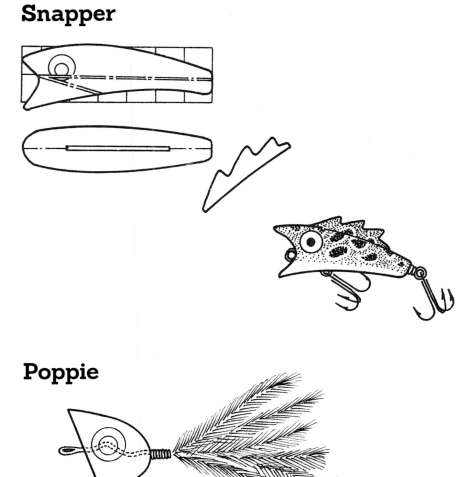

Poppie

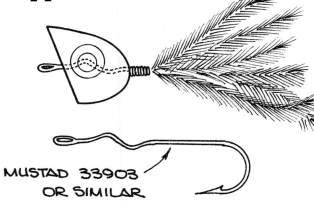

MUSTAD 33903
OR SIMILAR

Snapper

Here's another lure that has an action that is a pleasure to fish. The finned body "surfs" in an up-and-down motion during the retrieve but flops over on its side at rest, "dead in the water" so to speak. When you're fishing this plug, you are actually amazed if something doesn't strike on every cast!

When carving the slightly curved body, make certain the mouth is slightly rounded rather than a sharp "V" shape. The shape causes hydraulic pressure waves to be alternately pushed against the upper and lower jaw—each quickly transferring the pressure to the other. That gives Snapper the unique rocking motion. The back fin and tiny tail fin stabilize the plug on the forward course. Drill for a single-wire double rig and glue the plastic fins in place.

Finish with a yellow body, green spots over the back and sides, and spray the belly silver. The eye is large and sharp, and the mouth is red inside.

Poppie

A relic of the early days of surface plugging, Poppie has never really fallen from favor. Today's models are made of styrofoam or molded plastic as opposed to the early cork or wooden models…but the plastic and synthetic models are no more effective than the old-timers. In fact, I find that a popper with a softwood head of fir or mahogany is more stable and controllable than the modern plugs.

Cut the head from wood and sand to shape, keeping the face sloped as indicated. The head is ½–¾ inch long. Drill for a long-shanked "bug" hook and epoxy it in place. Paint the head a bright red, yellow, or green and tie a few bright feathers to the shank. It's incredibly simple and can be effectively cast and fished with a fly rod. Once you've had a bass on the end of a light fly rod you'll probably build several of these old standards, just hoping the more elaborate offerings won't work!

Frawg

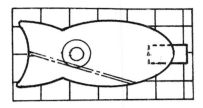

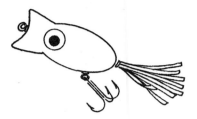

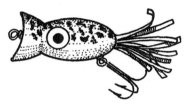

Butter Churn

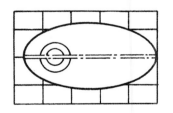

Frawg

This is a modification of another early popper that churns though the water like a demented dervish, calling attention to itself through action and noise more than form or color. The rounded mouth pushes a broken wave of water ahead of the lure, which then breaks through its own wake to create bedlam all out of proportion to its size.

The "double-egg" body of Frawg is 1½–3 inches long. Keep the mouth a rounded concave. Leave a round tag at the tail for attaching a skirt of rubber, plastic sheet, or rubber bands. The skirt is both cemented and tied to add strength. A lot of misdirected strikes will take their toll at the tail. Drill for a single wire rig with the hook just forward of the tail as shown.

Finish with a yellow or pale green body and a frogskin effect of random bright yellow and dark green speckles. The eye is large and conspicuous.

Butter Churn

A simple egg-shaped wooden plug, Butter Churn wears a large forward propeller device and a smaller propeller at the rear. The body skims the surface with little action, leaving the two buzzer blades to kick up a froth and make plenty of noise. This lure is quite effective in murky or discolored water.

Carve and sand the body to a length of 2–3½ inches and drill for a center shaft. Cut the spinning props from aluminum or other thin metal, bend and drill the tabs as shown. Rig the lure with a small bead behind the second propeller to act as a bearing. If the forward blade isn't spinning easily, you might have to add a bead there as well.

Paint the body a light color, adding contrast spots or some other pattern as required. The body may sometimes spin in the water, too—so you don't have to consider a back and belly in your paint scheme. The eyespots should be of high contrast, large, and prominent.

Clackerbug

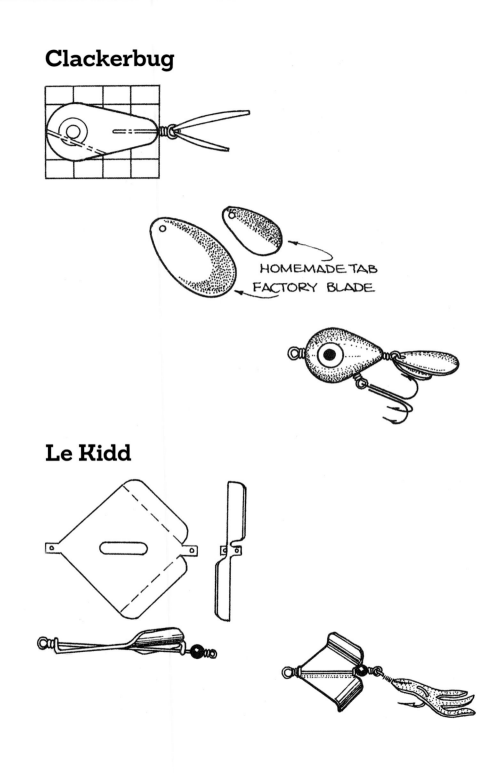

HOMEMADE TAB
FACTORY BLADE

Le Kidd

Clackerbug

This little lure is designed for very dark water where visibility is a definite handicap to bass angling. The small body provides buoyancy, but the lure is apt to sink at rest. In the kind of conditions the lure was meant to serve, movement is essential to attraction, so the lack of flotation isn't much of a handicap. The different tail blades flutter together on the retrieve, creating the noise and visual bubble signs that constitute almost the entire attraction of this lure.

Carve the little (¾–1 inch) rounded body as shown. Drill for a single-wire rig and for a separate tail anchor to hold the blades. The best combination is a horizontal Indiana blade (#1 or #2) above a small brass tab you've made at home. The small hook hangs below the lure.

Finish the body in silver or white with a black-on-yellow eye. The metal tab can be painted red to act as a close-proximity trigger.

Le Kidd

The delta-shaped buzzer blade is a fairly recent introduction to angling and has not yet been widely adapted to surface fishing. I designed this lure to take advantage of the enormous amount of splash and noise the delta can make when kept on the surface. To keep it there, I incorporated a flap of soft suede leather to act as sort of a "drogue chute." The soaked leather, while not exactly buoyant, tends to sink very slowly at rest. On the retrieve it offers a resistance to the line pull, keeping the lure at the surface. Once thoroughly soaked it is heavy enough to allow easy casting with even medium tackle.

Make the buzzer blade from juice-bottle plastic. If the plastic is dipped in boiling water for a couple of moments it will become soft and pliable, at which time you must bend the tabs and wings. The hot blade, properly formed, is then plunged into very cold water—ice water if possible. The plastic will set in the new shape. Without the cold-water bath it will eventually resume the old shape. The hot-and-then-cold treatment will erase the molecular memory of several types of plastic, allowing them to retain the shape we need for our lures. Once the blade is completed you need only bend the shaft as shown, insert a bead behind the blade to allow free movement, and add the glove-leather "pigskin" on the single hook. The leather, by the way, will accept water-based lure scents, improving the attraction value of the rig.

Fishing at the Surface

There aren't many game fish—other than largemouth or cruising pike—for which these lures will prove effective. But given the explosive excitement of a top-water strike, that's reason enough to make several and use them in the morning and evenings on a favored bass pond. As with all other lure categories, there remains a lot to be learned about surface rigs, and any of these designs can be endlessly altered.

chapter
· EIGHT ·

MAKING SPINNERS, SPOONS, AND BUZZERS

There seems little doubt that a reflective metallic lure was the first modern artificial lure, and it is likely that a primitive spoon—fashioned from clamshell—was the first artificial lure ever conceived. Admittedly, evidence indicates that some artificial flies appeared even before the clamshell spoon, but we've spent a lot of time already trying to separate flies from real lures, and I intend to maintain that distinction!

Actually, the spoons recorded by Captain Cook in Hawaii around 1700 were superbly developed lures and unquestionably caught plenty of fish. Several cultural anthropologists used some of the actual relics in a complex food-gathering experiment and succeeded in catching fish quite easily with them. Many of the spoons that were popular in the 1930s and 40s were coated with real mother-of-pearl and bore an amazing resemblance to the centuries-old Polynesian device.

Modern flashing attractors began around the mid-1800s when Julio T. Buell first began flogging the waters with a polished metal blade. Buell's prime contribution to the art was the scientific design that allowed a desired action to be reproduced by the hundreds and thousands. The development of the spinner—a blade that would rotate around a shaft for attraction but would not cause the strike—opened the field to practically every kind of fishing. The more recent "buzzers" and delta-shaped spinning blades are a modification of an older bit of tackle we've already discussed…the British Spin Harness.

These three principles—the wobbling spoon blade, the rotating spinner blade, and the whirling buzzer blade—offer the greatest latitude of any single type of artificial lure. It's pretty hard for the amateur to duplicate the polish and perfect curvature of the factory blade, but it really isn't necessary to achieve machine perfection in our efforts. Even the most lopsided blade will rotate or wobble as we hope—and our imperfection often introduces a sonic or erratic component that makes the lure especially effective.

We'll deal a little with the technique of cutting and shaping our own blades in this chapter—and it isn't terribly hard to do—but we will also consider the very practical notion that the blades are as easily purchased as made. In fact, factory blades are really very cheap…and I find it hard to justify the time and effort required to make my own, at least when I plan to build several dozen lures for an upcoming fishing trip or a long steelhead season!

Economics and the Factory Blade

Let's look for a moment at the argument that it's a lot more practical to buy your spinner and spoon blades than to make them. They are relatively cheap to begin with, and they are more uniform and better-finished than most of us could possibly make at home. Granted, we'll want to make special-purpose blades during the design of a particularly exotic lure, but for the day-to-day business of fishing the factory rig is the better choice.

We'll take a simple rig like the Duckabush worm rig as an example. I usually carry at least a dozen of these on a cutthroat excursion in three or four sizes and both brass and nickel finishes. I estimate it would take me around 30 minutes to cut, pound, and finish each blade. That would mean six hours of work just to produce a fairly common batch of blades. I can buy those blades from any of the suppliers in Chapter 14 for around $1 a dozen or less. Frankly, my time is worth more than twelve cents and hour (at least I think it is!) and I can use the six hours to tie rigs, build half a dozen bass plugs, and read my kid a bedtime story. More important, the final lures would be better than those with homemade blades.

The figures shown indicate the dollar-and-cents economy of buying the components for this worm rig. Multiplied by several years of scratching for cutthroat, it's a considerable savings.

There are other lures and even other blades that I always make at home. The experimental lures almost always require you to make you own, since the factories simply don't share our enthusiasm for the untested. There is no way to discount the fun of catching a fish on a totally homecrafted lure, either. But from the standpoint of economy, even if you built all your lures with nothing but factory components you would still save around seventy-five cents of every tackle dollar!

We've previously discussed the techniques for cutting and curving our blades at home, and we've looked at some of the castoff sources of metal that is already

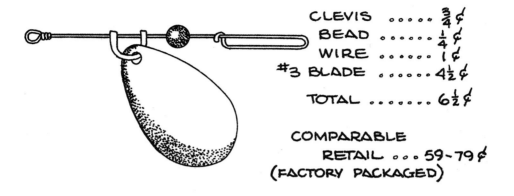

CLEVIS ..... $\frac{3}{4}$ ¢
BEAD ...... $\frac{1}{4}$ ¢
WIRE ...... 1 ¢
#3 BLADE .... $4\frac{1}{2}$ ¢

TOTAL .... $6\frac{1}{2}$ ¢

COMPARABLE
  RETAIL ... 59~79 ¢
(FACTORY PACKAGED)

curved properly for blade construction. Whether the blade is a factory rig or is made at home, the construction of the lure is identical—so let's get to the meat of this very interesting phase of lurecrafting.

Spinner, Spoon, and Buzzer Designs

Probably the most repetitive theme throughout this discussion has been that of variation. In every lure form thus far we've suggested that it isn't important to follow the design with any degree of precision. That's probably more true of the metal lures than any other single group. Dimensions and sizes are given as basic guidelines for the beginner. As you become more experienced in the science of luremaking and fish with your creations for a while, you'll begin fiddling with the design until it feels right, looks good, and catches a whole flock of fish. That's the way it ought to be!

Wobbler

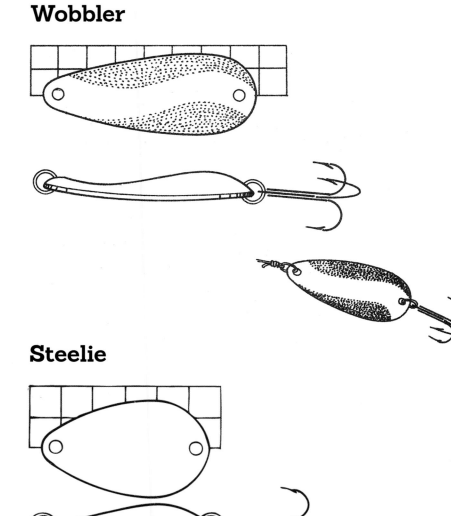

Steelie

Wobbler

This is a large, heavy spoon, ranging from ¾ inches in length, that can be cast, trolled, or spincast in both stream and lake. There are few fish that haven't been taken on some variation of this lure. The Wobbler is sold by virtually every lure company in a variety of sizes, shapes, and finishes. In various parts of the country is it known as "Shoehorn," "Daredevle," "Green Giant," and who knows what other names. It is effective in both fresh and salt water and is a standard fixture in most salmon and steelhead camps.

Blanks are available from many component suppliers, so you can finish a good assortment of these at relatively low cost. Rig the spoon with either a soldered ring or split-ring, to which you can attach a swivel when fishing the lure.

The spoon may be given either a nickel or brass solid finish, or the rounded back may be spray-painted in bright colors. Best combinations include red, fluorescent orange, and dark green. An unplated spoon may be dipped white and finished with red or orange patterns as shown on our design drawing.

Steelie

A modification of the Wobbler spoon style, Steelie is much shorter, rounder, and more deeply bowed. It has a rapid, fluttering action in the water that seems especially appealing to steelhead and other sea-run trout. It is also effective when cast or trolled in lakes where large trout and char can be found. It is 1–2½ inches long and weighs up to ¾ of an ounce.

Again, blanks can be purchased from component suppliers, but they are hard to locate and can be a bit more expensive. Finish exactly the same way as the Wobbler.

Duckabush Worm Rig

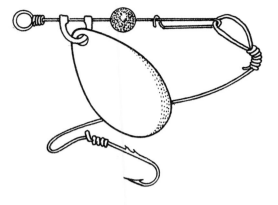

Ott-Six and Cocktail

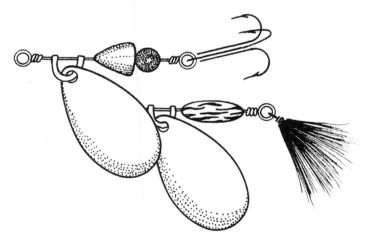

Duckabush Worm Rig

Named for a western river on which it was widely used in the 1930s, the Duckabush is just a spinner on a short shaft to which a bait hook is added. In practice, the hook is baited and the rig allowed to drift downstream over holding water. The spinner offers enough resistance to keep the rig off the bottom as it goes downriver, preventing serious snags. This rig is not a good choice for rivers with a lot of branches and debris underwater, but is excellent in gravel-bottomed trout streams.

Use an Indiana-pattern #2 to #4 chrome- or nickel-plated blade. Slip a clevis through the blade and thread it on a stiff length of stainless wire, followed by a bead. Bend an eye at the front and a typical "safety-pin" keeper at the rear. (An eye can also be bent at the rear but it's less convenient for changing hooks.) The blade requires no finishing and should retain only the reflective plating.

Ott-Six and Cocktail

Two of the most popular casting and trolling forms of the spinner-bar lure, these may be found in hundreds of slightly altered states with a variety of skirting effects. The lure is nothing more than a spinner blade on a shaft, followed by either a weight or an attractor device of some sort. Most often, an attractor is used that incorporates a weight factor as a physical component.

Begin these—and all bar spinners—by bending the hook on at the rear, and then building the lure as you go forward. The lure is then finished by bending the simple eye at the front.

Ott-Six was named for the bullet sinker used just behind the clevis. A bead behind the sinker acts as both a bearing and an added attraction device. These lures are very simple to make and can be produced in quantity for an extended fishing trip.

Cocktail differs in that it uses a heavy glass bead as both the weight and attraction component. I found these to be especially useful when trolled in bright sunlight. The glass acts as a prism to attract fish from long distances. A little time spent prowling arts and crafts shops can suggest literally hundreds of good lures built in this style. All finishing is done before assembly and usually consists only of painting the bullet sinkers when they are used.

Little Quil

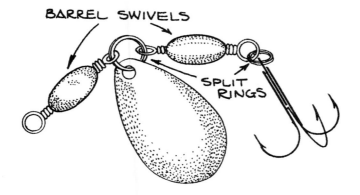

BARREL SWIVELS

SPLIT RINGS

Lemming

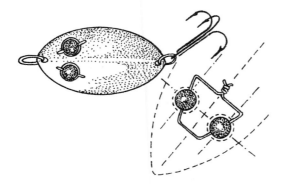

Little Quil

Little Quil is just my name for an almost universal spinner/attractor lure. This lure is so basic that it is often sold as an Indiana or Colorado spinner, named for the blade design that constitutes the basis of the rig. It takes no skill to put together and is constructed entirely of components that are probably already in your tacklebox.

Just assemble with two swivels, two split rings, a blade and a hook as shown. You can even bait the hook if you desire, but it will probably catch as many fish bare!

Lemming

This lure has been around for ages and is effective on bass, lake trout, char, rainbow, and a mess of other fish. The attraction elements include a good reflection component, well-conceived eye-triggers, and good motion. To make the rig effectively, you'll want to make the blade at home if possible. I know of no source of properly formed blades for this lure. Besides, this is one lure that's fun to make at home and catch something on.

Make the double-ended blade as shown. Drill two large holes for the red beaded eyes and four tiny holes for the brass wire rigging. Secure the eyes by twisting the brass wire tightly after all has been threaded. Finally, drill for a soldered or split-ring at the front and rear and add the hook.

The lure is usually left in a chrome or nickel finish, but it is effective when the belly is painted bright yellow and the back frogskin.

Dupont Beetle

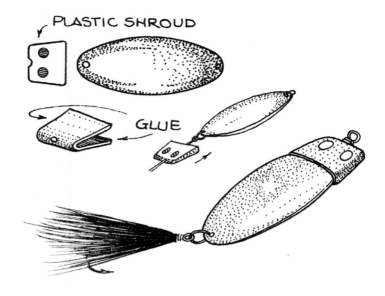

PLASTIC SHROUD

GLUE

Slinky

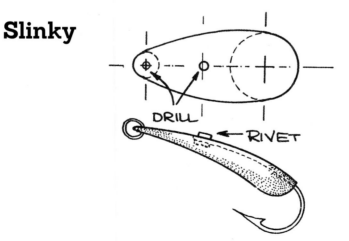

DRILL

RIVET

Dupont Beetle

The value of this modification of the willow leaf is that it provides a very soft swimming motion. The shroud significantly alters the action of the blade and prevents it from spinning upright. Instead, it will wobble softly, making it excellent for cast-and-retrieve fishing in very clear water near weedbeds and structure. The addition of a feathered or bucktail hook further softens the action and makes it attractive to a variety of game fish.

File the trailing edge of a large (#5 or #6) willow leaf blade. Drill a hole astern to receive the split-ring and hook. Take a folded piece of milk-jug plastic and trim to fit with household scissors. Epoxy or glue the shroud to shape and attach it to the blade as shown, then bend a nose-wire.

Paint the shroud only. It can be any bright color with contrasting eye or trigger spots.

Slinky

This is a more demanding spoon to construct, but is an excellent choice for lake trout, char, and any number of other game fish, depending on the size you choose to make. You may either make a blade or use a Colorado spinner blade that you've modified by deepening the belly curve.

Carefully center the hole in the blade and then rivet a short-shanked hook in place. It isn't necessary to secure the hook tightly to the blade, although many are quite tight. A loose hook will still trail properly and will add a noise component to the lure.

The lure is generally left in the polished finish of the original blade, but may be painted in any effective spoon pattern. Some lurecrafters add a stiff piece of stainless wire during the riveting operation to make the lure weedless.

Doctor Jim

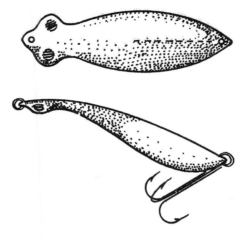

Ragtail

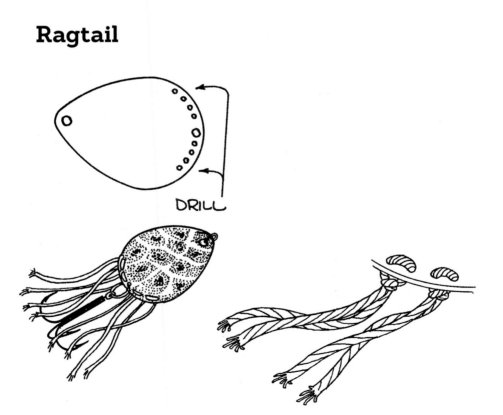

DRILL

Doctor Jim

Here's another traditional type of spoon that has taken a zillion fish since it first appeared on the angling scene. It would be impossible to limit this lure to any particular type of angling or to any species. It has been used successfully in salt and fresh water, in large and small sizes, to take almost every fish that swims.

You'll need to make a paper pattern in order to cut the blade in a reasonably well-balanced shape. It can be ¾–1½ inches long. Transfer the pattern to the metal stock, cut it out, and file/sand to final shape. Then shape it carefully over the anvil portion of a home vise or other matrix to achieve the multiple "mantis" kind of curve shown. Drill for rigging and add the hook and tow-ring.

The lure can be plain metal finish—especially nickel—or it can be painted in any of the spoon attraction patterns. The trigger spots should be of a very high contrasting color.

Ragtail

This is an original design that I'm rather proud of. Years ago I was looking for a lure that provided a lot of attraction but could be fished in the kind of clear water that keeps fish "spooky." It needed to swim naturally but not flash brightly or create too much suspicious motion. It further needed to be a reasonable representative of a natural food source. This modification was the final result of a lot of experimentation.

Drill a rigging hole at the rear center of a large Colorado blade as shown, then drill eight carefully spaced little holes—four on either side of the rigging hole. Paint the blade in a frog finish or other good attraction pattern. Once the paint has dried, rig the lure as normal and add four 4-inch strands of fuzzy yarn—preferably rug-hooking yarn—in shades of olive, yellow, green, or any combination. My most effective lure has been a frog finish with the four inner strands of pale yellow and the four outer strands of dark green.

The appeal of this lure lies in the very quiet swimming pattern created by the drag effect of the wet yarn at the tail. On the retrieve the strands really look like the legs of a swimming frog—and the fish respond!

Ingram Ring

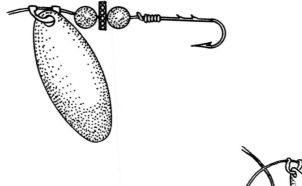

Loppsider

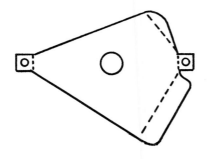

Ingram Ring

This is a bait-and-spinner rig that has become enormously popular in many western lakes and streams and is finding great favor in the upper Midwest. It will work anywhere and will attract most game fish. It is ridiculously easy to make—as soon as you can find the little jeweled discs that go between the red beads. A little prowling around thrift shops and garage sales should solve the problem…and most crafts shops have a selection for home costume- jewelry makers.

Just thread the components as shown on a snelled hook, add a worm or bit of porkrind, and fish in almost any fashion. This is one of the very few lures that can be stillfished to advantage.

Loppsider

This is a small flashing lure that is still another modification of an older piece of tackle—the buzzer blade. It can be fished as a separate lure, or the hook may be replaced with a short snelled bait hook and a natural attractant added. Either way it is an effective lure and one of the few that can claim any degree of success as a trolled lure for largemouth bass. It isn't as gaudy as many of the present bass lures, but can be deadly when trolled slowly along the margins of weed cover. In that regard, it is a great "prospecting" tool when searching for scattered schools of fish.

The added attraction is the eccentric action of the blade as it rotates about the shaft, creating very strong hydrosonic waves that may coax a fish out of hiding. The sonics may be more important than the visible movement.

It's a very easy lure to craft at home. Cut the off-center blade as shown from metal or plastic and bend the tabs into a propeller design. Run either a bearing bead or a split-shot behind the blade. It can be painted in a light color or any a combination of red-and-white or other highly contrasting designs.

Meadow Bug

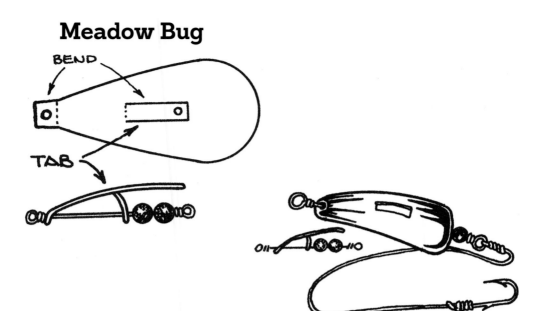

Chern

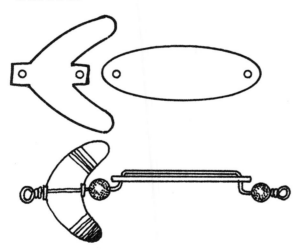

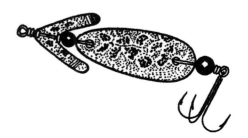

Meadow Bug

This lure has a long history in the streams and lakes of North America and is one of a handful of lures accepted by British anglers—who have a decidedly provincial attitude toward most lures that were not developed in England. We note that most fishermen will quickly adopt any lure that has proven itself useful, and you'll see a lot of your old favorites in New Zealand or Greenland…but not on the runs of Britain. The Meadow Bug, in one of many adaptations, is an exception to that rule.

The lure is really only a spinner blade that has achieved a controlled reflection pattern through the use of a "strut" that establishes a fixed angle from the shaft. The blade is cut from metal or plastic and the tab cut along three sides and bent downward as shown. Some of the very early models featured a separate strut that was soldered to the inner surface of the blade. It might be fun—in the interest of fishing tradition—to make a few of the old-style blades, but our method works quite nicely. The finished blade is put on a shaft and followed by a couple of beads, while the business of catching the fish is left to a snelled hook and some bait following the attractor.

The lure is generally finished in nickel or red-and-white.

Chern

This is another lure that came about as a response to a specific set of angling circumstances. I needed something that could be cast easily on light tackle to lake-bound rainbows in their spawning shallows, would provide a high degree of visual annoyance to prod them into a strike, and would create a lot of noise to draw them out of the weedy redds where they were guarding their territory. The Chern does all those things quite nicely.

Make the propeller as shown and slip it onto a shaft to which an eye has been bent. Add the bead, then bend the first pair of right angles. Slip the painted body plate in place, add the second set of right-angle bends, and finish with another bead and another eye. A short-shanked hook follows the lure, which is fished unbaited.

The body will tend to rotate slowly as the lure is retrieved, turning shaft and all. It's important to attach this lure to the line with a snap swivel to prevent tangles. I prefer to paint the body red on one side and leave the other side a bare metal color. The propeller may be painted or left plain.

Walleye Wim

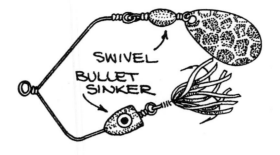

SWIVEL

BULLET
SINKER

Flapper

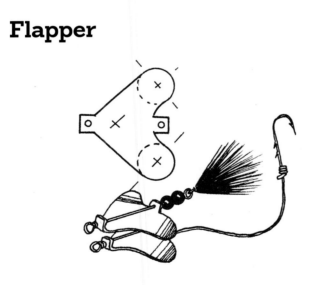

Walleye Wim

This is a very common lure for walleye and has proven quite successful for smallmouth bass. Even a few largemouth anglers will use this lure after it has been modified by lessening the lower weight. The lure is made mostly of factory components, wire-bending being the chief task of the luremaker.

Assemble the components as shown in the sketch. The lower leg has a definite upward bend to compensate for the weight of the bullet sinker during the retrieve. The configuration is excellent for walleye and for char, since both tend to strike from below. Once attracted by the flasher blade, they'll move below the lure and be exposed to the skirted hook. It's easy to make this lure too bright to be effective, so be sure to use a small blade of hammered brass or colored to lessen the reflection. Skirting material should be white, yellow, or bright red.

Flapper

Here's another design that utilizes a moderate flash and a lot of hydrosonics for attraction. The modified propeller has rounded tips to generate a wide sound pattern as it flashes through the water. The skirted or bucktail hook acts as both attractant and trigger. Two small beads are placed ahead of the skirt as blade bearings and colored tail-spots.

I have had little luck with this lure when the propeller was made of plastic. I think it needs weight to generate sound waves and to make it practical for light-tackle casting. Even when I substituted painted shot for the beads (to add the necessary weight) the lure wasn't very effective. Moments later, with a metal-bladed lure, I got successive strikes on several casts. I'm not completely certain why it happened, but it sure cured me of messing with plastic blades.

Paint the lure red-and-white or use a bright reflective finish. A dark skirt or bucktail seems to be more effective than a light one.

Blaster

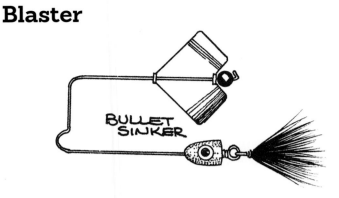

Scurry-Bug

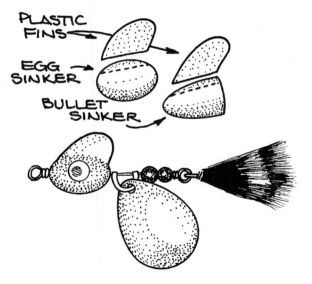

Blaster

This lure is remarkably similar to the walleye lures that have been favorites for so long, but it attracts different fish in a very different way. The buzzer blade creates both visible and audible attraction components and tends to draw fish from alongside—rather than from behind—the moving lure. Because of the expected angle of strike, you'll note that the bucktail and hook are well behind the trailing edge of the buzzer. Effectiveness is reduced if the hook lies below or ahead of the blade.

Cut the blade from metal and bend the shaft as shown. Add a painted sinker as counterweight and add the hook well behind the blade. The blade will spin, but the entire lure will not rotate on even the fastest of retrieves. The action is best if the line is tied directly to the half-circle tow-point, without snap or swivel to alter the action.

Red or yellow is a good choice for the head color, the blade is left shiny, and the skirt should be a medium to dark color.

Scurry-Bug

This wonderful little midwater lure catches a lot of fish. It sells for about three-dollars but costs a dime to make. Scurry-bug casts easily without fouling, can be trolled deeply without added weight to diffuse the fight, and attracts char, lake trout, winter bass, smallmouth, and pike.

Make the head by sawing a slit in an egg sinker and fitting a plastic rudder to the top. Dip the head three or four times in bright paint to soften the outline at the joint and add contrasting eyespots. Then bend the head onto a shaft with a small Indiana or Colorado blade with clevis, a couple of beads, and bend a bucktail hook onto the end.

Hothead

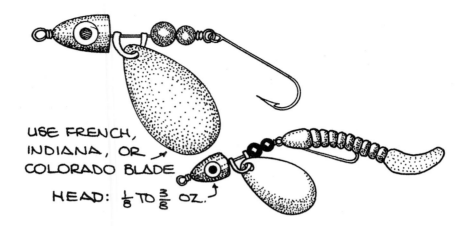

USE FRENCH, INDIANA, OR COLORADO BLADE

HEAD: $\frac{1}{8}$ TO $\frac{3}{8}$ OZ.

Dubbul-Delight

Hothead

Here's a lure that looks great and is made with factory components, leaving the wire-bending as the only task of consequence at the bench. Dip the bullet head several times in red, yellow, or other bright paint and add eyespots. Bend a wire eye, add the head, flasher arrangement, a couple of different sizes of beads, and bend on a worm hook. Finish with a rubber worm or piece of porkrind.

We can modify this midwater lure for surface angling for bass by simply using a disproportionately small head. The worm or rind will give it sufficient body for light-tackle casting, yet it won't sink fast in shallow water.

In either shallow-water bassin' or in midwater trout and char fishing, the head color has a pronounced effect on any given day. Most anglers carry several models in different colors, even adding a skirt in place of the worm on some lures. Thus fitted it becomes a good walleye lure in many waters.

Dubbul-Delight

This simple lure is absolutely deadly at times for rainbow and kamloops trout in the larger lakes of the North. It is very light and must be trolled behind a flasher string or small trolling sinker. It is extremely reflective and works best quite deep and on overcast days. The great degree of visual attraction is enhanced by the polar-bucktail hook.

I built the first of these lures while on a week-long fishing trip into the Canadian Cariboo, a land of big fish in big lakes. Our usual offerings weren't getting a lot of response because of a very dark, rainy week of weather. The big fish were sulking deep and it appeared a very bright lure was needed that would provide sufficient attraction and still approximate the prey fish the bigger fish wanted. The combination of a small Colorado and a medium willow leaf suggested itself as a possible answer…and it worked.

The lure is simple to make. Just drill a hole in the trailing edge of a #3-#5 willow leaf for rigging, bend on a short shaft at the head, and rig a Colorado (#2-#4) with a clevis and a bearing bead. Finish with a towing eye at the front. The body and blade are left chrome or nickel.

Lake Trolls

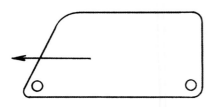

A VARIETY OF ATTRACTION EFFECTS ARE POSSIBLE THROUGH THE CHOICE OF BLADE TYPES, SPACING OF BLADES, AND COMPONENT SIZES. THE FULL ATTRACTOR STRING MAY BE CUSTOM-TAILORED TO SPECIFIC ANGLING NEEDS.

THE RUDDER MAY BE CUT FROM PLASTIC OR METAL, ABOUT $1\frac{1}{2} - 2\frac{1}{2}$ INCHES LONG.

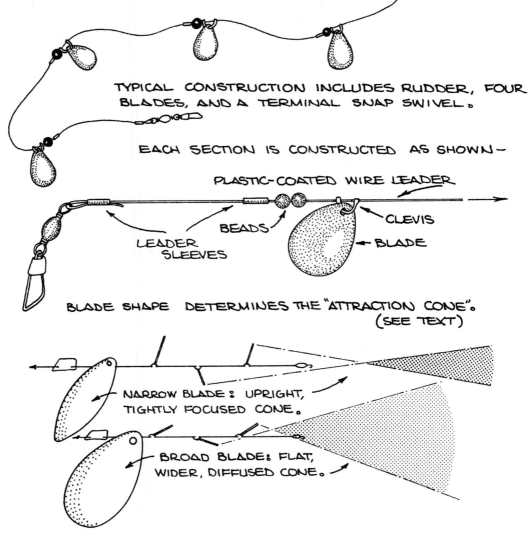

TYPICAL CONSTRUCTION INCLUDES RUDDER, FOUR BLADES, AND A TERMINAL SNAP SWIVEL.

EACH SECTION IS CONSTRUCTED AS SHOWN —

PLASTIC-COATED WIRE LEADER

BEADS

CLEVIS

BLADE

LEADER SLEEVES

BLADE SHAPE DETERMINES THE "ATTRACTION CONE".
(SEE TEXT)

NARROW BLADE: UPRIGHT, TIGHTLY FOCUSED CONE.

BROAD BLADE: FLAT, WIDER, DIFFUSED CONE.

Lake Trolls

These are, of course, the backbone of lake trolling. The flasher string provides the attraction necessary in a large body of water where fish are scattered from heck-to-breakfast. We must remember that the string provides only the attraction element. The strike trigger and the means of hooking the fish must be provided by whatever secondary lure we attach to the working end of the rigging.

The string is assembled from components as shown. The average string is around 30–36 inches, but you may find situations in which a shorter string (seldom any longer) will be more effective. We discussed the construction and theory of the lake troll in Chapters 2 and 3 at length, and I think an understanding of the blade spacing, modifications, and attraction cones is important before you build very many. But we have reviewed the essentials in the accompanying sketch. The trolls are easy to build from either homemade or factory components and your rigs will be every bit as effective as the factory-made units. The homecrafted trolls, by the way, will cost around ten-percent of the cost of a factory outfit.

chapter
· NINE ·

FRESHWATER JIGS

Jigging is a rather limited angling method in which a lure is lowered deep into the water—often to the bottom—is quickly jerked up and allowed to settle back down. If the technique is limited, its application surely isn't. Jigging is effective in fresh and salt water for a great variety of game fish. There are few fish, in fact, that cannot be taken with a jig. It is a particularly popular means of catching fish through ice, where space restrictions prohibit most other forms of fishing.

Lures for jigging have some pretty definite characteristics. They must be relatively heavy with respect to size, should have a lot of attraction packed into a little space, and usually are fitted with some means of providing a fluttering action as they fall. Since nearly all jigs are intended for use in deep, low-light situations, they are generally finished in light, bright colors.

The technique of jigging—and the lures required—was developed quite early in our fishing history. We have precious little actual information on the beginnings of this fascinating angling style, but we have found relics of primitive jigs that were used by the Eskimos and northern Indians about 200 years ago. The lures were developed almost exclusively in the far North, where the water was ice-bound for much of the year.

Many of our jigs can be trolled in deep water or can be fished in the characteristic up-and-down motion from a stationary point. In a great many cases it is possible to modify the individual lure design to make it exclusively a trolling or casting lure by simply substituting a bead or a smaller weight for the heavy jigging weight. A few lures that were designed for jigging—the Slab is a good example—are now more widely used as spinning lures than for the purpose for which they were invented.

Building jigs is not the easiest of all tackle crafting. Some require a degree of mechanical dexterity and a few demand some fly-tying skills. None of our designs require a lead melting process, although some of the heads are admittedly better if they have been cast directly on the hook. Bare jigheads are available in most tackle shops and can be purchased in an enormous variety from the tackle catalogs. Many home luremakers find it better to buy a few inexpensive jigheads than to take time to crimp or cement the heads to their hooks.

Many of our designs have been simplified so common egg and worm sinkers can be used in place of bonded heads. The wire work required in these designs usually very simple. The wire-shafter jigs, moreover, provide a degree of falling action that cannot be duplicated by the commercial jigs with their one-piece construction. Most lurecrafters make plenty of both in order to meet any fishing situation.

If jigging is a type of fishing you enjoy often, you may want to invest in a lead melting outfit and a few molds for making your own one-piece jigs. The equipment is easy to use and not terribly expensive when compared to buying a lot of jigs. (The nature of the fishery almost guarantees you'll lose lots of them!) Most of the suppliers listed in Chapter 13 have lead supplies, which are furnished with full instructions for use.

There are a few places where the jigging technique has been adapted to fishing a small area of fast water for passing fish. It is not much different from jigging in a lake or bay, but the lure is necessarily much heavier than an equivalent calm-water device. The lures don't require as complex a design, since the current takes care of motion on the downward cycle of the lure. In the following collection you'll find examples of these styles in Haff-Hip and Floot, lures I have built specifically for this emerging fishery. They have worked very well for me in fast water.

As we look at the construction steps involved in building these lures, remember that practice and patience will quickly transform the sometimes awkward effort into a very satisfying part of your luremaking activity.

Egghaid

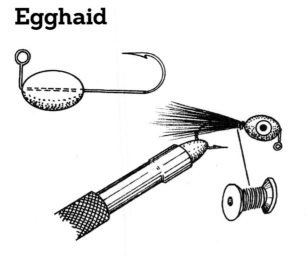

Hotchkiss

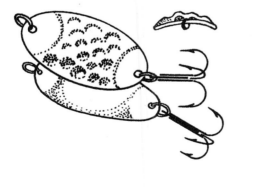

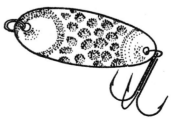

Egghaid

Egghaid is an incredibly simple jig that is effective for bottomfishing in shallow lakes and slow-moving rivers. It isn't a terribly active lure, but it catches more than its share of fish. It can be made weedless by adding a guardwire or building it around a commercial weedless jighead. In the muddy or gravelled bottoms that I usually encounter, the feature hasn't been necessary.

First, crimp or cement an egg sinker to a jig hook. Dip the sinker in white or silver and apply contrasting eyespots. Tie the skirt directly to the shank and cover the wrapping thread with a coat of cement or lacquer to prevent it from coming untied during use. Fingernail polish is a good choice for securing the wrap. The skirt should be white bucktail or some other light hair. I have had success with natural bucktail colors and with artificial fur fabrics as a tail.

Hotchkiss

This old standard has found favor among trout anglers as a heavy casting lure, but is probably best-known as a winter bass and icefishing lure. Lots of southern bass anglers rely on this great old lure during the cold winter months to coax a strike from deep-running, lethargic bass. It is suitable for almost every jigging technique. The construction of Hotchkiss begins with a small chunk of sheet lead, brass, or even steel. With a hacksaw and file, make an oval blank and smooth the edges with emery cloth or a burring stick. Using a bench vise as an anvil, hammer both ends down thin and flat. Shape the jig into a slightly concave shape over the end of the anvil. It will leave the lure with the characteristic hammered finish. Brass jigs need no further finishing, but either lead or steel lures should be thoroughly dipped in several coats of paint after final shaping.

Rig the lure with split or soldered rings and a bare treble hook. This jig relies on the slightly rounded belly curve for action and it is less effective if fitted with a skirt or bucktail hook. The painted jig may be sprayed with chrome paint for better visibility in deep water.

Slab

Chenille Jig

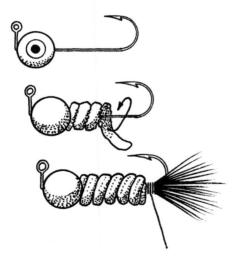

Slab

Slab is a diagonal chunk of metal bar that behaves very well when it is jigged. On the upstroke it tends to wiggle a little, then flutters down wildly on the downward release. It has become very popular among trout anglers as a medium-weight casting lure.

The process of constructing this lure is physically demanding and takes a bit of time, as it is sawed from a metal bar. We have fully illustrated the process in the description of the lightweight cousin Deadeye Dick in the next chapter. Please refer to those drawings for tips on hacking this lure out of heavy metal bar.

Slab should be dipped in primer and then spray painted with chrome or metallic gold. I have had some success with white lures and with a double-dipped red-and-white model, but chrome and gold seem to be best for most jigging applications. The shape of this lure is excellent, but I think there is a lot of room for further experimentation with regard to painted finishes.

You'll need to drill either end from the flat side in order to align the holes. Rig with split or soldered rings and a bare treble. Any tags or skirt will negatively affect the action of this lure.

Chenille Jig

This is an outstanding midwater jig for spiny-rays. It probably wouldn't be an overstatement to suggest that more crappie have been taken on this jig than on all other lures combined.

This lure requires nothing more than a ⅛–½ ounce cannonball sinker and a length of appropriate fabric. Chenille (available at tackle shops and sewing-notions counters) is the preferred material, but successful lures are also made from rug yarn, pipe cleaners, and ravellings from old sweaters.

You can make your own jighead as shown or buy a handful cheaply, but in either case use a soft Aberdeen gold hook. The jig is usually fished around cover and submerged brush where it is snagged as often as not. The soft Aberdeen will bend to free the lure, at which time it can be easily bent back into shape.

Cement or crimp the sinker to the hook. Tie the chenille directly behind the head and run the thread along the shaft, wrapping the fabric around both shank and thread as you go. The thread can then be used to secure the rear end of the wrap. Trim the chenille and tie on a few pieces of bucktail, hair, or skirting fabric to complete the lure.

The most common finishes include a white or yellow head, green, yellow, or blue body, and dark bucktail skirting.

Ol' Bullet

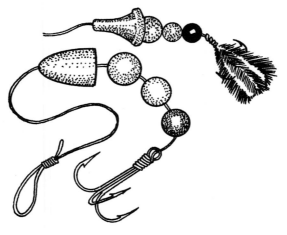

Paddle-Tail

Ol' Bullet

This is a modification of a saltwater rig I use often. It had such a great success rate with black rockfish and greenling it seemed judicious to build a couple of smaller models for freshwater. Both as a jig and a casting lure this configuration has worked very well. A model with two pearls and a grape-purple bead behind has proven to be a deadly attractor for walleye in the Columbia river in Oregon. Since it is also effective when trolled, it's pretty difficult to classify this simply as a jig, but we have to stick it someplace!

Begin construction of this threaded lure by tying on a feathered treble hook, leaving at least 18 inches of heavy monofilament to act as body and leader. Thread a colored bead and two pearls onto the line and finish with the leadhead. The head should be painted and eyespots added if desired. In some fishing situations, particularly if you are jigging for char, the eyes seem to be very important. The eyespots seem to have little effect on walleye, but they should be added if you are going to cast or troll the lure in a lake.

Paddle-Tail

This is unquestionably a gimmick lure, yet it has worked very well in a few fishing situations. It has been stream-jigged for shad with some success, but has been dynamite for some lake species. The design was given to me by an angler who concentrated on Burbot (freshwater ling cod) in the Pacific Northwest. It is admittedly an odd-looking gadget, but it works very well in a limited fishery.

The body is simply a piece of pencil lead through which we have run a length of stainless wire, preferably a bit heavier than that used to tie spinning lures. The tail section of the lure is gently pounded flat with a hammer and smoothed round with a file and burring tool.

When the body has been formed and smoothed, dip the lure in primer and paint it a light or bright color. The bucktail hook can be bent on and a bright bead or pearl and a towing eye added up front. A trigger spot should be added near the tail to finish the lure.

This is primarily a jigging device, but it can serve well as a deepwater troll for lakers and char. The very soft body can easily be bent into a "ripple" to give the lure an excellent side-to-side swim pattern. The softness can be something of a handicap when jigging in hard, rocky areas, but the body can be returned to normal with the fingers.

Dunce

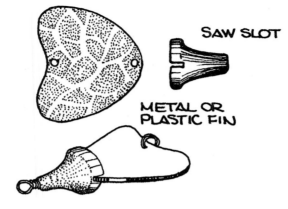

SAW SLOT

METAL OR PLASTIC FIN

Willie-Wobl

Dunce

This cute little jig is a surprising success in the ice-fishing arena. The broad finned body tends to flutter wildly on the downstroke and darts upward on the retrieve in a motion that is quite appealing to many game fish. The action would lead one to believe that the lure should be effective for winter bass in some of the shallower impoundments, but I don't know that it has ever been so tested.

The rig is fairly simple to build from a few benchtop parts. The fin may be either metal or plastic and the head almost any kind of worm sinker. Saw a slot in the head (sinker) as shown, bend a wire onto the leading edge of the fin and connect the parts together. Twisting the towing eye will cinch the two parts firmly, leaving only the rear eye and hook to be rigged.

The head and fin should be painted separately. The fin can be detailed in frogskin or any other pattern, but one side should be left light. Small eyespots should be added to the head after assembly.

Willie-Wobl

This is one of the most active and attractive of deepwater jigs and is especially well suited to the darkness under winter ice. The weight is nearly all in the head, so the lure tends to create a "feeding" illusion as it is fished. The head pops up and down with the rod tip but the body tends to lag behind, much the same as one of a feeding school of minnows might. The lure will work on most fish but is especially good for kokanee, walleye, and char.

The body is simply an oval cut from a sheet of brass or other heavy metal. It can be built with a plastic or aluminum body, but the action is not nearly as good. The head is a cannonball or egg sinker. The head should be primered and dipped in a light color and the eyespots added before assembly. The body is dipped and detailed with any pattern. If both head and body are dark, the jig becomes a good springtime bottom rig in shallower areas where it will take bass. The lure in a darker motif resembles a pollywog if jigged slowly.

Rig by bending a wire to the front of the body, threading it through the head, and forming a towing eye. The head and body should be loosely coupled to add a noise component. The hook is affixed with a split or soldered ring.

Thomas Clapper

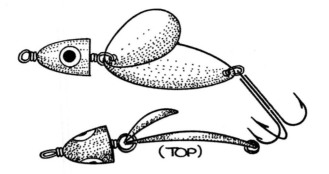

(TOP)

Bug-Eye

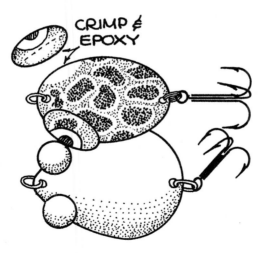

CRIMP & EPOXY

Thomas Clapper

Thomas Clapper is another migrant from the saltwater wars, modified to add a noise component, a simple rattle that calls attention to the lure in murky water. This design is also an exciting visual stimulator, due to the unique falling action of the jig. As the head bobs up and down with the rod tip, the vastly differing blades tend to "parachute" on the downward cycle, flashing and clattering as they do. On the upward move they quickly streamline behind the head, nearly disappearing at any distance.

Thomas Clapper is made from factory components, although the ambitious luremaker could make his own blades if he wishes. I prefer a large (#4) willow leaf and a #2 or #3 Colorado as body components. I paint a bullet sinker any color as long as it's light and add a contrasting eye. The body blades are in a nickel or chrome finish. This lure is fitted with a bare single or treble hook.

Bug-Eye

I have experimented with two models of this mid water jig, both of which have caught fish with surprising regularity in a lot of diverse waters. It hasn't been particularly good when bottom-bumped like most jigs, but works best just 10 or 12 feet down. The most consistent results were obtained with lures measuring just over an inch long.

The body is cut from either metal or plastic and two small egg sinkers crimped and epoxied in place. You can substitute a small Colorado or Indiana spinner blade that has been drilled for a rear hook. Either lure will work, but the swim pattern is greatly altered with a commercial blade. By and large, the homecrafted body with only a light curve seems to work a great deal better.

The lure should be completely assembled (but not rigged) before the finish is applied. Because of the extreme angles at the point where the sinker joins the body, the lure is best dipped three or four times in the base color before a pattern is added. The paint layers tend to "soften" the hard angles and make the lure look better.

After painting, add split or soldered rings fore-and-aft and rig with a bare treble hook.

Golf Tee

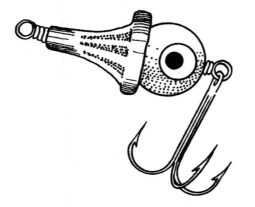

Tubeworm

Golf Tee

There was a very popular spinner around a few decades back that used the upper end of a fluorescent golf tee as an attraction element. The lure was used in both salt and fresh water for all sorts of fish and was quite effective. The fluorescent dye used in those golf tees is one of the best refraction agents ever discovered and it did wonders in the silt-green salmon and trout streams of the West.

The jig has virtually no built-in motion and makes no noise. It relies purely on an ability to break low-level light into components that can be easily seen by deepwater fish. The lure, by the way, is equally effective in saltwater.

Dig through the junk box or grandpa's golf bag for a handful of these fluorescent orange plastic tees. Cut off the pointed shaft, leaving the collar-and-nose shape as illustrated. Select a cannonball sinker of an appropriate size for the water you'll fish and dip it in primer and a medium color. Add a high-contrast eyespot before assembly. Bend a treble hook onto a shaft, adding the finished leadhead and the golf tee, and bending on the forward eye.

Tubeworm

This is a simple jig that can be built in a few moments from stuff left over from other lure projects. It is exclusively a bottom-bumper when jigged, and becomes a fine trolling rig when it follows a flasher string at midwater depths. It is technically an impressionistic design that seems to be representative of a lot of natural food elements along a lake or river bottom.

Cut the tail of a 3-inch length of ¼-inch surgical tubing into the flared skirt, using a hobby knife or razor blade. Paint a bullet sinker and add an eyespot. Rig with a treble hook bent onto a wire, slip the tubing down until the hook is inside the skirt section, and then add the bead and head. Finish with a forward eye as shown. Only the head and bead are colored. The tube is left the natural brown or whitish-brown color that it comes in.

Zingo Gig

Haff-Hipp

Zingo Gig

One important part of Zingo's success is the eccentric vane at the top. It whirrs rapidly on the upstroke and then reverses direction to send out a different set of reflections as it drops. The blade is kept in a moving attitude by the weight, which hangs below it throughout the jigging motion.

Begin construction by bending a treble hook (bucktail or bare) onto a shaft; add a bead and a painted bullet sinker. Add a trigger spot of red. Just ahead of the sinker—and this is important to the continued smooth function on the downstroke—add a half-inch of plastic tubing, perhaps a bit of insulation stripped from a piece of radio hook-up wire.

Above the tubing add another bead and finish by bending a forward eye. At this point, hold the lure upside-down and spin the blade. If it tends to hang up on the wire wrapping, adjust the eye wraps to get smooth rotation. The lure may be 1½–3 inches long.

Haff-Hipp

Here's one of the heavyweights that was designed for jigging the pools in large, fast-flowing rivers.

Paint a large trolling sinker by dipping it in primer and then giving it several coats of white paint. The weight may be sprayed with chrome paint, if desired, to increase the reflectivity of the lure. Paint a very high contrast eyespot on either side and rig with a medium-to-dark bucktail and a sawed off willow leaf blade. The lure is generally built in the ¾- to 1-ounce range and can be increased to as much as 3 ounces for fishing holes in deep, swift rivers.

Maribou/Bull Maribou

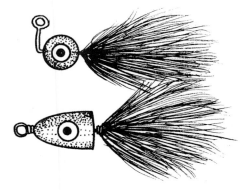

Pigfuzz

Maribou/Bull Maribou

Maribou is a relative antique among the jigs. The first lure was built for commercial tuna fishing. The scaled-down sport version isn't much more complicated than the cob-rough commercial jig…but it catches a lot of different kinds of fish in many different fishing situations.

Paint the head by dipping in primer and coating with white paint. Add a red or black eyespot over a yellow circle. The feathers are tied directly to the hook shank.

The only significant difference between the two jigs is the size. Bull Maribou is a half-ounce or larger and tied on a #2 hook. It is better fished in moving water.

Pigfuzz

This is a standard jig that is excellent for deepwater bass, especially in winter impoundments. It can be used for a variety of game fish, but bass seem to respond to this configuration best. It works well on smallmouth in those waters that lend themselves to jigging techniques.

To build this lure, paint a cannonball sinker and detail with eyespots. Bend a wire to a single plain-shanked hook and run it through the head. Tie a rubber-band skirt around the rigging wire at the back of the head and thread a "porkskin" (made from an old soft leather glove) onto the hook. The resulting lure is especially good for fishing deeper structure because the leather can be impregnated with a commercial scent to enhance the appeal. Many anglers fish this jig as either a pure jig of a semi-casting rig. This technique requires casting the lure out over a relatively clear bottom and bumping it along during the retrieve.

Silverside

Floot

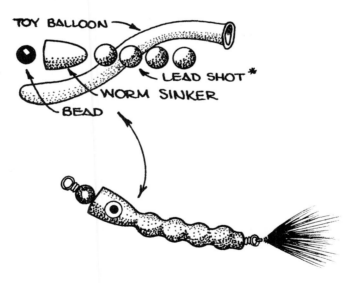

TOY BALLOON

LEAD SHOT *

WORM SINKER

BEAD

Silverside

This lure is another variation of a saltwater rig that has been adapted to a specific freshwater situation. It's another of the fast-water jigs that are finding new favor with a lot of anglers who traditionally fish the heavy rivers of western North America. It is very heavy for the size and can be successfully jigged in considerable current.

A ¼-ounce head and a ½-ounce egg sinker should be primed and dipped white, then sprayed with a chrome finish. A contrasting eyespot is applied to the head.

Assemble the lure on a high-test stainless shaft by bending a feathered treble at the end, adding the body, bead, and head. Finish with the forward eye.

Floot

This is a lure that got its start as a saltwater jig that was very effective in shallow water for a number of rockfish species. It was modified for winter bass and other bottom fish, and is effective in fast rivers.

Build Floot by first putting all the weights on the central shaft and bending the eye at the tail. Don't bend a hook directly to the shaft; you'll need all the access you can get to pull the tubing over the sinkers!

Once you've stuffed—and that's a considered choice of words!—the lead into the rubber casing, add a bright bead at the head and paint eyespots directly on the tubing. Finish with a forward eye and attach the hook with a split-ring.

Toy balloons are a good choice for the body material. They come in a lot of bright colors and are thin enough to coax over the lead without too much trouble.

Hopper

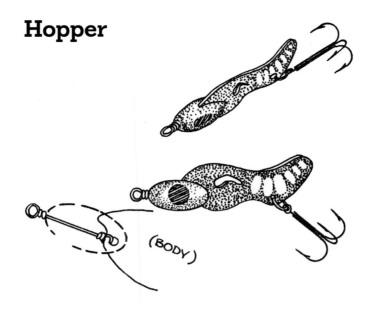

(BODY)

Rattler

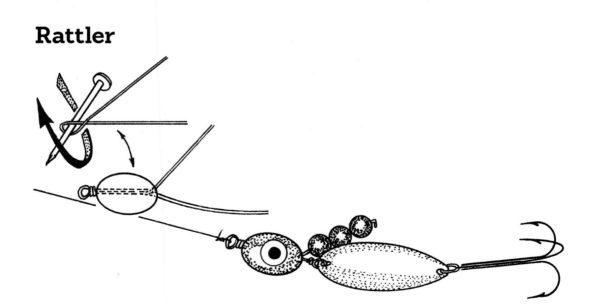

Hopper

If some of the jigs we make are rather limited in their usefulness, Hopper is just the opposite. It is probably the closest thing to a universal lure in the entire field of jigging. It is a lightweight that is at home in large or small lakes, rivers, ponds, and the farmyard creek. It will attract almost every known game fish and quite a few nongame species as well.

Cut the peanut-shaped body from a piece of thick plastic, the kind your morning milk or juice comes in. The body is painted with a spray-and-mask process as explained in Chapter 5. Note the little notch cut from the front of the body. That allows a wire rig to be tied to the body before the head is crimped in place. Even though the head is epoxied to the body, this mechanical connection helps make a reliable lure. Complete the rigging by adding a split-ring and a small treble hook.

Rattler

I built this lure especially to fish a group of western lakes that suffer from a thick algae bloom every summer. The trout are still there, but there is absolutely no point in fishing for them with conventional tackle. Surface visibility is about an inch and the fish cruise in a thick soup about thirty feed down. Even at that depth the visibility is no more than a foot, and the fish must be attracted by a lot of light and as much noise as you can generate with a slow-moving lure. Sonic attractors are out, because they require trolling speed to work and anything moving through algae-laden water is out of range before a fish can find it.

Rattler can be fished in the traditional jigging manner; and the extended beads will constantly bang against the flasher blade, giving the fish something to home in on. Once the fish is within a couple of feet the modified willow leaf will bring him the rest of the way.

Build Rattler by drilling a second hole in a large willow leaf blade and preparing an egg sinker with a dipped, bright paint job. Twist an eye onto a double-rig shaft and run both wires through the head. Bend one wire onto the leading end of the willow leaf; fit the other with three or four fluorescent red beads and crimp the end. Finish the lure by adding a split or soldered ring and a treble hook.

chapter
· TEN ·

BUILDING TROUT LURES

The angling fraternity has spent an enormous amount of time and effort trying to cloak the act of catching a trout in a certain mystery. We've been bombarded with articles, learned dissertations, even entire volumes that credit the trout with cunning and judgment that simply aren't supported by fact. It's been like that ever since Izaak Walton—an admitted ne'er-do-well —wrote the first of an ad infinitum of finny fairy tales. The process of natural selection and eons of pursuit have made the trout a bit skitterish, but that certainly doesn't justify the literary inventions that surround the intelligence of a trout. In point of fact, the average rainbow is on an intellectual par with a rutabaga! On the other hand, the persistent legends surrounding the trout give us a plausible alibi for spending an inordinate amount of time actually catching a couple.

When we strip away the fabric of fiction and view the trout in the harsh light of reality, we find a fish that is wholly guided by instinct and is incapable of making even the most basic of decisions. We can use its predictable behavioral responses as a scientific basis for designing and building the lures we'll use, and on those occasions when it fails to respond properly we will simply add another footnote to the mystical bibliography of the trout. There's a certain paradox between the trout's written history and its actual performance, but the dedicated angler is the beneficiary of this confusion. On the one hand we have an enormous body of wonderful art and literature and on the other we have a trophy that can be caught quite easily when it is presented with a good lure.

From a practical point of view, the trout angler faces the distinct disadvantage of working in a strange environment, seeking a quarry that is perfectly adapted to it. Those drawbacks are balanced by the behavioral traits that cause the fish to strike at a variety of preposterous gadgets that can be tossed into his habitat. As long as they possess the proper attraction components and incorporate some sort of response trigger, the trout usually will try to chew on them.

In all of the preceding projects we have discussed the latitude that is available in building lures. The trout lures included here are rather small and have been quite carefully designed to incorporate the proper attraction in less space. I encourage departures from set design, of course, but there probably isn't as much room for modifications in this group as in most others. The inventor in each of us, however, can be satisfied by allowing a given lure to suggest an entirely different way to put the same attractors on the end of a line. In pure creativity, the trout lures can offer the greatest of freedom and an unlimited opportunity to thrash the waters with the product of your imagination. As always, the designs are meant to catch fish and feed the imagination.

Parker Minnow

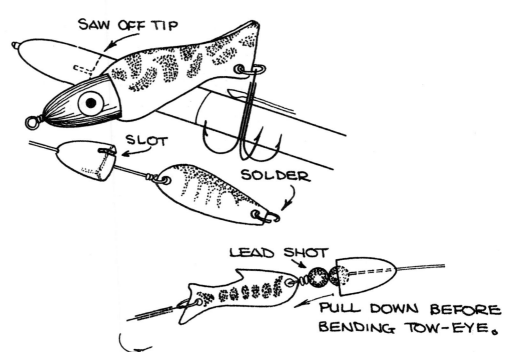

SAW OFF TIP

SLOT

SOLDER

LEAD SHOT

PULL DOWN BEFORE
BENDING TOW-EYE.

Ghost Minnow

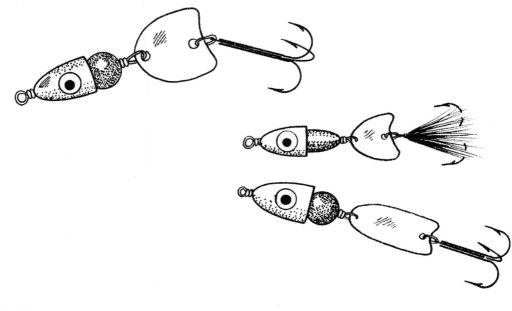

Parker Minnow

The Parker is a lightweight lure that can be fished as easily with a fly rod as with spinning or trolling tackle. It's a semibuoyant floater that is excellent for fishing shallow streams or the upper two feet of a lake. When a shot is added to the line ahead of the lure it serves the same purpose in deeper streams and lake levels. The lure is especially good for lake trout, char, and large native trout in streams.

Cut the head from an old ballpoint pen and add the eyespots. Cut the body from either aluminum or from a plastic juice or milk container. You can either cut the body from the flat part of the plastic or from a curved portion to add a variety of swimming actions.

Attach a wire shaft to the front of the body, slip the head over it, and bend the forward eye. If the body is plastic, the tail should be rigged with a split-ring, which is less likely to cut through the body under the stress of a fight (or a snag) than a soldered ring. If you add one or two split-shot to the shaft and pull them inside the head during assembly, you can change the floater to a free-troll or casting lure.

The body is finished by dipping in a light color and either brushing or spraying the detail. Frogskin, ghost ribbing, or parr marks are excellent pattern choices.

Ghost Minnow

Many prey fish fry are quite transparent during their immature phase, and this lure capitalizes on that physical characteristic. It is a wonderful representative lure that can be used in almost all kinds of habitat for trout.

Cut the ½-inch tip from the clear barrel of a ballpoint pen. The body should also be of very clear, flat plastic, a material that can be found at any thrift shop or garage sale. Cut the body, thread a wire through the hole, add a bright bead, then slip on the head and bend the forward eye. Finish with a split or soldered ring and a treble hook. A bucktail or feathered hook will enhance the upright action and may add another attraction element.

To modify this lure for free-casting or trolling, add a split-shot or egg sinker in place of the bead. Dip in white and then paint with a bright spray or fluorescent coat.

Deadeye Dick

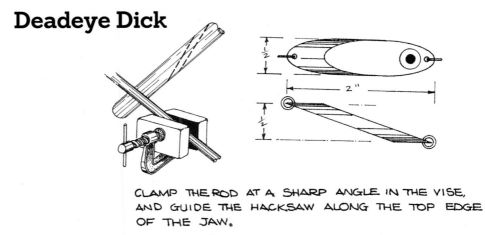

CLAMP THE ROD AT A SHARP ANGLE IN THE VISE, AND GUIDE THE HACKSAW ALONG THE TOP EDGE OF THE JAW.

DRILL HOLES ABOUT $\frac{1}{4}$" FROM EITHER END ~ RIG WITH SPLIT RINGS.

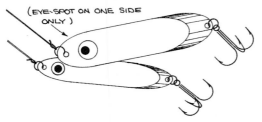

(EYE-SPOT ON ONE SIDE ONLY)

Snapper Grub

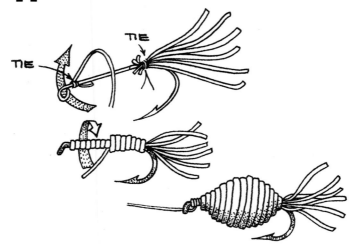

TIE

TIE

Deadeye Dick

This fine lure is cut from a lucite or other clear, plastic rod. A discarded plastic towel holder provided enough material for a couple of dozen of these. The design was suggested by a popular metal casting lure that has had great success in a lot of trout lakes in the North. My experiments with this clear plastic version were very satisfying in both lakes and streams.

Construction is simple but requires careful sawing to cut the slab from the plastic rod. Once the right angle has been found, it is simple to move the bar up a quarter inch in the vise to cut another blank. Once started, it's a good idea to cut a half-dozen or more blanks in each sitting.

After the blank has been cut and drilled, smooth each side with very fine sandpaper. The initial smoothing—even with 150-grit paper—will leave the sides dull and opaque. A final sanding with wet 250- or 400-grit emery cloth will make the lure transparent and very smooth. It takes a little elbow grease, but the results are very satisfying.

Paint the eyespot on one side of the forward end and rig it with split or soldered rings. Use pliers as a heat sync if you solder to prevent burning or melting of the lure.

Snapper Grub

This lure is very nearly a fly in terms of construction. It is tied on a plain shank hook with long strips of rubber band, preferably bright yellow ones. It is a representative lure that is especially effective in streams that host the caddis fly, apparently looking enough like an overgrown caddis larva to elicit a strike.

If the lure is tied with common household ribber bands, it will require several, which must be either tied together or snubbed to the body as you progress. A better alternative is to peel an old golf ball. You'll find an unbroken strand about a mile long inside some brands…enough to tie a few dozen of these lures in one swoop.

To build Snapper, just put the hook in a vise, tie on the tail strands, and fasten the body material at the head end of the shaft. Wrap the rubber around the shaft, moving end-to-end until the body is built up to the desired shape. It doesn't seem to matter if the body is plump or fairly skinny—fish will still hit it.

Finish the lure by spraying with bright yellow paint. Some acrylic enamels are flexible enough to be fished without cracking, but common enamel should only be applied lightly to prevent any cracks.

Keno King

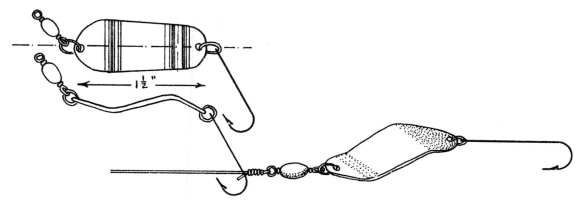

#12 SWIVEL

1½"

Sly Pete

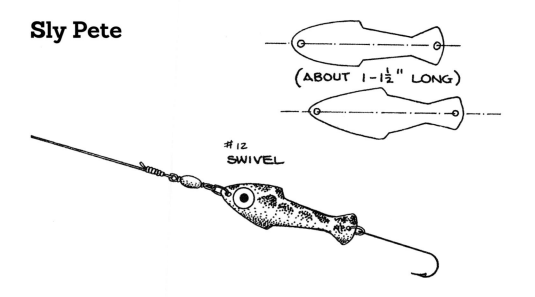

(ABOUT 1–1½" LONG)

#12 SWIVEL

Keno King

This is an incredibly simple lure that can be cut and formed in just a few minutes. There are a lot of these on the market, speaking well of the effectiveness of such a simple design.

The blade is cut from plated metal and can be either fished in the shiny form or painted. A heavy grade of metal is preferable, as long as it can be easily cut with tin snips. If it is so heavy that it requires a hacksaw, it's probably too heavy to fish very well.

Most trout lures in this pattern are around 1 ½ inches in length. Somewhat smaller versions are effective in mountain streams and small lakes, while models up to 4 inches are used in saltwater and large rivers for big trout and salmon.

If the lure is cut from chromed or plated metal and is to be fished as is, it should be dipped in clear lacquer or varnished to prevent rusting along the cut edges and holes. Unplated lures can be dipped in white and double dipped with a bright red or yellow diagonal half. The lure can be dipped and masked, sprayed with frogskin, spots, or other pattern.

Sly Pete

This is simply a shape variation of the Keno King that happens to include a slight curve along the long axis of the body to produce a more pronounced wobble on the retrieve or troll. It is effective in streams or lakes for trout up to a couple of pounds, but doesn't appear to attract many really large fish. I know of a couple of real trophies taken on a 2½-inch version in western Canada, but the occurrence is rare. The commercial models are produced only in the 1–1½-inch models, which should give us a clue as to what sizes are most effective.

The lure can be cut from chromed or plated metal and dipped in a clear finish or can be painted in a variety of designs. The eyespot is normally added only to the outside curved surface. Most models of Sly Pete are only finished on one side, the other being chrome, red or white.

Twistee

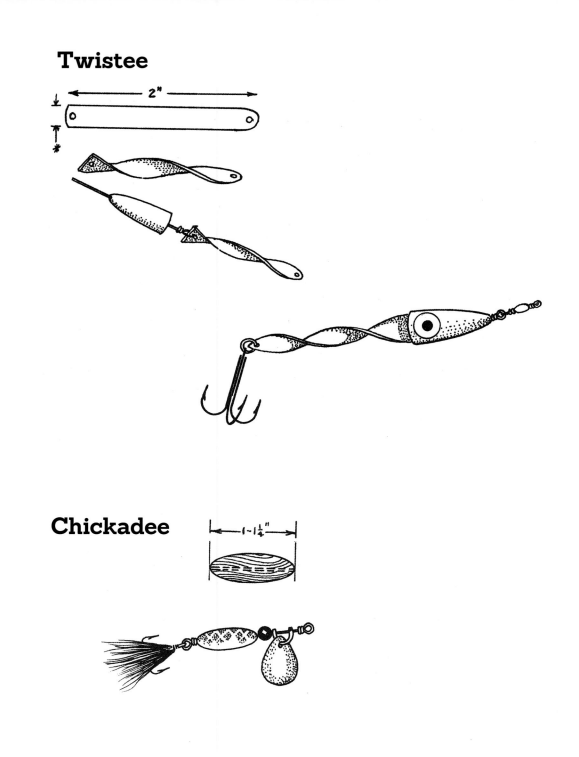

Chickadee

Twistee

This interesting lure is patterned after a commercial rig that appeared briefly in the early 1950s and soon retreated into deserved obscurity. The original had a corkscrew strip of metal that revolved around a thick shaft. The concept was good, but the execution of the original was truly preposterous. I think this lure solves the problems of the first while maintaining the sound attraction concept it attempted to execute.

Cut the tip from an old ballpoint barrel as a head. Paint the eyespots and set it aside. Cut the body from metal or milk-jug plastic. A metal body can be twisted into the proper shape by simply holding one end in place with pliers and gripping the other end with another pair of pliers and giving it a 360-degree twist. The metal will hold its shape with no further effort. A plastic body is formed in the same manner except that the plastic must be immersed in boiling water for about a minute, the body twisted to shape, and then it is held in cold water for a few seconds to allow the material to set in the corkscrew shape.

Once the body has been formed it can be sprayed in a solid color, dipped in some color, or sprayed. Assemble the finished components by bending a wire to the leading end of the body, pulling it through the head, and bending a forward eye. Complete the lure by adding a split ring and single or treble hook.

Chickadee

This is among the more popular lures for western trout, having found success in every kind of trout water known. It is commercially manufactured in every color and pattern in angling and is fitted with every blade type.

The wood body can be whittled and shoeshine sanded in a minute or less with a little practice. About the only problem the novice will have is making his first few bodies a trifle too large. It won't take long to get the hang of making them the right size and shape.

Dip the body in almost any color and finish with any standard pattern. Bend a bare or skirted (bucktail) hook onto a wire. Add the body, a small bead, and any kind of spinner assembly as shown. Finish with the forward eye and it's ready to catch trout and a variety of other game fish.

River Jool

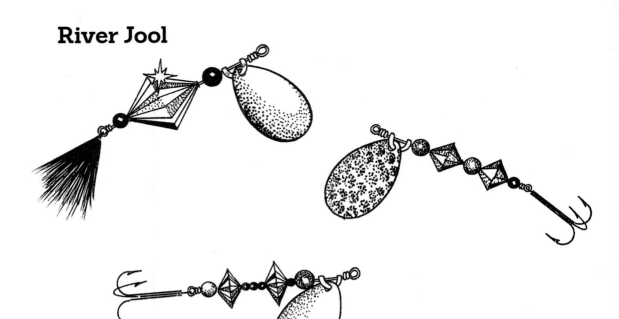

Flipspoon

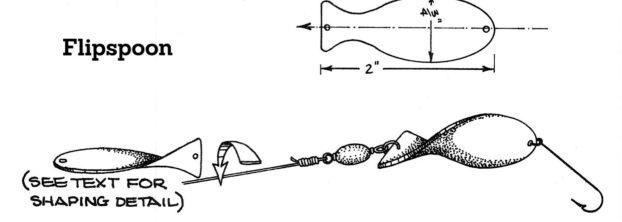

2"

(SEE TEXT FOR
SHAPING DETAIL)

River Jool

Jool is a traditional spinning lure on which we have substituted a faceted costume jewel for a more standard body. The lure is especially effective in dark waters that have been colored by runoff or glacial silt. It is perfectly suited to many of the western trout and salmon streams, where the refracted colors and bright facet reflections draw immediate attention.

There are a lot of spinning lures that are built like the Jool, and construction is very simple. Bend a buckskin or bare hook onto a wire, add the jewel— flanked by bright, small beads—and put on a #3 or #4 spinner assembly as shown. Finish with a forward eye.

Flipspoon

Flipspoon is a simple variation on regular spoon bodies that provides a swirling motion rather than the expected wobble of a conventional rig. It works best on a very slow troll or retrieve, the kind of technique we would normally use in very cold or dark water. I've tried it in a variety of colors, but the silver-and-red of my first model seems to be best.

Construct this lure by cutting and drilling the blank from a piece of chrome or nickel-plated steel. Aluminum lures of this design are too light to be very effective. Rig the lure as shown with either split or soldered rings and with a single hook.

Finish the unplated side with a spray of red, gold, dark green, or another proven attraction color. Because it is a steel lure, you will need to dip the finished blade in clear lacquer or varnish to prevent rust. This is a design that has never appeared on the commercial market to my knowledge, a surprise considering how effective it can be.

Glow-Worm

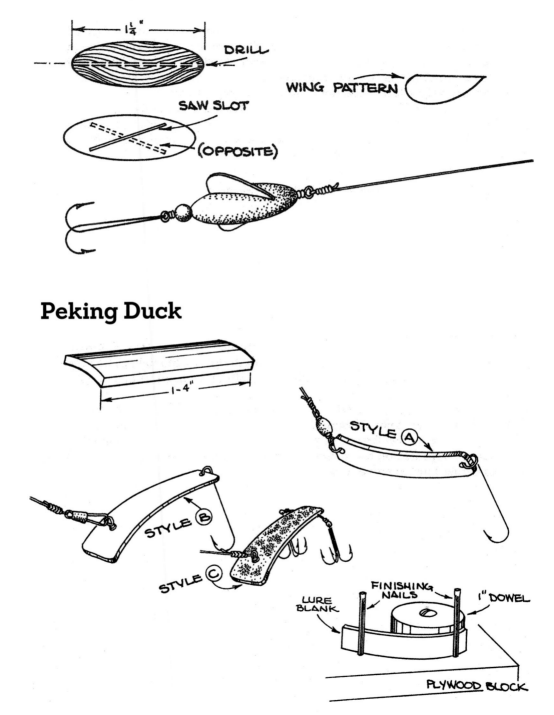

DRILL

WING PATTERN

SAW SLOT

(OPPOSITE)

Peking Duck

STYLE A

STYLE B

STYLE C

FINISHING NAILS

1" DOWEL

LURE BLANK

PLYWOOD BLOCK

Glow-Worm

This is a home version of a trout and salmon lure that can be found in any tackle shop under all sorts of local names. Most of the commercial models are an unrigged plastic device that is so exceedingly overpriced as to keep it out of many tackleboxes. The commercial version probably costs no more than two cents to produce but costs a dollar or more. Fortunately, we can make this little gem on the home bench for the cost of a hook and a bead—little more than a manufacturer's factory cost…and his is unrigged!

Whittle and sand a small wooden bead as shown. Drill for a center shaft and saw the diagonal cuts on either side. Cut a couple of plastic wings from any flexible piece of plastic (a milk jug, for example) and cement them in place. Bend a couple of hooks onto a wire, slip a bead and the painted body on the shaft, and finish with a forward eye.

The body is dipped in white and can be finished in any proven attractor pattern. I like to overspray the back with red fluorescent paint and the belly with yellow.

Peking Duck

This is an adaptation of an old lure I saw in a Taiwan museum a few years ago. To build it, you need only cut a few pieces of bamboo to the desired size. Make sure the grain runs the long way. Drop the pieces in one of those kitchen steamer baskets with a little water under it and allow them to steam for about an hour or longer, until the wood is soft and pliable. Put the strips into some sort of jig that will hold them at the desired curve until they dry. I have illustrated one rough jig; there are several ways to hold the piece as it dries and any will work.

Once the wood has dried it will be "set" in the new curve indefinitely. Drill the blank, paint it, and rig as shown. I like the upside-down style A for tiny fly-rod models, the downcurved style B for larger lures, and the hip-hooked Flattie, style C, for big lake models. The rigging depends more on the thickness of the blank than on the length.

Peking Duck is outstanding for some fish in any size and finish. I can think of no finishing scheme that won't work…and none that aren't available on the commercial models. Just thumb through a tackle catalog for finishing suggestions.

Pearl Van Gogh

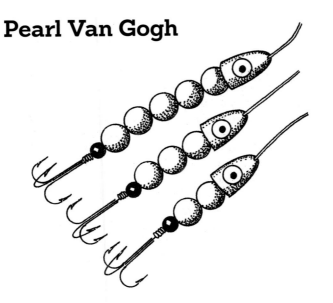

Leech

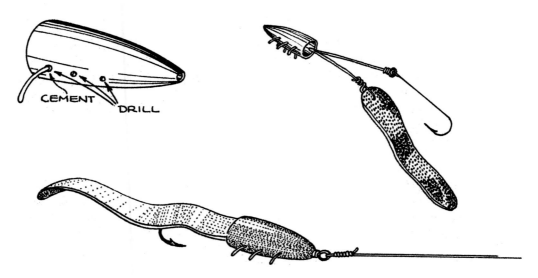

CEMENT

DRILL

Pearl Van Gogh

Here is a lure that has so many fishing applications that it could be considered a universal type and should be in every angler's tacklebox. Cut the tip off a ballpoint pen (which should be second nature by now!) and paint on the eyespots. Select a few beads and line them up on the tackle bench until you find a configuration that meets your approval. You may use any kind of bead, of course, but I find that costume pearls are among the best of choices. Once satisfied with the lineup, just slip them—in order—onto a heavy snell ahead of a bare or skirted treble.

Leech

This is a straightforward lure that represents a leech or other food source of large fish in a lake or slow river. It can be successfully fished in those waters that don't host leeches, since the attraction is a representative shape and motion that duplicates a number of potential prey animals. It is deceptively easy to build and produces a nice-looking and good-fishing lure for deeper trout water.

Drill the point of a ballpoint pen as shown and cement a half-dozen plastic scrub-brush bristles into the holes. This feature is optional, but the tiny legs tend to kick up mud and sediment from the bottom, more closely duplicating a bottom feeder.

Attach a ¼-by-2-inch strip of soft, black leather to a length of wire with a rather loose twist, to prevent the wire from cutting through the leather. Bend the hook onto the other end of the same wire, allowing around 2 inches between those components. Bend the wire at center as shown and thread it through the head. Hold the hook and body in place as you twist a forward eye at the front of the lure with a nail or other object.

Cispus

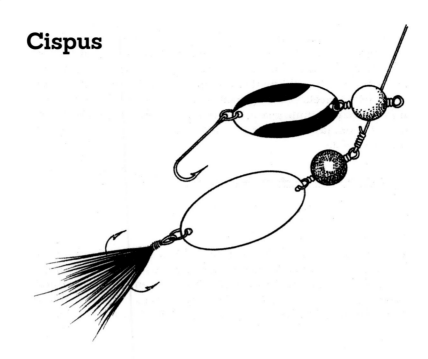

Cispus

This is another example of how simple an effective trout lure can be. It is nothing more than a flat oval body of metal or plastic, a pearl or large, bright bead, and a bit of wire. As simple as it appears, Cispus is an effective lure that behaves nicely in either lake or stream and will catch plenty of fish.

The bead should be quite large with respect to the body, preferably nearly as great in diameter as the body is from top to bottom. The large bead creates a uniform hydraulic current as it moves through the water and the flat body tends to wiggle from side to side within that current pattern. For that reason it is important that the body not be curved or bent.

Cut the body from metal or plastic, dip in paint (except plated metals, of course) and add a finish design. Almost any finishing scheme will work on this body, but because of the length I don't recommend eyespots. The strike trigger—if it is the eye—is simply too far from the hook. A plated body should be dipped in a clear finish to prevent rust.

This group of lures has been classified as trout lures in order to separate them from those few lures that don't work on trout. You will find dozens of other lures among the various categories that will be equally effective on trout but are primarily designed for other species. More importantly, you will find a great many other designs that you can adapt to trout fishing if you wish, just as many of these can be adapted to bass, walleye, salmon, or anything else.

When we look at a lure that incorporates solid attraction components, an effective mechanical configuration, and a working set of response triggers, we are looking at a lure that should catch any kind of fish. It may need to be scaled down or built up to fit the species involved, but the components of attraction will work anywhere. A case in point is that of salmon and steelhead lures. They are usually a little larger than other trout lures, but there are only a few designs that cannot be quickly and efficiently adapted to smaller trout. We'll look at those lures next.

chapter
· ELEVEN ·

BUILDING STEELHEAD AND SALMON LURES

It would seem at first glance that the separation between (a) trout lures, (b) steelhead and salmon lures, and (c) salmon and lake trout lures is a very fine distinction. The assumption is quite correct. We find salmon lures that readily take trout, steelhead lures that will catch salmon, and trout lures that might take all three. It is impossible—and undesirable—to build a lure exclusively for one of these species. And so I have classified our lures according to the type of water for which they're best suited rather than the species. The lures in this chapter are intended for use on anadromous fish in rivers and streams. The designs that will be discussed in Chapter 12 are specifically meant for salmon, lakers, and char in lakes and bays.

If you are an experienced freshwater fisherman, you'll quickly recognize salmon lures that can be adapted to trout fishing and will make the necessary adjustments at the bench. You'll look at a steelhead design and see the potential it offers for a favorite trout stream. It is from this kind of imagination and experimentation that the very best lures are conceived.

There are hundreds of lures that will take both steelhead and salmon in the coastal rivers of North America when the runs are thick. We have selected from this mass just a few lures that have proven they could catch fish from less-populated streams. These lures possess the highest level of attraction, either through motion, appearance, or a combination of both. None is difficult to build, but the tolerances are somewhat less than in other lure categories. For that reason we have given more detailed construction information for each. There is still plenty of latitude and room for individual adaptations, but we have faithfully copied the actual lures so that the novice can produce an effective lure for a demanding angling technique.

Finishing and detailing are probably more important in this set of artificials than in any other. The steelhead and salmon for which we search are bound by a different set of behavioral traits than are lake fish, and their habitat is usually a crystalline, high-visibility environment. Any aberration in the finish will be detected by these well-traveled individuals and the lure will be detected. The steelhead is more selective than other trout and is more wary of a poor presentation than even a veteran brown in the high rivers of Montana. The steelhead's passage to adulthood has included a long stint down his home river and years evading the superb predators of the sea. He has run the gauntlet of irrigation structures, hydroelectric dams, sea lions, otters, killer whales, and countless anglers. The steelhead is a survivor! Catching one requires an excellent presentation with a good lure and a measure of good fortune. We can learn the techniques required and we can feel assured that sooner or later we'll have luck on our side. That leaves the lure as the remaining variable. If we follow a proven design and build our offering with great care, we will have balanced the intricate formula and the steelhead will strike.

The strike of a steelhead and the subsequent powerful runs cannot be adequately described in words or pictures. It is a display that must be experienced to be fully understood. For half an hour, the successful steelhead angler lives in glory. He fights for every inch of line, guides the fish away from rocks and submerged brush, and makes dozens of on-the-run decisions before it ends. When the fish finally comes to hand and he lifts his prize from the water his eyes quickly scan every curve and scale. It is a moment from which he will never quite recover. It may be his first fish or his hundredth…it really doesn't matter. It is a cherished moment that depended on his skill, his ability to read the water, and a lure that was perfectly made and finished. He may have released a thousand such fish in his career, but he will not build his lures carelessly. He will paint them with patience and skill, rig them with attention to each turn of the wire, sharpen each hook, and present them with pride. He will never let a moment of sloppy work at the bench rob him of his half-hour of greatness.

These lures should reflect the best of your skills…a lot depends on them!

Beedie Diver

CARVE AND SAND A SMALL EGG-SHAPED
BLANK. SAW IT FROM THE STICK AT AN
ANGLE AS SHOWN. SAND THE FACE HOLLOW
TO FIT A #2-4 "INDIANA" SPINNER
BLADE. EPOXY AND TACK THE BLADE
WITH A SMALL ROUND-HEAD SCREW.

THE BLADE MUST
EXTEND BELOW THE
BODY TO ACT AS BOTH
A DIVING PLATE AND
KEEL.

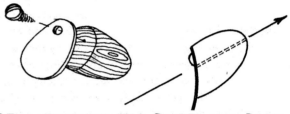

DRILL THROUGH THE BLADE AND BODY
JUST BELOW THE SCREW BUT AS HIGH
ON THE BODY AS POSSIBLE.

THE LURE MAY BE
RIGGED ON A WIRE
FOR CASTING AND
TROLLING....

OR THREADED ON A SNELLED
HOOK FOR DRIFTING IN FASTER
WATERS.

COSTUME PEARLS

Beedie Diver

Beedie Diver takes advantage of the habit of salmon and steelhead to lay right on the bottom of a clear, daytime river. These species spend the hours of light in "holding water," tucked behind rocks or in shallow depressions in fastwater riffles. The lure must be equipped to dive down into those spots on the retrieve and project a good representative image as it does. Beedie serves this purpose well.

I first built this lure a good many years ago to fish a coastal stream that comes down to the Pacific from Mount Olympus in the Washington Olympics. I believe it was the first homemade lure on which I caught a steelhead. It wasn't a big fish by any means, but I remember it as clearly as any I have ever taken. It was as clear and bright as the crackling winter morning on which it was taken…and it made every hour at the tackle bench worthwhile.

Dip the body in white paint and completely finish it before adding the blade. It may be finished with a dark back and red or yellow oversprayed belly. One good finish scheme is an all-black body with reflective silver glitter sprinkled over the back and sides. A dark green body with green glitter is excellent for some water conditions. Glitter can be found in a variety of colors in craft shops.

The lure can be effectively fished behind a dropper in very fast water.

Hambone

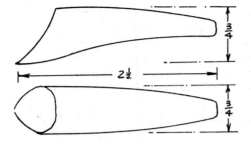

CARVE AND SAND THE BODY TO THE DIMENSIONS SHOWN, THEN USE A RASP TO HOLLOW THE FACE AS DEEPLY AS POSSIBLE.

USE A ROUND OR HALF-ROUND RASP TO HOLLOW THE FACE.

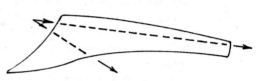

DRILL THE BODY FOR RIGGING WITH TWO HOLES. THEY WILL BE $\frac{1}{8}$-INCH APART; PLACE ON THE U<u>PP</u>ER HALF OF THE FACE.

AFTER PAINTING, RIG THE BODY AS SHOWN. IF THE EYE LOOP IS TOO LONG, BEND ONE OR TWO TWISTS. THIS WILL PULL THE ANCHORS TIGHT AGAINST THE BODY.

EYE-SPOTS AND TRIGGERS MAY BE ADDED AFTER THE LURE IS RIGGED.

Hambone

This is a river plug that is excellent when fished from a drift boat or cast downstream into a flowing pool that might hold salmon or steelhead. It is a good free-diver, bumping the bottom on the retrieve or when held against the current. It is a bit larger than traditional steelhead lures and is better suited for salmon. It can, of course, be scaled-down to meet the requirement of fishing steelies or smaller jack-salmon.

The body should be formed carefully to insure good balance. It is a good idea when rigging to leave the forward eye rather long so the lure can be tuned for a good wobble as it dives. Bending the eye to one side or the other will allow the swim pattern to be adjusted as required.

After the body has been smoothed and drilled as shown—or drilled for a single wire rig in the smaller versions—it should be dipped in white and sprayed with a shiny chrome finish. The back can be lightly oversprayed with blue or dark green. After rigging, add contrasting eye spots and a trigger spot at the caudal area.

Willow Wobbler

THE WILLOW WOBBLER
MAY BE MADE OF HOME
COMPONENTS OR FROM
FACTORY PARTS...

CUT AN ELONGATED BLADE FROM
METAL AND DRILL A HOLE NEAR EITHER
END. IF USING A FACTORY BLADE, DRILL
A SECOND HOLE AND FILE THE TIP ROUND.

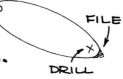

FILE

DRILL

BEND A $\frac{1}{8}$-$\frac{1}{4}$ OZ. BULLET SINKER
AND A SMALL BEAD TO THE
HEAD END OF THE BLADE.

AT THE TAIL END, INSTALL A SPLIT-RING
OR SOLDER A RING AND HOOK.

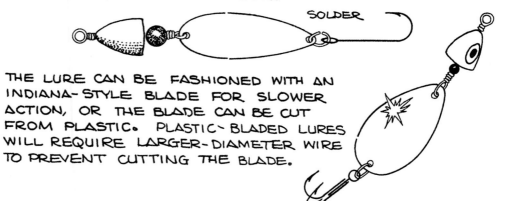

SOLDER

THE LURE CAN BE FASHIONED WITH AN
INDIANA-STYLE BLADE FOR SLOWER
ACTION, OR THE BLADE CAN BE CUT
FROM PLASTIC. PLASTIC-BLADED LURES
WILL REQUIRE LARGER-DIAMETER WIRE
TO PREVENT CUTTING THE BLADE.

Willow Wobbler

This is a simple lure that reacts well to fast water and is especially suited to fish the hard-running flats of the larger steelhead and salmon rivers. It is heavy enough to cast well and will run along the bottom on a retrieve or drift over the flats. It seems to be just about as effective on salmon as on steelhead.

I modified this lure slightly from the drawings by using a big #6 willow leaf blade and a ⅜-ounce bullet head for fishing big water. I gave a couple to a pair of young anglers on Canada's fabled Thompson River one winter and was gratified to see a locally produced model—exactly the same—the next season in several tackle shops. I hope the lads earned some college money (or at least a new graphite rod) from their enterprise.

The head should be either silver, white, or a bright solid color with contrasting eyes. Red and yellow are good choices for salmon, white and silver for steelhead.

Hot Stuff

CARVE THE SMALL, PEANUT-SHAPED
BODY TO ABOUT THE DIMENSIONS
SHOWN. NOTE THE FLAT "TAIL"
AND THE FLAT 45° NOSE.

CUT THE DIVE PLANE FROM
MILK-JUG PLASTIC TO ABOUT
THE DIMENSION SHOWN.

$\frac{3}{4}$

$1\frac{1}{2}$

$\frac{5}{8}$

EPOXY THE DIVE PLANE
IN PLACE BEFORE
DRILLING THE BODY.

$1\frac{1}{4}$

$1\frac{1}{4}$

THE BROAD "LIP" WILL
HELP THE LURE DIVE
DEEP WHEN HELD
AGAINST A CURRENT.

DRILL FROM HEAD TOWARD TAIL.

DRILL THE HOLE FOR THE BELLY
HOOK WELL FORWARD OF CENTER.

THE LURE WILL "SWIM" IN A NOSE-DOWN
POSITION WHEN RETRIEVED RAPIDLY. WHEN
HELD AGAINST THE CURRENT IT WILL
VIBRATE AS IT DIVES ALONG THE BOTTOM.
"TUNE" THE LURE BY TRIMMING THE DIVE
PLATE. (SEE TEXT)

RIG AS SHOWN. TIE THE
LINE DIRECTLY TO EYE:
DON'T USE A SWIVEL!

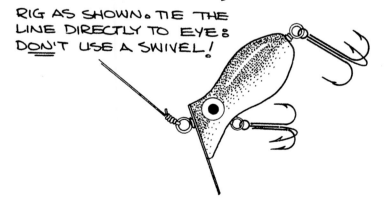

Hot Stuff

This is an exceptional diving lure that is best fished from a drift boat or held against the current in good, fast holding water. It is primarily a steelhead rig but has taken a lot of salmon in the Pacific coastal rivers. The lure dives hard as it maintains the characteristic "tails up" stance and really roots down among the rocks where the big fish lie.

There are two ways to install the dive plane. If soft milk-jug plastic or metal is used, epoxy the plane before painting the body. If you choose clear plastic, paint the body first, then cement the plane in place, allowing the clear plastic to transmit the color along the edges. Either method is effective.

The body is usually sprayed white and detailed with a faint dark back and a tint of red, pink, or yellow on the belly. Due to the unique swimming position, the fish will likely see the belly first and will catch the dark back color as an undersurface reflection.

Salmon models of this lure can be considerably larger than shown. Some commercial equivalents are as long as 3½–4 inches. An effective salmon finish would be hot pink, black with black glitter on the back, or black with white brushed rib lines or spots.

Goose Egg

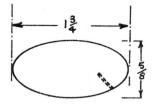

CARVE AND SAND THE SIMPLE LITTLE
BODY TO ABOUT THE DIMENSIONS
SHOWN. CUT THE "JAW" TO ACCEPT
A #2-3 COLORADO SPINNER
BLADE.

DRILL THE BODY TO ACCEPT THE
CENTRAL WIRE AND DRILL A ¼"
HOLE FROM ONE END AS SHOWN.

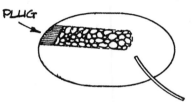

(SEE TEXT)

CEMENT THE BLADE IN PLACE.
PACK THE LARGER HOLE WITH
"BEADS" OR STYROFOAM.

CEMENT A ¼" PLUG IN THE
HOLE AND SAND SMOOTH.

RIG AS SHOWN: THE METAL BLADE PULLS THE HEAD
DOWN AS THE FOAM "FLOTATION" LIFTS THE TAIL. THE
RESULTING "HEADSTAND" POSITION COPIES MANY
BOTTOM-FEEDING PREY SPECIES.

THE LURE WILL DIVE
MORE DEEPLY IN
CURRENT OR WHEN
TROLLED.

Goose Egg

This lure is similar in some respects to the popular Hot Stuff just described. It dives quickly into the rocks and is especially effective when fished from a drift boat or held against hard-flowing current. The tails-up attitude is enhanced through the addition of some styrofoam beads inside the tail. The beads don't add to the buoyancy of the tail as much as they prevent water from seeping into the cavity and reducing the tail lift.

Finish the body with a dipped light color and apply a screened or patterned overspray to the back. The belly can use a faint overspray of red. This body as adaptable to almost any kind of finish pattern and seems to be quite effective in both light and dark overall color schemes. It is worth experimenting with several patterns on different days, depending on sky and water conditions.

The lure doesn't need to be made any larger for salmon attraction. The small model seems to be more useful for both steelhead and salmon than a larger configuration.

Eggbeater

THE SEVERAL VARIATIONS OF THIS LURE BEGIN WITH A BALL OF WOOD RANGING FROM ABOUT $\frac{3}{8}$ TO $\frac{3}{4}$-INCH IN DIAMETER.

DRILL A SINGLE HOLE THROUGH THE CENTER, WITH THE GRAIN.

CLAMP THE BALL IN VISE AND SAW A DIAGONAL CUT ACROSS THE SIDE ABOUT $\frac{1}{8}$" DEEP. (SEE TEXT)

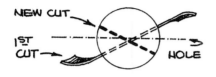

NEW CUT
1ST CUT
HOLE

USE A PIECE OF CARDBOARD OR PAPER TO MARK THE CUT, THEN MAKE A SECOND CUT OPPOSITE THE FIRST.

CUT TWO "WINGS" FROM PLASTIC. TRIM TO FIT AND CEMENT IN THE CUTS. THEY SHOULD HAVE A "PROPELLER" EFFECT WHEN VIEWED FROM THE END.

GLUE

←18"→

BEARING BEAD

THE LURE IS RIGGED ON A MONOFILAMENT SNELL & FISHED BEHIND A DROPPER STYLE SINKER.

Eggbeater

This lure is a standby for salmon fishing and has taken a good share of steelhead from northwest rivers. It isn't terribly popular in Alaska, but can be seen on virtually every river south of the Queen Charlotte Islands. A half-inch foam plastic version of this lure is immensely popular on the salmon and steelhead streams of the Great Lakes.

The lure is completely buoyant and is fished behind a lead dropper. The weight keeps the rig down along the bottom of the streams, but the buoyant lure tends to whirr along above the rocks and gravel, tempting the fish to detach and rise to meet it. It is customarily cast broadside to the current flow and allowed to bump along downriver, covering a lot of good holding water as it progresses. Meanwhile it is spinning rapidly, presenting the alternate bright colors it has been painted.

Dip the assembled lure in yellow paint, allow it to dry thoroughly, and overspray one side with fluorescent red. There are lots of color combinations, but the red-over-yellow scheme is far and away the most popular.

The lure should be quite small, perhaps a ½–¾-inch in diameter. Some salmon models will be an inch or more in size and are usually double-dipped in red-and-white or red-and-yellow to produce a striking contrast between the sides.

Hyponose

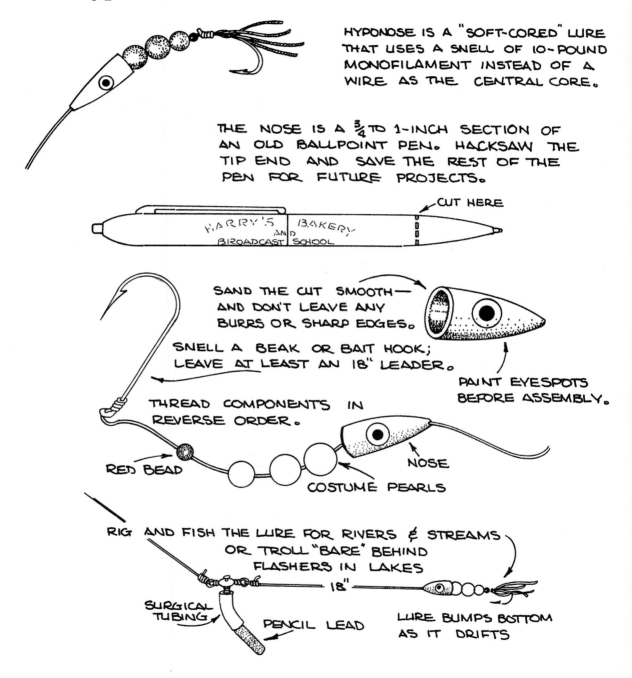

HYPONOSE IS A "SOFT-CORED" LURE THAT USES A SNELL OF 10-POUND MONOFILAMENT INSTEAD OF A WIRE AS THE CENTRAL CORE.

THE NOSE IS A $\frac{3}{4}$ TO 1-INCH SECTION OF AN OLD BALLPOINT PEN. HACKSAW THE TIP END AND SAVE THE REST OF THE PEN FOR FUTURE PROJECTS.

CUT HERE

HARRY'S BAKERY AND BROADCAST SCHOOL

SAND THE CUT SMOOTH — AND DON'T LEAVE ANY BURRS OR SHARP EDGES.

SNELL A BEAK OR BAIT HOOK; LEAVE AT LEAST AN 18" LEADER.

PAINT EYESPOTS BEFORE ASSEMBLY.

THREAD COMPONENTS IN REVERSE ORDER.

RED BEAD

COSTUME PEARLS

NOSE

RIG AND FISH THE LURE FOR RIVERS & STREAMS OR TROLL "BARE" BEHIND FLASHERS IN LAKES

18"

SURGICAL TUBING

PENCIL LEAD

LURE BUMPS BOTTOM AS IT DRIFTS

Hyponose

We used the barrel of a ballpoint pen to make yet another dynamite lure. The truth of the matter is that this is the first lure I ever designed using a ballpoint as a foundation. It was not my first steelhead lure to register a catch, but it sure has been the most consistent producer of searuns.

Hyponose is a semibuoyant lure that combines the best features of the fully buoyant drifters and free-casting lures. It can be fished bare or behind a dropper. I generally fish this lure behind a dropper when I am wading or bank fishing and as a bare lure when I am working from a drift boat. It works admirably in both situations.

The only finishing required is the addition of eyespots. I simply make the head in whatever color the original pen barrel happened to be and use pearls and a red bead to complete.

We have illustrated the Pearl Wasp as a means of showing the variations that are possible with this basic lure. You may want to make longer or shorter bodies or even substitute fluorescent beads for the pearls. I would gauge the body size roughly on the size of fish I expect to encounter; the larger the fish, the longer the body is the rule. I move to a red-beaded body if the water is particularly milky or dulled by runoff silt.

Lucky Lulu

LUCKY LULU DIFFERS FROM MOST SIMILAR STEELHEAD & SALMON LURES IN THAT THE CENTER SHAFT IS THE HOOK SHANK.

THE LURE IS BUILT ON AN ABERDEEN OR HEAVIER O'SHAUGHNESSY JIG HOOK. USE A #2, #1 OR #1/0.

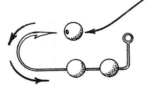

YOU MAY NEED TO DRILL A LARGER CENTER HOLE IN THE BEADS SO THEY WILL SLIDE OVER THE BARB. ALWAYS THREAD BEADS FROM THE POINT, NOT THE EYE.

PUSH THE BEADS FULLY FORWARD: TIE STREAMER FEATHERS, YARN, MYLAR, OR RUBBER AS A SKIRT.

SEAL THE WRAP WITH PAINT, CEMENT, NAIL POLISH, ETC.

SAW A SLIT TO THE CENTER OF A CANNONBALL OR SLIDING EGG SINKER. FILL THE CUT WITH EPOXY AND PINCH FIRMLY IN PLACE.

EGG SINKER

WHEN EPOXY IS HARD, DIP THE LEAD HEAD IN PAINT, LET DRY: ADD EYE SPOTS IF DESIRED.

THE UNWEIGHTED LULU LITE USES A PEARL OR SILVER BEAD FOR A HEAD. (SEE TEXT)

Lucky Lulu

This simple little lure has probably accounted for as many spring chinook and early-run steelhead in certain years as any other. It is an annual fixture on parts of the Columbia River system, where it continues to produce solid fish season after season.

The lure is really nothing more than some beads on a brass hook, headed with a weighted sinker in some instances. A tail is tied on as both an added attraction component and a practical means of keeping the beads from falling off! You can vary the head style as desired, depending on what sinker you can find in the goodie-box. The sinker doesn't really need to be painted (a commercially-produced version uses a plain sinker without eyespots) but I find that a light-colored head and eyespots improves the catch numbers.

In shallow steelhead streams you might choose to fish the unweighted Lulu Light behind a dropper. The lure isn't precisely buoyant, but it is light enough to follow above the gravel and present an inviting target to holding steelhead or salmon. In either version, Lulu is good for both salmon and steelhead. It is especially good for the jack-salmon that follow the spawning schools upriver.

Flasheye

THESE LURES ARE THE TROUT
ANGLER'S EQUIVALENT OF A
POPULAR BASS RIG. THIS
ADAPTATION IS VERY
EFFECTIVE IN STREAMS.

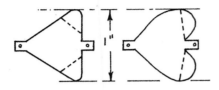

MAKE EITHER OF THESE BUZZ
BLADES FROM METAL OR PLASTIC.
THEY MAY BE PAINTED OR PLAIN.

PLASTIC BLADES WILL REQUIRE
BOILING WATER TO "SET" TABS.

PLUNGE THE DRILLED BLADE IN BOILING
WATER FOR 30-SECONDS, BEND TAB
UP, AND DOUSE WITH COLD WATER. THE
PLASTIC WILL PERMANENTLY "SET" IN
THE DESIRED SHAPE. USE PLIERS!

BEND &
COOL

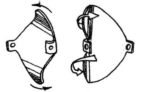

USE THE SAME TECHNIQUE
TO BEND THE PROPELLER-LIKE
"EARS" ON THE BUZZER.

WHEN ASSEMBLING THE LURE, ALWAYS FOLLOW THE
BLADE WITH A SMALL BEAD — IT ACTS AS A BEARING.
THE BODY STRUCTURE MAY BE ANY NUMBER OF SMALL
BEAD CONFIGURATIONS.

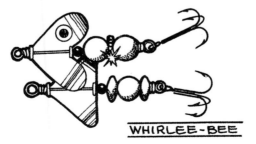

WHIRLEE-BEE

PAINT EYE ON
ONE SIDE ONLY.
(SEE TEXT)

Flasheye

Flasheye takes a cue from the popular buzzer and dart blades, providing a means of adding a lot of attraction to a lure in slower-flowing salmon and steelhead rivers. One of the problems in such a habitat is building a lure that can be cast easily but still creates plenty of flash on a slow retrieve or when held against light currents. Flasheye accomplishes the task admirably.

Cut the blade from metal or plastic and bend up the tabs and tips as shown. I find plated metal—dipped in clear lacquer to prevent rust—by far the superior choice. The blade is put on a central stainless shaft ahead of a beaded body. It can be almost any combination of beads or jewels, depending on the amount of attraction you wish to add. For dull or dark water, use a refractive, faceted jewel; for clear water, a brightly colored bead or rhinestone ring. There isn't any set rule regarding body construction. The blade provides most of the attraction, leaving the body to give us the response trigger that will prompt the strike.

Paint an eyespot on one side of the blade as shown. The eye will "blink" as the blade spins, creating a very powerful stimulus. Rig as shown with bare hooks.

Dimwit

THIS VERSATILE LURE WILL REQUIRE SOME CAREFUL CUTTING AND WIREWORK TO ACHIEVE THE PROPER ACTION.

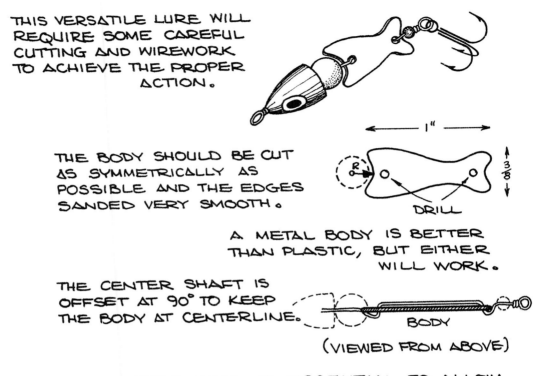

THE BODY SHOULD BE CUT AS SYMMETRICALLY AS POSSIBLE AND THE EDGES SANDED VERY SMOOTH.

1"

DRILL

A METAL BODY IS BETTER THAN PLASTIC, BUT EITHER WILL WORK.

THE CENTER SHAFT IS OFFSET AT 90° TO KEEP THE BODY AT CENTERLINE.

BODY

(VIEWED FROM ABOVE)

THE SMALL REAR BEAD IS ESSENTIAL TO ALLOW THE BODY TO VIBRATE FOR SONIC ATTRACTION... IT IS ALSO AN EFFECTIVE STRIKE TRIGGER.

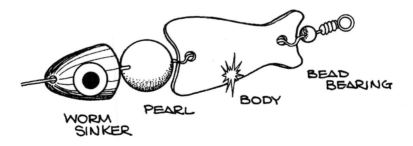

WORM SINKER

PEARL

BODY

BEAD BEARING

Dimwit

Dimwit is a free-casting lure that is effective for salmon, steelhead, jacks, and Dolly Varden. The body of this lure will rotate slowly, wobbling and clacking as it does. There is no indication that noise plays a significant part in the attraction process in fast-moving water, but the action this lure provides attracts fish very well. It is especially effective when fished as a spinning lure on the broad flats of larger rivers. I have used it with grand success in the middle sections of Oregon's Deschutes river, on the Kenai in Alaska, and almost everywhere in between. I find the lure to be a real bother in small streams, though. The weight ratio is such that the lure tends to hang the bottom with disgusting regularity. I suppose a clever lurecrafter might find another material for the head that would solve the problem, but I haven't fooled with it much.

The body should be dipped in clear lacquer or varnish to seal the cut edges and prevent rusting. The bullet head should be dipped in primer and then dipped in a light paint color. It can be further sprayed silver or detailed as preferred. Eyespots can be added before or after assembly.

Pom-Pom

A SIMPLE BUT EFFECTIVE "SOFT" DRIFTING LURE. THE SPUN POLYESTER BODY CAN BE FOUND IN FABRIC SHOPS.

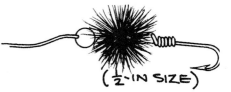

(½-IN SIZE)

THE POM-POM MUST FIRST BE SPRAYED WITH A SILICONE WATER-PROOFING PRODUCT. (DO SEVERAL AT A TIME.)

WHEN FULLY DRY, THREAD A SNELLED BEAK HOOK THROUGH THE HARD "CORE" OF THE POM-POM. (HEAT THE TIP OF A NEEDLE AND USE PLIERS.)

ADD AN ATTRACTOR BEAD AHEAD OF THE FUZZY BODY.

RIG THE POM-POM BEHIND A "DROPPER" AND FISH IT SO IT BUMPS THE BOTTOM AS IT DRIFTS. ALWAYS USE A SCENT ATTRACTANT... SEE TEXT.

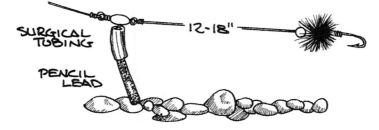

SURGICAL TUBING

12-18"

PENCIL LEAD

Pom-Pom

I developed this lure in response to a series of observations we made of steelhead and feeding jacks that would hit the hard drifting lures that are widely used on the Pacific Slope rivers. Our experiments showed a lot of fish weren't hooked because they quickly rejected the drifter, perhaps because of its hard, foreign feel. I assumed that a lure that would allow the fish to chew without resistance would be held in the mouth longer, allowing the angler time to set the hook against the strike. The solution turned out to be a spun acrylic ball of fabric that held a round shape, could be made buoyant, and was soft enough to maintain contact long enough for the fisherman to react. It is sold in fabric and hobby shops under the generic name "pom-pom".

Buy a package of half-inch pom-poms at a hobby shop. They come in yellow, red, pink, white, and a number of other colors less suited to fishing. Spread a few on a piece of newspaper and spray them with a quality waterproofing product containing silicone. Turn the dried pieces over and spray again. The waterproofing agent keeps them buoyant.

Rigging the lure requires penetrating the hard core with a permanent hole to allow a leader to be pulled through. Some of these gadgets have a core that is soft enough so you can thread the leader through a medium-sized needle and just "sew" it through; others will require the needle be heated.

Once the pom-pom has been thus threaded, simply slip an attractor bead down the leader and the rig is ready to fish. Treat each lure with a fish scent to cover the characteristic odor of the silicone waterproofing agent. Rig behind a dropper, cast directly across the current, and allow to bump the bottom.

Rattler

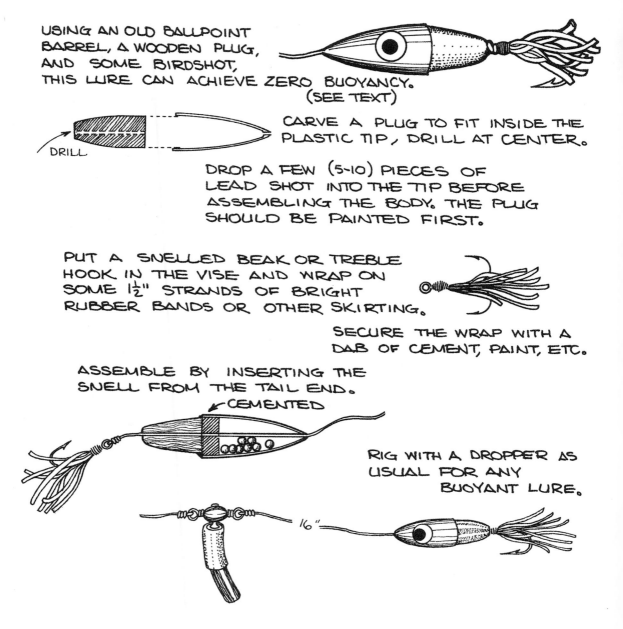

USING AN OLD BALLPOINT BARREL, A WOODEN PLUG, AND SOME BIRDSHOT, THIS LURE CAN ACHIEVE ZERO BUOYANCY. (SEE TEXT)

DRILL

CARVE A PLUG TO FIT INSIDE THE PLASTIC TIP, DRILL AT CENTER.

DROP A FEW (5-10) PIECES OF LEAD SHOT INTO THE TIP BEFORE ASSEMBLING THE BODY. THE PLUG SHOULD BE PAINTED FIRST.

PUT A SNELLED BEAK OR TREBLE HOOK IN THE VISE AND WRAP ON SOME 1½" STRANDS OF BRIGHT RUBBER BANDS OR OTHER SKIRTING.

SECURE THE WRAP WITH A DAB OF CEMENT, PAINT, ETC.

ASSEMBLE BY INSERTING THE SNELL FROM THE TAIL END.

CEMENTED

RIG WITH A DROPPER AS USUAL FOR ANY BUOYANT LURE.

16"

Rattler

Rattler is a noisy lure that fits a narrow niche in the salmon and steelhead inventory. It was designed to be fished as a free-casting lure in the slower holes of any river and can be rigged behind a dropper for use in the faster sections of the stream. Rattler can be built to have "zero buoyancy," meaning it will remain at rest anywhere in the water. When free-fished in a big hole, it will rise slowly in increased current and fall in slower currents.

Finish the head by dipping, spraying with silver or a light color, and adding eyespots. The lure should be finished in a light color. It can be screened and oversprayed with a dark back and faintly sprayed along the belly. I generally paint the body a solid color, since the lure will rotate as it swims. There is no keel or shape component to keep it swimming in any particular attitude, so there is no practical distinction between back and belly. I have found a silver lure with a white and black eyespot and a yellow tail to be excellent.

This group of lures can provide a lot of enjoyment at the bench and on the river. They are all good choices when fishing for big fish in moving water. They are not designed for lakes, bays, and coastal estuaries. These lures rely on the current to produce the action that catches fish. To attract fish in still water, we must build lures that get their action from their own movement or have attraction components incorporated in themselves.

The big Stillwater lures are a class unto themselves. The demands may not be as great as for river lures, but the fish we seek are those that have survived their environment for a long time. We will find that lake lures require a lot of thought and care, too. In the next chapter, we'll examine salmon and lake trout lures that have been specifically designed for big water.

chapter
· TWELVE ·

MAKING BIGWATER LURES

It wasn't so long ago that every angler considered size the only criteria for judging fishing success. It was a relative thing that depended on the individual piece of water and the species involved, but the universal goal was to catch the biggest fish in that particular place, regardless of the tackle or technique involved. Fishermen gained their reputations on the basis of huge specimens or enormous numbers of fish. Almost no consideration was given to understanding the fishing environment or pitting skill and experience against a delicate fishing resource.

Things have changed a little in the past couple of decades, but probably not as much as we'd like to think. We have been the beneficiaries of the development of ultralight tackle and we have come to regard the challenge as an important part of our enjoyment. Still, the televised bass tournaments and the big-money salmon derbies are judged on the size or accumulation of fish. There aren't any alternative ways of keeping score.

Let's admit, though, that there lurks within all of us the desire to carry home a fish of such astonishing proportions that neighbors will troop from miles to view the creature. In truth, this pervasive fantasy is born in every kid who affixes a garden worm to his first rusty fishhook—and it dies hard!

The lures in this section have proven an ability to attract large fish. They are big lures, compared with those we have built for smaller trout, bass, and other game fish. The designs are adaptable to smaller specimens, of course, and can be scaled down to meet other fishing requirements. They are, however, lures that have been successfully built in the big-model format required for trophy waters and have taken their share of heavyweights.

Big lures are a little easier to make than some of the smaller rigs. They offer a greater latitude for error and are easier to shape and handle. It should be added that, even though they are larger, the finish and detail steps must be accomplished just as carefully. Those big fish didn't get that way by snapping at any lure that came along. They aren't intelligent, by any means, but it is generally conceded that large trophy specimens have responded to their instincts more accurately than those who fell prey at a younger age. Your finish, detail, and lure presentation must be careful and accurate if you are to coax one of the biggies to strike.

Flatypus

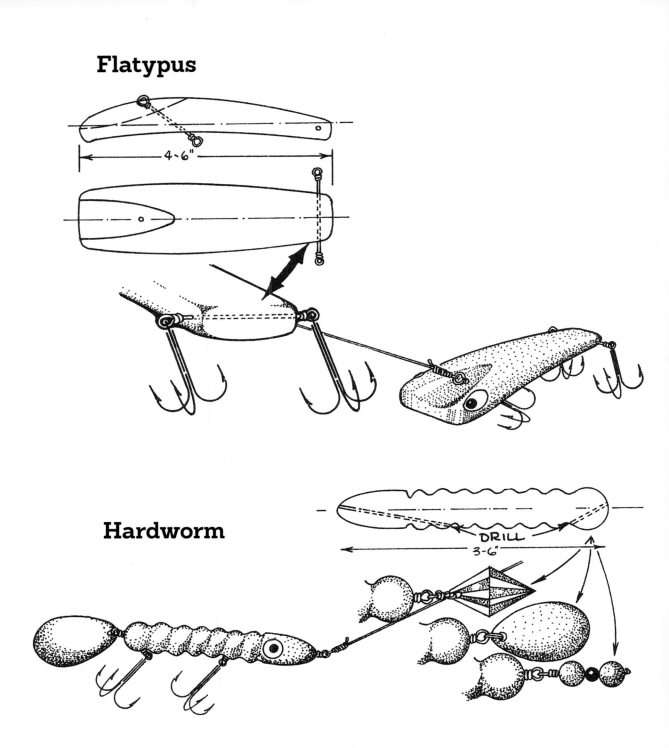

4-6"

Hardworm

DRILL

3-6"

Flatypus

This is one of the most successful plugs ever built for bigwater angling. I know of one individual plug—not mine, darn it!—that has taken sockeye salmon, rainbow in the 10-pound class, and a Canadian laker just a shade under 40 pounds.

Carve and sand the gently curved body as shown. The hollowed nose should be roughed out with a pocketknife and then rasped to shape and sanded smooth. This indentation must be perfectly regular in order to provide good swimming action, a regular wobble, and not dart side-to-side. The complete lure can be tuned by bending the towing eye to one side or the other, up or down. Bends in the eye will significantly change the action.

Drill the body for a single-wire rig up front and for a hook hanger astern. The lure should always have a double-hooked tail.

Flatypus can be finished in silver, white, or any light color. A good finish is a white or silver body with the back oversprayed through a screen to produce a scale effect and the belly lightly oversprayed with bright red. Sometimes I've added a small trigger spot to the underside, right between the hooks.

Hardworm

Hardworm has been proven in a great many bigwater situations and has become a popular lure in the larger lakes of the upper Midwest. It has been known to take trout, pike, and muskies in the same general area, presumably in the same lake.

Carve and sand the slim body with a number of grooves around it. The head is finished in a torpedo shape and the tail is rounded to a terminal ball. The blank is drilled for rigging as shown. Obviously, a fairly tough wood should be chosen since the tail anchor is quite short. I almost always use dry fir for the blank and I would avoid spruce, pine, or cedar…they could split under the strain of a heavy fish.

The rear rig is quite unique; the attractor at the rear can be a nickel blade, a costume jewel, or a string of beads. The rear rig can be tied with 40-pound mono instead of wire if you wish.

The body should be finished and detailed before rigging. The lure is often pale yellow, white, or silver and oversprayed along the back with dark green or blue. The belly can be lightly oversprayed with pink or red. Eyespots should be added, but no trigger spot.

Lake Leech

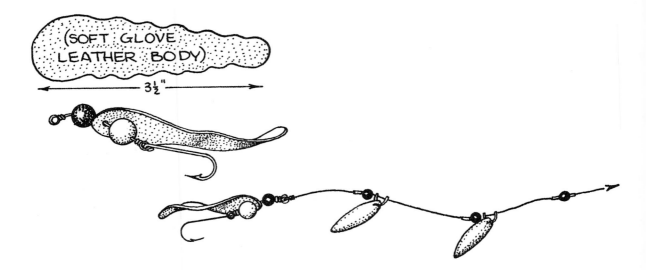

(SOFT GLOVE LEATHER BODY)

3½"

Scoundrel

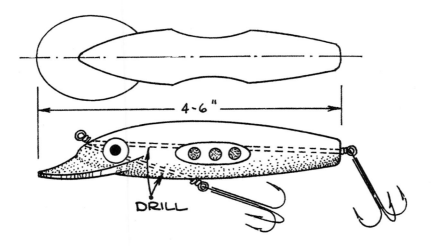

4-6"

DRILL

Lake Leech

This simple lure came about as a result of a desperate need for a big-bodied leech on a Canadian trout lake. Some decent fish were taking a big #2 leech fly and when I changed to a trout leech I had made the size rating went up. It seemed to be one of those situations where "bigger is better,'" so I rigged this lure in camp that night, exactly as it is shown here. It was a case of the first design meeting the need nicely and I didn't have to fool with it after it was completed. We fished it slowly behind a two-blade troll, letting the body glide easily just off the bottom. The first fish taken on this leech probably should have been sent home via the taxidermist, but optimism got the better of me and I released it. None of the subsequent fish matched the size of the first, but success with this lure was consistent.

Cut the body from soft, dark glove leather, the edges rippled to provide some light action on the troll. The white or pearl lower bead gives the impression of an underbelly and it allows the leather to maintain a spread shape in motion. The red forward bead is a representative head that the fish apparently respond to. The forward bead also helps brush aside the small weeds and aquatic grasses along the bottom. The body can be doused in a water-based scent compound before fishing.

Scoundrel

This is a grand bigwater plug that attracts a lot of attention. It tends to swim in a head-down position and wobbles well against the troll. It requires some fine-tuning of the towing eye to get the right kind of rapid tail action. The indentations on either side seem to increase the wobble rate, and provide a good surface for prismatic tapes.

Carve and sand the wooden body to shape. Be careful to balance the diving lip so the lure will trail fairly straight. An imbalance will result in the lure pulling violently to one side and will badly dampen the wobble as it swims. Drill for a simple single-wire double rig.

The body should be dipped in white paint and then oversprayed with silver, yellow, white, or another light body color. The back may be textured with a screen or a brushed vermiculation. The belly should be lightly oversprayed with red or yellow and the eyespot added. The side panel is painted a contrasting color and the dots are added. If you'll take a piece of prismatic or reflective tape and punch it with a common paper punch, you can use the little circles that have been cut out. Just peel the backing off the little punches and stick them on.

Needle

Squamish

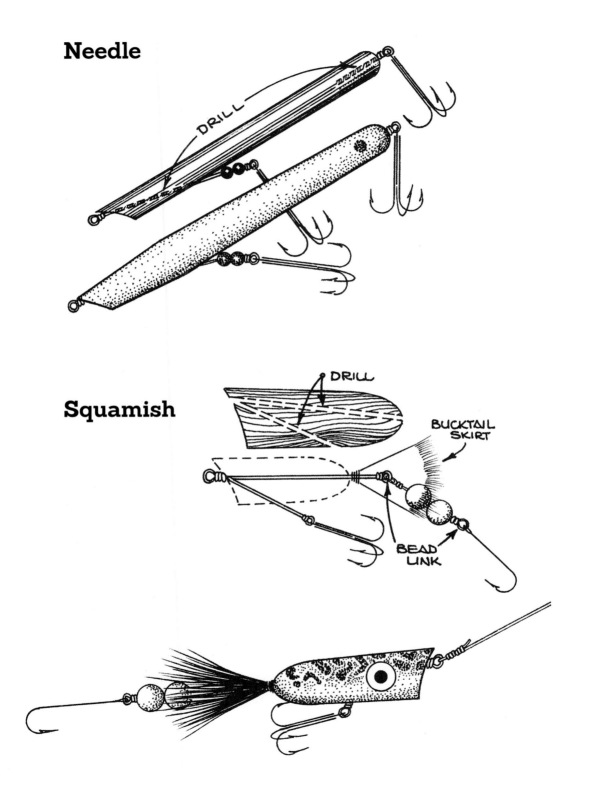

DRILL

DRILL

BUCKTAIL SKIRT

BEAD LINK

Needle

Needle is a very popular lure for many big lakes and for the saltchuck. It's about as simple as a lure can get, yet it attracts fish because it represents the shape of a lot of different prey animals.

Carve the body or simply trim the ends of a piece of dowel and sand it smooth. The lure is generally in the range of 5 to 7 inches long, so drilling through is pretty risky. Drill the front for a single-wire rig and attach the rear hook with a separate anchor. We have elsewhere described the anchor that incorporates mechanical "ears" to help it hold, and this is certainly recommended in the case of the Needle. Note that the belly hook is rigged with a couple of beads above the eye. The beads help with the overall attraction, but they are most important as a rudder.

The body is fully finished prior to rigging. It should be dipped, and can be as simple as an all-silver or a double-dipped red-and-white scheme, or it can be a brushed and detailed pattern. It seems quite efficient when oversprayed and screened to produce a scale effect on the back. The lure seldom incorporates eyespots but does have a bright response trigger at the tail.

Squamish

A solid performer among the bigwater lures, even though it isn't as large as some of the others, Squamish achieves the effect of size through its composition of several components. The body is about 3 inches long, the bucktail another 2 inches or so, and the bead link adds another inch.

Squamish is specifically designed to be towed behind a weight or flasher string. The upcurved face actually tends to make the lure try to climb to the surface and the trolling tackle is necessary to keep it down.

Carve the wooden body and drill for a single-wire double rig. The body should be fully painted and detailed before it is rigged. The central rigging wire should extend about a half-inch behind the body to allow a bucktail or hair skirt to be tied directly to the shaft. A second shaft is added behind the main and a couple of pearls bent onto it. The hook is attached directly to the bead link or a split-ring is added for the hook. The belly hook can also be attached with a split-ring.

The body is dipped white and may be oversprayed and detailed in almost any standard brushed pattern.

Ghost Glider

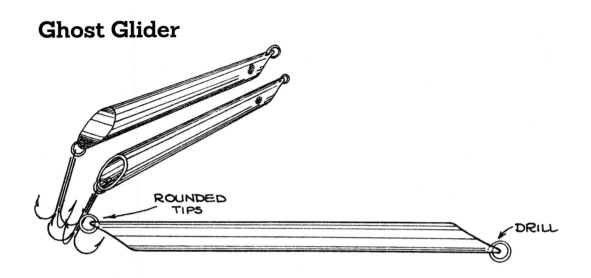

ROUNDED TIPS

DRILL

One-Eyed Jack

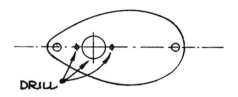

DRILL

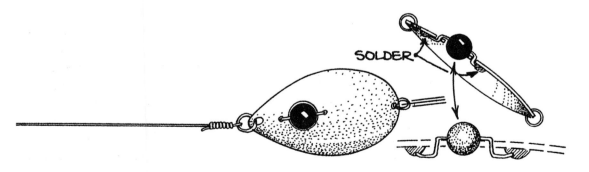

SOLDER

Ghost Glider

Here's a large lure that is especially adapted to the very clear water in spring and early summer. Many small prey fishes have little or no color during their early juvenile stages so that they are less visible in the clear waters of spring time. The big predators are conditioned to strike at the less-visible targets quickly during this period…and this lure capitalizes on that instinct.

The lure is just a piece of clear plastic rod about a ¼ inch in diameter or a stiff plastic tube about the same size. The two look quite similar in the water but serve a different purpose. The solid rod is relatively heavy and can be used for a cast-and-retrieve fishery or can be trolled bare in clear water during the search for real slabs. The hollow tube looks the same underwater, but is excellent for trolling behind a flasher string at moderate depths. The heavier solid rod is a poor choice for slow trolling, since the weight tends to drag the flasher string along at a diagonal, reducing the reflection pattern and making the lure rather hard for the fish to spot. You will probably want two or three of each in sizes ranging from 4 to 7 inches.

Cut the blank from the bar or tube as shown, slightly rounding the cuts at head and tail. To prevent scratches, the bar or tube should be padded with leather or an old cloth while it is held in the vise for sawing. An unblemished surface is quite important if the lure is really going to represent a prey species in its colorless juvenile phase. Apply a red or yellow eyespot (no pupil).

One-Eyed Jack

This is a heavyweight trolling spoon that borrows from the bass angler's famous Lemming by using a bright red bead as an instinctive target for the bigwater trophy. It is a much narrower blade than the Lemming and is thus better suited to a fast, deep troll. The lure is especially good for deep water rainbows during the hotter summer months. It should be trolled quite fast and without a flasher string. It isn't very effective on char because of the faster speed it is designed for, although it accounts for plenty of lake char when dragged slowly along the bottom. It is also an excellent lure for coho salmon in either fresh or salt water.

The blade should be from 3 to 5 inches in length and quite heavy. Many commercial brass blanks can be used in the production of this lure. Drill the body to accept a large (6–8 mm) round bead and put a tiny rigging hole directly fore and aft of the large hole. Run a brass wire through the bead and down through the rigging holes. The loose ends of the wire could be brought together and twisted to secure the bead, but soldering the ends separately as shown is a better technique.

My experience with this lure indicates a nickel or pure white finish is unbeatable.

Shimmy Spoon

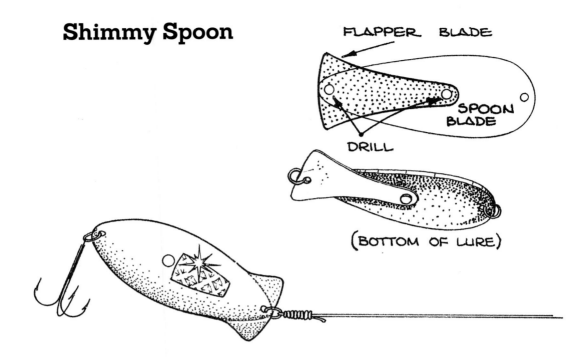

FLAPPER BLADE

SPOON BLADE

DRILL

(BOTTOM OF LURE)

Kokanee

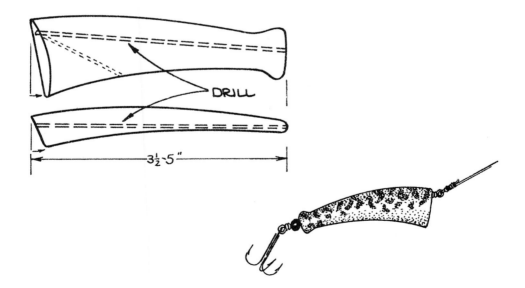

DRILL

$3\frac{1}{2}$-5"

Shimmy Spoon

This is a standard spoon that has been modified to dampen the wobble a little and to add a sonic component that is very useful in fishing deep, dank water that is discolored by algae, silt, or the mud of a fall runoff. The lure has the reflective power of the original blade but has been slowed in an effort to allow the reflections to be more stable—to penetrate toward a given spot in the water for a longer period of time. The sonic attractant helps guide the curious fish toward the target and the prismatic tape on the back acts as a good response trigger.

The secret to this lure is the flapper blade that is riveted to the underside of the standard spoon. It is the device that modifies the wobble into the desired slow shake, and it is the cause of sonic generation on the troll.

Cut the flapper blade to the approximate shape shown and long enough to reach from the center of the blade to the leading edge. Drill the flapper and the spoon at the same time and loosely rivet the two pieces together. I invariably use a brass spoon, a very thin brass flapper blade, and a brass rivet. The use of dissimilar metals will sometimes set up electrolysis between the components, ruining the lure and driving fish away because of the current generated.

Drill the front of the flapper to correspond to the forward hole in the spoon. The front split ring goes through both pieces to secure the flapper in the proper position.

Finish the lure with a piece of prismatic or day-glo tape on the back. The lure should be left nickel or painted a solid light color.

Kokanee

This is a standard cut-plug artificial that finds a lot of use in angling for big fish in either fresh or salt water. It is almost a fixture on the inland saltwater of the West Coast and is very popular in the northern and western bigwater lakes.

Drill for either a single-wire or a single-wire double rig, depending on the size of the lure you've made. As a general rule, I single-rig any Kokanee under 4 inches and double-rig the larger ones. I often rig this lure with a red bead just forward of the hook to act as an external trigger spot.

The body should be dipped, before rigging, in at least two coats of white to produce a very smooth surface. The sides are sprayed silver and the back is oversprayed with blue or dark green through a screen to produce scales. The belly is lightly oversprayed with white to represent the herring or adolescent minnow species. The back can be detailed in black or deep green with well-defined vermiculations.

Warclub

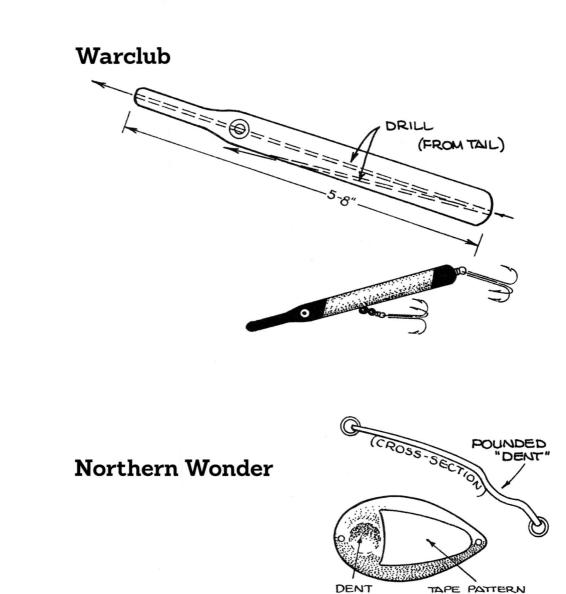

DRILL
(FROM TAIL)

5-8"

Northern Wonder

(CROSS-SECTION)

POUNDED
"DENT"

DENT   TAPE PATTERN

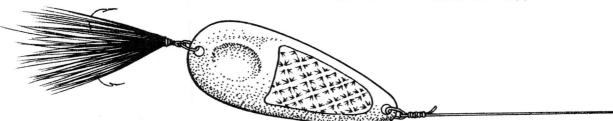

Warclub

To be quite honest, the first time I saw a lure that looked like this I really thought somebody was pulling my leg. The original was considerably fatter than my final modification and it looked remarkably like an old-fashioned ale bottle. The lure was a homemade affair that a friend had used in Alaska, insisting it was the hottest thing in the country for big char. My first models were a bit slimmer than the original and further experimentation produced the rig illustrated here.

Drill from the tail end for a single-wire double rig. Smaller models can be fitted with a single rig, which most of mine are.

I have only finished this lure in the one way shown. I have dipped the body and sprayed it an all-over silver, then dipped the head and tail in bright red. The eyespot is black on white and the thing works very well. I have seen similar commercial rigs in a variety of colors.

Northern Wonder

Here is a consistent performer that has been seen on almost every kind of trophy water in North America. Commercial versions are popular in saltwater for salmon and other game species, on large lakes for char and trout, and in smaller versions on the big rivers for salmon, steelhead, trout, and Dolly Varden. It would be hard to find a single lure that has been so well received in the world of bigwater angling.

The spoon has been modified to give it a side-to-side hula-hipped shake instead of the traditional wobble. Almost any spoon can be thus altered by pounding a shallow depression at the back as shown. Some of the more rounded designs can be modified in this way with some success, but the narrow, heavy "devle" spoons seem to work better.

The spoon can be altered by simply pounding the depression with the back of a ball-peen hammer. A more precise job can be done by holding a steel ball bearing with pliers over the exact spot and hitting the bearing—quite hard —with a hammer.

There have been a number of experiments with alternative finishes for this lure, but none has been as successful as a plain nickel blade and a shaped piece of dayglo or prismatic reflective tape. The commercial versions come in almost every known color of reflective tape, but always with a basic silver finish on the spoon.

Jacque's Special

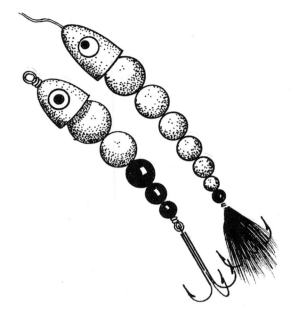

Pullman

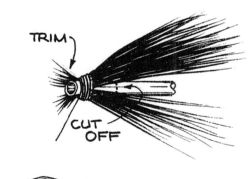

TRIM

CUT
OFF

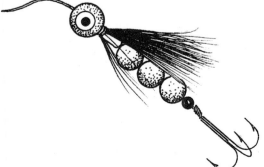

Jacque's Special

This lure is named for the lake where it was conceived, an off-again, on-again trophy spot in the Canadian Cariboo. We were drifting along the shore waiting for something—anything!—to start rising. Along one of the deeper shorelines I noticed some feed fish darting about near the bottom. I couldn't see them clearly and had no idea if anything was chasing them, but I kept getting a consistent visual impression of those fish. It was a tapered figure, light-colored at the front and with a hint of color at the hindmost third. I went back to camp and built some beaded bodies very like those illustrated. Equipped with a handful of 3-inch lures exactly like the upper one, my partner and I caught and released a couple of dozen trout in the 3- to 5-pound class, noticing that another party on the lake was getting only the pan-sized stuff. The lure has continued to produce very well in lakes all over the Northwest. I don't know that this design has ever been tried in the bigwater lakes of the rest of the country, but I have no doubt it will be just as good anywhere.

The construction of Jacque's Special is simple. The head is made from the top of a ballpoint pen. Thread the beaded components on a shaft or snell as shown. The forward beads and head should be light colored, pearls, or silver costume beads. The tail section must be one or more bright red or orange beads. The lure can be finished with either a bare hook or a skirted rig. Both work in some circumstances. The lure is trolled behind a flasher string.

Pullman

This is a freshwater variation of the Coho fly, a salmon lure used widely in the Pacific. The lake version shown here has been modified by the addition of a large pearl head and a shortened bucktail collar. The lure was designed to be trolled behind a flasher string. It is usually trolled quite fast in shallow to moderate depths in trophy lakes, where it attracts just about every kind of fish that swims.

Tie the bucktail collar on a tiny brass or plastic tube. The hair can then be inserted onto a snelled or wire shaft. The little tube you'll need is nothing more than the inside of one of those ballpoint pens we've been wrecking all the way through this book. Once the bucktail or other hair collar has been tied, trim the tube to about a half-inch so it won't seriously separate the other components.

Thread the components onto the snell in reverse order, beginning with a tiny red trigger bead at the tail. Add three pearls or white beads, the collar, and finish with the head. Eye spots can be painted on the head if desired.

Magnum

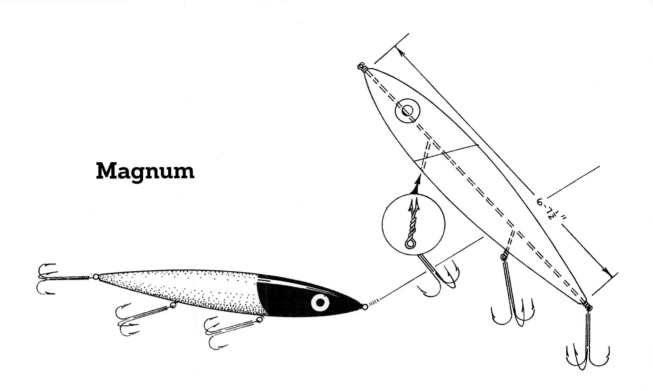

Silver Craw

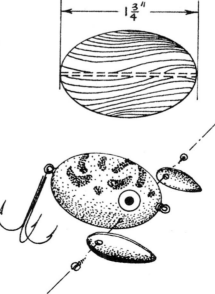

Magnum

This is probably the most famous bigwater lure in the history of fishing, and there is little point in telling anyone about it. It has seen more water and caught more fish than any other…and it will probably remain a favorite as long as people search for big fish.

Carve and sand the big, regular body as shown. Drill for a single through-wire rig and for two belly hooks. The belly anchors are "eared" to add mechanical strength to the epoxy bond.

The body is white or silver and has been double-dipped to produce the characteristic red head. There are variations in the color scheme, but almost nobody uses them.

Silver Craw

This might be the only lure in this group that can be considered a gimmick, but it is extremely effective in the limited trophy fishery for which it was designed. The lure was built nearly fifteen years ago, but it is a rig that I have kept pretty well under my hat. It was, in fact, a bit of a hard decision whether to include it in this book…but here it is.

The lure came about after a naturalist friend of mine reported on the feeding habits of very large, landlocked cutthroat trout. He had been observing a number of fish in the twenty-plus class that had developed in a large series of stream-fed ponds. They didn't have the feeding options of their counterparts in Pyramid or Flaming Gorge Lakes, but they had evolved into very opportunistic feeders. It takes a lot of protein to maintain a landlocked twenty-five pounder, and these fish would take anything that happened along. During the observation period, my friend noted that the food of choice, when available, was swimming field mice. When this lure was introduced into the water he had studied, the big cutts struck without hesitation. In the years that followed, I found this lure effective in every cutthroat water I fished, but it didn't seem to tempt rainbow or other trout. I haven't tried the lure against any other species, reserving it for the cutthroat waters where I know it to work.

Carve the oval body as shown and drill it for a through-wire rig. Finish the body before rigging or adding the wings.

The body is finished in medium gray or green with brushed patterns on the back. The belly is lightly sprayed white. The blades are added after the finish, first screwed in place and then epoxied at the inside junction.

Silver Craw can be fished at the surface in early morning or late evening, but is better trolled at a shallow depth in deep water. It isn't large as bigwater lures go, but it attracts the attention of cutthroat from quite far away.

chapter
· THIRTEEN ·

USING FACTORY COMPONENTS

We have suggested the use of factory components for home lurecrafting as a good means of makings some very professional pieces. It is also a way to save a lot of money, compared with purchasing ready-made lures at the local tackle shop. The lures that have been built—at least in part—with factory components often work more smoothly than home-fashioned rigs and they are much less time-consuming.

There are a few components that simply cannot be made efficiently at the home bench. These are usually the little, inexpensive bits of gear that are built by impossibly complex machines at such an enormous rate that the cost to the consumer is just pennies. Among these are snaps, swivels, clevises, split-rings, sleeves, and a number of other pieces.

Let's look at the cost of making a typical spinning lure from factory components and compare it with a similar rig fashioned from scratch. The illustration points up the advantage of using some factory-made gear instead of roughing it out at home. The lure is a simple brass-bodied spinner, the kind that will be found in any tackle shop in the country.

Using factory components from the supply catalog, we will spend a total of about 19 cents on the rig, we will build it in a matter of moments, and we will produce a slick, professional-looking lure. It only requires bending a forward eye on a wire, threading on the components, and looping the tail-wire through the hook and back up the body.

The handmade equivalent requires us to cut and pound a blade, finish the blade with paint or clear lacquer, drill a piece of metal rod for the body and paint it, and to bend a little clevis out of wire. In both cases we will use a costume bead as a bearing. (Did you ever think about making a glass bead? Impossible!) We will have built the rougher lure for only the cost of the bead, but it will have taken us nearly an hour.

We must recognize that both lures will exhibit about the same degree of attraction and would probably finish dead-even in an angling contest. The primitive lure doesn't look quite as slick to our eye, but the fish would probably see the two about equally. The factory lure would probably spin a little better, but the difference is not in the fishing. It is in the cost—in time and money—to the luremaker.

The lure that has been made with factory components is unquestionably the better choice for most of us. The cost is small and the time requirement is little. For less than two dollars (about the cost of a ready-made equivalent lure) we can outfit ourselves with ten variations, enough to meet the angling demands of several days of fishing—and it has only taken half an hour! I believe this to be a great trade-off.

There are a great many lures that will be built largely from scratch, and those are the lures that provide the greatest satisfaction. Many others, though, are better fashioned from factory parts.

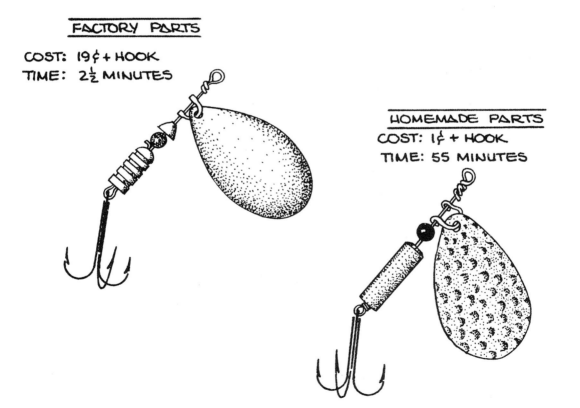

FACTORY PARTS

COST: 19¢ + HOOK
TIME: 2½ MINUTES

HOMEMADE PARTS
COST: 1¢ + HOOK
TIME: 55 MINUTES

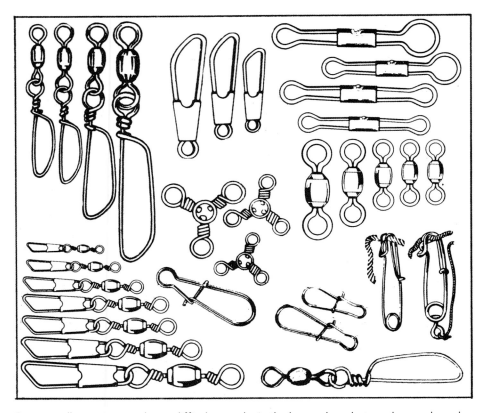

Some small parts are much too difficult to make in the home shop, but can be purchased through the catalogs at low cost.

One component that we need to consider from a slightly different viewpoint is the common spinner blade. It can be made quite well and cheaply by an experienced amateur luremaker, but the time demands are fairly great. The homemade blade cannot be plated at home without extensive equipment and must be dipped in lacquer or varnish to prevent rusting. If we were concerned only with cost and effort, we would choose factory blades for all our crafting. But there are two other factors of importance that make the homemade blade a good choice in some situations. First, you may want to make an experimental blade of your own design or of a size not commonly handled by the commercial outlets. You may want to try an altogether new concept in spinning rigs—and that will require a blade made on your own workbench. The second reason is less rational, but just as important to most of us. It is simply a lot of fun to catch a nice fish on a lure that has been completely built with our own hands and skills. It isn't the kind of reason that can be easily measured or defended, but it makes sense to most amateur lurecrafters!

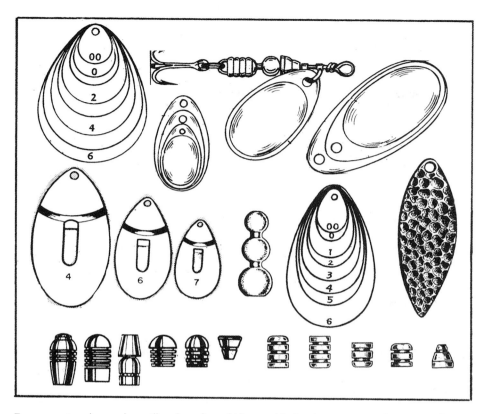

Every amateur luremaker will make a few of his own blades, but most production work will utilize factory blades and bodies.

For most "production" lures and when you are getting a bunch of gear laid aside for a week of backcountry fishing, you will probably want to use factory blades. They are inexpensive and are of a uniform good quality. Almost the same arguments can be advanced in behalf of spoon blades.

The Component Catalog

One of the handiest items on the home tackle bench is the commercial component catalog. There are all kinds of fishing items in the books, of course, but several suppliers have set aside large sections of their catalogs for the homecraft smart. As you thumb through the colorful pages of readymade lures, you'll undoubtedly get a lot of ideas for good lures you can make and you'll find all sorts of finishing suggestions for the lures you have already built. It's a handy information source and a supply point for a great many specialized items you might not even know existed.

There are a number of tools available through the mail-order catalogs that will prove especially valuable on the home bench, pieces that you won't find in the local hardware store or in many tackle departments. There are split-ring pliers, crimping tools for leader sleeves, inexpensive hook vises, wire-bending tools, snelling tools, and an intriguing selection of fishing gadgets and tools.

The catalogs generally include several pages of fly-tying supplies, many of which are suitable for luremaking. It is in this section you will find the bucktail and other hair products that are important to several of the lure designs in this book. You may also decide to use special fabrics, tubings, mylar, or feathers for your luremaking tasks. Most of these can be found in any well-stocked tackle shop, but the prices might be a little better from the mail-order suppliers.

A couple of the catalogs include a fine selection of specialized lure parts and supplies. Most have spinner and spoon blades, clevises, hardware, and such, but the specialists include hook hangers, lure bodies, special cements for lurecrafting, epoxy paints, prismatic materials and day-glo tape, and a lot more. It's enough to warm the heart of any enthusiast!

One of the more fascinating items that has turned up in the catalogs is a special kind of acetate floss that, when wound into almost any odd shape and treated with a chemical solvent, will harden to the shape intended. It is one of the better new products for the lure designer, and you'll probably want to get some for your bench.

Working with Lead

If you are going to become really involved in home lurecrafting, you will eventually start making cast lead items on your home bench. The first pieces will probably be lead jigheads, but you'll soon expand to sinkers, diamond jigs, and all sorts of other heavy components. The process is a lot easier than most people realize and the supplies and equipment are not prohibitively expensive. The catalogs offer electric furnaces (a really efficient way for the amateur to work with lead), melting pots that require an outside heat source, lead ladles, and a huge array of molds.

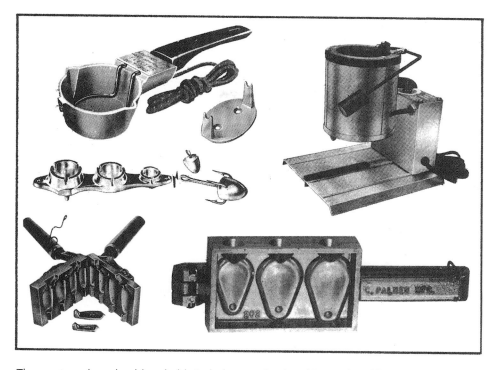

The amateur shop should probably include some lead-melting and molding equipment. Small pots or furnaces can be found at moderate cost. Molds are available to make many components.

The tackle catalogs list, for example, jig molds that will allow you to make three or four sizes at a single pouring—and they supply the correct hook for each size and design. Other molds are available for trolling sinkers, downrigger weights, surfcasting sinkers, and even tiny split-shot. The amateur with a small electric furnace can even put melted lead into holes and hollows in his wooden lure bodies to provide the internal weighting that is essential to some designs. Saltwater anglers are particularly apt to include leadwork in their luremaking activity.

A good lead pot is an essential tool for the home luremaker who becomes deeply interested in original design. He can cut and form a wooden pattern for a new concept in jigs, make a simple plaster-of-paris or concrete mold, and immediately pour his new invention in lead. A great many of the most popular jigs on today's markets began as a wooden pattern in a home lurecrafter's shop. It is through this kind of experimentation that progress is made in the science of angling—and you'll find all the lead supplies you will need in the component catalog.

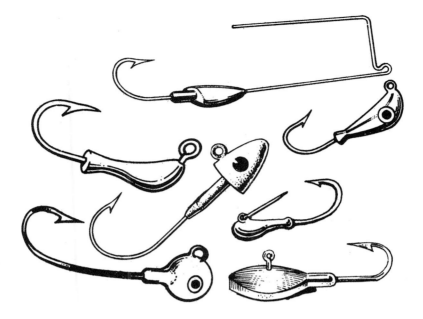

The lurecrafter who doesn't mold his own can buy molded jigheads that are unfinished and quite inexpensive.

Entering the Plastics World

The home lurecrafter today can expand his skill into the area of live-rubber and plastic lures with a minimum of equipment and at relatively low cost. Some suppliers offer jugs of plastic material that can be heated in an old saucepan and poured into a mold to produce all sorts of soft-bodied lures. Molds are available at very low cost to produce rubber nightcrawlers, shrimp, scampi-tails, waterdogs, salamanders, and dozens of other designs.

This material is another wonderful opportunity for the home designer. A mold can be made from almost any pattern and the melted plastic poured in. If you don't like the result, you simply remelt the plastic and try something else. It is a great medium for experimentation. I've made some pretty bizarre bodies while looking for a special design, and they've been a lot of fun. I finally found that I could freeze a minnow or a worm and use it to make a plaster mold. By mixing several colors of melted plastic I could make some really incredible lures. The colored dyes are available from the same suppliers that offer the basic material.

I can't encourage any amateur enough to invest in lead and plastic molding equipment. It is enormously satisfying to make a batch of top-grade lures and then take them out and catch a number of fine fish with them. You can provide lures for friends or even sell a few to local fishermen. (We'll talk more about that in a few minutes.) The tackle market will introduce several thousand new lures in the next few years, and I believe that most of those will be born at the workbench of amateurs who understand the principles of fish attraction and build their models with skill and imagination. A knowledge of lead and plastic techniques will allow you better to meet the demands of tomorrow's angling.

Designing with Factory Components

Not long after you start making your own lures, you'll probably get the itch to design them, too. When you're determined which attraction components you need, lay out the design on paper. The drawing—however rustic—isn't necessary for visual corroboration or mechanical construction details. Those are usually pretty well fixed in your mind, anyway. The sketch provides a checklist of attraction components in the design. It allows you to consider how each part of the lure will appeal to the behavioral instincts of your prey. Those parts that are based on sound principle are left, those that are superfluous are deleted. When you're satisfied with the sketch, you can reach into the parts box and actually lay out all the parts, in order, on the sketch pad. At this point you can determine the visual value of the lure and check the functional appropriateness of each part. The lure is built; all that remains is to test it against the actual reaction of the fish. The fun part! When you're sitting in your boat, hefting a respectable bass that has fallen for a lure that began as a vague glitter in your mind, you have collected a trophy shared by very few of your peers. It is the very best part of home lurecrafting.

A Cottage Industry

At some point in your progress, you'll sit at your bench, idly fingering an excellent lure you have just finished. It is polished nicely, the wire is perfectly wrapped, and the beads are in precise proportion to the blade and shaft. You're enormously pleased with yourself—and you should be. It occurs to you that there are probably fishermen all over the place who would pay you for lures just like that one. Fortunately, you're right. There are fishermen who would buy that lure, particularly if it will catch fish.

The commercial manufacture of fishing lures is a business that can be successfully conducted from the home workshop. There are probably one or two cottage lurecrafters in every community in America…and there is always room for another. I have no intention of talking anyone into—or out of—the notion that he can make some extra money by making lures at home and selling them through local outlets. I'm not going to talk about packaging, markup, promotion and advertising, or anything else related to the industry. I've known a few hundred amateurs who have entered the business. Some have succeeded beyond reason; most haven't. From their experience I will pass along a couple of observations that seem germaine. The rest is up to you.

First, try to be a cottage industry, not a tackle giant. Produce a few lures that work well in your area and that you understand fully. Buy the components at a level that will allow you to realize a decent profit for the time you spend. Second, use the simplest packaging and labeling method you can find. A copy-machine label stapled to a cheap plastic bag is standard among home industries…and it is usually enough. You won't be able to compete with the big industries in packaging or promotion, so don't try.

Most of all, guarantee your product fully. You'll notice that the major manufacturers have a policy that provides for instant replacement of a lure that fails for any reason, no questions asked. You'll have to do just as well. If you don't have enough confidence in your own tackle to offer a complete, no-question guarantee, you'd best stay out of the business. And remember that the buyer won't treat your tackle as gingerly as you do. He bought it to fish with, not gently coax across a riffle!

You can make some extra money with your lurecrafting if you wish, or you may decide to try to make a living at it. It's going to work for some people and it won't for others. Most of us will allow the thought of a business connection pass and file it away with that light-tackle world-record we're going to catch and those Sunday luncheons with Charles and Di. A few will actually try to sell their lures, some will be successful, and a couple of you might become millionaires. Lotsa luck!

Getting the Catalogs

The component catalog will open a lot of doors. They will expand your ability to produce fine lures, teach you new techniques, and make your fishing more fun. That's a pretty good return for something that is either free or a terrific bargain at a dollar or two. Believe me, you're going to want to send for every one you can find, and you are going to use them.

You can get the addresses of several suppliers from the classified section of many outdoor magazines. Many of these are old, established firms that have earned a great reputation among the thousands of amateur lurecrafters in this country. I have never had a bad experience with any of them. I am including the names and web addresses of a few that I have dealt with and I recommend them to you without reservation.

CABELA'S
www.cabelas.com

JANN'S NETCRAFT
www.jannsnetcraft.com

BARLOW'S TACKLE
www.barlowstackle.com

These suppliers are often generous with information as well. I've corresponded with some over the years and have gotten my questions answered quickly and with genuine interest.

You'll find the catalogs a fine source of information and a way to keep up with changes in the world of artificial lures. They will suggest many adaptations on your bench, they'll give you good knowledge of what a lure should cost, and they will provide a lot of enjoyment on a winter evening. Send for them. They are going to make you a better home lurecrafter!

INDEX

More Great Books from Fox Chapel Publishing

Cooking Fish & Game
ISBN 978-1-896980-77-5 **$12.99**

Making Wooden Fishing Lures
ISBN 978-1-56523-446-8 **$19.95**

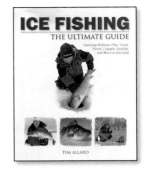

Ice Fishing: The Ultimate Guide
ISBN 978-1-896980-72-0 **$24.99**

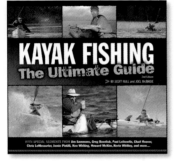

Kayak Fishing: The Ultimate Guide, 2nd Edition
ISBN 978-1-56523-638-7 **$24.95**

The Paddling Chef, 2nd Edition
ISBN 978-1-56523-714-8 **$16.95**

Camp Cooking in the Wild
ISBN 978-1-56523-715-5 **$19.95**

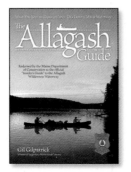

The Allagash Guide
ISBN 978-1-56523-488-8 **$11.95**

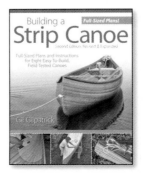

Building a Strip Canoe, Second Edition, Revised & Expanded
ISBN 978-1-56523-483-3 **$24.95**

Building Wooden Snowshoes & Snowshoe Furniture
ISBN 978-1-56523-485-7 **$19.95**

Building Outdoor Gear, Revised 2nd Edition
ISBN 978-1-56523-484-0 **$19.95**

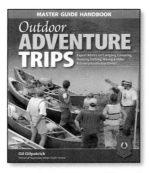

Master Guide Handbook to Outdoor Adventure Trips
ISBN 978-1-896980-75-1 **$19.99**

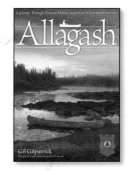

Allagash
ISBN 978-1-56523-487-1 **$19.95**

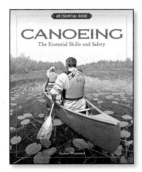

Canoeing: The Essential Skills and Safety
ISBN 978-1-56523-634-9 **$19.95**

The Little Book of Whittling
ISBN 978-1-56523-772-8 **$12.95**

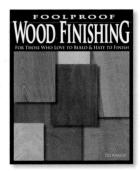

Foolproof Wood Finishing
ISBN 978-1-56523-303-4 **$19.95**

More Great Books from Fox Chapel Publishing

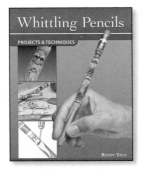

Whittling Pencils
ISBN 978-1-56523-751-3 **$12.99**

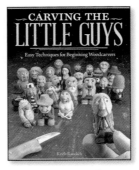

Carving the Little Guys
ISBN 978-1-56523-775-9 **$9.99**

Carving Fantasy Characters
ISBN 978-1-56523-749-0 **$16.99**

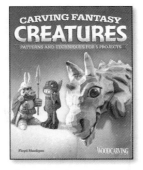

Carving Fantasy Creatures
ISBN 978-1-56523-609-7 **$12.99**

Big Book of Whittle Fun
ISBN 978-1-56523-520-5 **$12.95**

**Complete Beginner's
Woodcarving Workbook**
ISBN 978-1-56523-745-2 **$12.99**

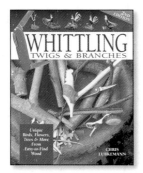

**Whittling Twigs &
Branches, 2nd Edition**
ISBN 978-1-56523-236-5 **$12.95**

Whittling Little Folk
ISBN 978-1-56523-518-2 **$16.95**

Tree Craft
ISBN 978-1-56523-455-0 **$19.95**